Colin Powell
and
Condoleezza Rice

Foreign Policy, Race, and the
New American Century

Clarence Lusane
Foreword by Kwame Dixon

Westport, Connecticut
London

Library of Congress Cataloging-in-Publication Data

Lusane, Clarence, 1953–
  Colin Powell and Condoleezza Rice : foreign policy, race, and the new American century / Clarence Lusane ; foreword by Kwame Dixon.
    p. cm.
  Includes bibliographical references and index.
  ISBN 0–275–98309–9 (alk. paper)
  1. United States—Foreign relations—2001– 2. United States—Race relations—Political aspects. 3. Powell, Colin L. 4. Rice, Condoleezza, 1954– 5. Bush, George W. (George Walker), 1946—Friends and associates. 6. African American diplomats. 7. Iraq War, 2003—Diplomatic history. 8. World politics—1995–2005. 9. Hegemony—United States. I. Title.
  E902.L87 2006
  327.730092'396073—dc22   2006006630

British Library Cataloguing in Publication Data is available.

Library of Congress Catalog Card Number: 2006006630
ISBN: 0–275–98309–9

First published in 2006

Praeger Publishers, 88 Post Road West, Westport, CT 06881
An imprint of Greenwood Publishing Group, Inc.
www.praeger.com

Printed in the United States of America

♾™

The paper used in this book complies with the Permanent Paper Standard issued by the National Information Standards Organization (Z39.48–1984).

10 9 8 7 6 5 4 3 2 1

To the hundreds of thousands who have lost their lives or had them ruined by the policies of the Bush administration. And the millions who continue to resist being marginalized, forgotten, and exploited. May Bush and his top officials always be held accountable for the destruction they brought to the world.

Contents

Foreword

Race is a social construct and a powerful sociological metaphor; it unfolds and operates on multiple levels, at times, intersecting with other variables (Crenshaw 1995 and Delgado 2001). Currently, the intersection of race, gender, class, power, and hegemony as conceptual tools is central to the study and investigation of international relations and foreign affairs. Race and its intersectional consequences, like race and gender, as well as race and class, have contributed significantly to conceptual and theoretical models that advance our understanding of the world. Now, critical race theory is influencing the study of international relations like never before.

Race as a social construction, and its influence on international relations is gaining currency; and the study of race as an aspect of international relations and U.S. foreign policy is more common. In international affairs and human rights, issues such as genocide, immigration or migration, the death penalty, displaced peoples, torture, rape, and other violations, may at times, have a distinctly racial or ethnic dimension. In particular, events such as the genocides in Cambodia in the 1970s, Iraq in the 1980s, Rwanda and the former Yugoslavian republic of Bosnia-Herzegovina in the 1990s, and now the Sudan, are powerfully grim reminders of the ways in which race and ethnicity act as destabilizing factors in international relations. Given these events, it is easy to understand why race and ethnicity are central to the study of international affairs.

In the United States, the study of race and foreign policy, as currents within international affairs, are enjoying a renaissance as more and more scholars are examining the ways in which race influences U.S. decisions, actions and conduct in international affairs. This is due to several factors, one being the U.S. civil rights movement, on the one hand and the centrifugal role African Americans have played in influencing U.S. foreign policy considerations, on the other. Major events of the nineteenth, twentieth, and twenty-first centuries illustrate the role of African American social movements: from the anti-slavery campaigns of the late nineteenth century, to the black participation in the Abraham Lincoln Brigade that fought in Franco's Spain; from the question of colonialism and formation of the United Nations, to the war in Vietnam; from the liberation struggles in southern Africa to the role of black activists and intellectuals at the World Conference against Racism (2001), speak to the crucial role that African Americans have played in international affairs. Oftentimes their views have been diametrically opposed to the official policies of the United States.

Within the social sciences—history, sociology, political science, international relations, African American Studies, and Women's Studies—race and its intersectional consequences, when properly used as a conceptual tool, provides a unique understanding, a deeper interpretation, and a more nuanced critique of social relations. More recently, scholars have widened their understanding of the constituencies that influence foreign policy making. In particular, they have come to realize that U.S. foreign relations are embedded in complex social, economic, cultural, and political factors of domestic as well as foreign origins. The race relation approach offers practical assistance in dealing with international issues, and it helps to broaden awareness that race itself is a salient factor in international relations (Plummer 2002, 3).

Race and International Affairs

In a 1969 article in *Foreign Affairs*, "Color in World Affairs," Harold Isaacs argued that the modern world was created as a racially hierarchical polity, globally dominated by Europeans and North Americans and that the world as of the late 1940s was by and large white and Western dominated (Isaacs 1969, 235). Unfortunately, this still holds true even until today. While the old structures of formal colonialism and de jure colonialism, have been dismantled through the painful processes of decolonization, national liberation movements, social revolutions, civil rights movements, and anti-apartheid struggles, the fundamental nature of Western control—read as mainly as white—over the rest of the world—read as mainly as nonwhite—is largely intact. This control was ensured and based on a series of institutions elaborated in the aftermath of World War II.

These post–World War II political institutions—some inter-connected and overlapping and other not—were designed based on the social and political power of the United States and the old Soviet Union. The United States as a main hegemonic power would take the lead in the establishment of a new post-war framework that would include: the United Nations and the Security Council, the Bretton Woods System, the World Bank and the International Monetary Fund, the North Atlantic Treaty Organization, and other multi-lateral institutions; these leading hegemonic actors, would preside over the world making decisions for the whole of humanity, the majority of which being nonwhite.

Within this context the concept of a racialized social system is quite useful for the study of international relations. Its application to foreign policy and international affairs establishes a framework to better understand and analyze the role of racialized social systems. For example, the trans-atlantic slave trade; colonialism in African, Asia, and Latin America, which were part of the field of international relations, as they were clearly subjected to the rules, laws, interpretations, and conventions of international treaties; and apartheid in the United States and South Africa were in fact racialized social systems. A racialized system refers to societies or systems in which economic, political, social, and ideological levels are structured by the placement of actors in racial categories. These systems are structured or conditioned by race because social systems articulate two or more hierarchical patterns (Bonilla-Silva 1996, 469).

In short, all racialized social systems place peoples within racial categories and differential hierarchies that produce particular social relations between or among the groups. The group or groups placed in the superior position (i.e., usually as defined by their position within the political economy) tends to have more access to the political process, higher levels of income and capital, access to land, better education and health care, and is granted more social value (e.g., smarter or better looking); and has the power to define social boundaries between themselves and "others" or what W.E.B. Du Bois called the psychological wage. The totality of these racialized social relations and practices constitute the racial structure of a society (Bonilla-Silva 1996, 470).

In the aftermath of World War II, the United States apartheid framework systematically excluded blacks from voting rights and effective political participation to jobs within the federal bureaucracy. As a consequence, few blacks were employed by the U.S. foreign policy establishment. Although blacks were sharp critics of U.S. foreign policy from the outside, few were able or allowed to a get foot inside. In *Black Diplomacy: African Americans and the State Department, 1945–1969*, Michael Krenn points out that historically blacks were excluded from positions within the foreign policy establishments and the important posts at the State Department. He argues that in 1950, of the thirty-three blacks in the Foreign Service, two-thirds were employed in traditionally black posts in Liberia. Except for the newly appointed ambassador, Edward P. Dudley, nearly all held low-grade positions (Krenn 1999).

He posits that institutional racism and elitism—the "old boy's club" mentality—explains why blacks and other outsiders were excluded or not recruited and employed in the foreign policy bureaucracy. The preference for white men who were southern bred and/or Ivy League–trained to serve as career officers remained unchanged over the second half of the twentieth century. He contends that, however, during the Truman years, "Department of State officials slowly came to the conclusion that race would play an important role in the postwar world" and realized "that America's domestic racial problem was now a foreign policy problem" (Krenn 1999).

Krenn also points out in the *African American Voice in U.S. Foreign Policy since World War II*, that social scientists are starting to examine the intersection of race and U.S. foreign policy. New questions are being raised: Does racism influence U.S. policies toward people of color (at home and abroad)? What was the role of racism in specific policy actions and formulations: Manifest Destiny and the wars with Mexico, the war in the Pacific against Japan, and the decision to drop the atomic bomb? How did African Americans in the United States develop a foreign policy framework, and how did it affect issues such as the occupation of Haiti, the Italo-Ethiopian War, attitudes toward decolonization of Africa, and relations with South Africa (Krenn 1988)? These are crucial questions.

Krenn argues that in the aftermath of World War II, one the most significant development in terms of race and U.S. foreign policy was the emergence of a much stronger and vocal African American voice in U.S. foreign relations. African Americans understood intuitively and intellectually that the organic forms of oppression at home were tied or linked to the situations of other oppressed peoples abroad. Moreover, African Americans saw the concrete links between their own struggles for human rights at home and the struggles of peoples of color across the globe.

Similarly Mary L. Dudziak's seminal study, *Cold War Civil Rights: Race and the Image of American Democracy* (2000), explores the impact of foreign affairs on U.S. civil rights policy during the early years of the Cold War (1946–1968). After World War II, the United States took on the mantle of world leadership, yet, at the same time, found itself subject to increasing international criticism. According to Dudziak (2000), American racism was seen as the nation's Achilles heel. U.S. allies, as well as critics, questioned whether civil rights abuses undermined the international image of the United States and interfered with its leadership of the free world. How could American democracy be held out as a model for others to follow, particularly newly independent nations in Asia and Africa, when within U.S. borders persons of color were lynched, were segregated in schools and public accommodations, and were disenfranchised? When the Soviet Union made American racism a principle anti-American propaganda theme in the late 1940s, civil rights in America became the terrain upon which an important Cold War ideological battle would be waged.

Dudziak (2000) argues that concerns about the impact of race discrimination on U.S. foreign relations led presidents from Truman through Johnson to pursue civil rights reform as part of their broader Cold War strategies. While foreign affairs was only one of the factors motivating civil rights reform during these years, it was crucial in understanding why a period of domestic repression, such as the Cold War, was simultaneously, also a period during which some civil rights reform would take hold. According to Dudziak, for nearly twenty years, countering the problem of race was an important issue in America's Cold War policy. The government tried—however unsuccessfully—to portray the story of race in democratic America as one of progress. Consequently, civil rights reform was uneven, if not sporadic, as Washington had to bring reality more in line with its ideological rhetoric. Thus, she argues, civil rights reform was in part a product of the Cold War.

Brenda Gayle Plummer's edited volume, *Window on Freedom: Race, Civil Rights, and Foreign Affairs, 1945–1988* (2003) explores how race mediated freedom in the foreign relations of the United States. She argued that Gunnar Myrdal's *An American Dilemma* (1944), was a high watermark in the history of race relations as his work broke new ground in making what had been an insurgent view within the social sciences normative in the academy. Despite the work that black scholars had been producing for years, the new view of race gained legitimacy only when underwritten and rubber-stamped by a scholar anointed by the mainstream academic leadership. One of the derivative benefits of Myrdal's study is that it legitimated a discourse that explicitly linked racial reform with the desired world order.

In stark contrast to the traditional power relations or realist approach that emphasizes power struggles among nation-states this volumes offers a pluralist view on international affairs. It examines the full range of political, social, and ideological behaviors as well as the role of non-government actors and how they influence foreign policy. According to Plummer (2003), in the post–World War II period, racism undermined U.S. global leadership and strained its relations with countries that had a stake in achieving global racial equality; likewise, racial discrimination in the United States had implications for relations between European states and their former colonies. By linking U.S. domestic politics to international affairs, it is argued that the overall struggle for human rights by racial and ethnic minorities is best understood within the context of competitive international relations.

There are, of course, other works that critically explore race and the intersection of U.S. foreign policy and international affairs. The scholarship on the convergence of race; civil rights; the Cold War; African Americans and human rights; McCarthyism; and the impact of black radicalism on U.S. foreign affairs is flowering. Gerald Horne's classic work *Communist Front? The Civil Rights Congress, 1946–1956* (1988), to Penny Von Eschen's *Race against the Empire: Black Americans and Anti-Colonialism, 1937–1957* (1997)—and many more—demonstrate the full range of works now emerging on race, foreign policy, and international relations.

Powell and Rice: The New American Century

Colin Powell and Condoleezza Rice: Foreign Policy, Race, and the New American Century examines race, gender, and the construction of U.S. foreign policy. It is an impressive work: It adds to the scarce literature on the intersection of race, gender, and international relations, and it magnifies our interpretative power regarding the ways that African Americans have influenced foreign policy and international affairs. How have African Americans—churches, the media, intellectuals, activists, non-governmental groups, trade unionists, congresswomen and men—framed, articulated, and implemented foreign policy issues and strategies? Is it even possible to speak of a uniquely African American foreign policy? These questions set the stage for an interesting analysis and critique of Colin Powell and Condoleezza Rice as leading foreign policy architects. Given the body of materials by Powell and Rice—speeches, interviews, articles, and public pronouncements—to date there is little systematic and detailed analysis reflecting their views as key foreign policy strategists. This book fills this void nicely.

The rise of Colin Powell and Condoleezza Rice as U.S. foreign policy architects raises a number of substantive and complex questions regarding U.S. foreign policy. It is clear that their appointments served to place race as well as gender firmly within the fluid parameters of international relations and U.S. foreign policy. The year 2000 was a watershed year for black political power as Colin Powell became the first black secretary of state, and Condoleezza Rice became the first black national security advisor, thus making her the first black and woman to hold this post. Subsequently, Rice in 2004, was named secretary of state, making her the second black to be named as secretary of state and the first black woman to hold this post. It could be argued convincingly that as persons of color, a black man and a black woman, that holding these positions has served to place race and gender squarely at the center of international relations and foreign affairs. It could be further argued that their rise to the highest and most powerful positions within the U.S. foreign policy establishment serves to spotlight the role of African Americans in the area of international affairs as never before. Before their appointments, blacks had never held such high posts within with the U.S. foreign policy establishment. However, a black foreign consensus—the attempt by African Americans to influence U.S. foreign policy—has existed for years.

Moreover, the fact that they were appointed by an extremely conservative Republican administration that lost the popular vote in the 2000, and with little or no ties to a black constituency, only serves to raise more thorny and complicated questions. While there have been black ambassadors and a handful of blacks operating within the State Department machinery over the years, there had never been any black Americans—before them—with such important roles in constructing, articulating, and representing the United States in foreign affairs. In fact, with their appointments they became the highest ranking blacks in the U.S. government ever. It should be pointed out, however, that long before Powell and Rice, African Americans (as outsiders and insiders) historically had played important and crucial roles in shaping U.S. foreign policy interests and considerations.

This is one of the first books to examine the intersection of race, gender, and the politics of U.S. hegemony. It analyzes the roles, influences and, more important, the social construction of U.S. foreign policy by Colin Powell and Condoleezza Rice as African Americans within the framework of international relations. Few African Americans have played such key roles in the social construction and implementation of U.S. foreign policy as Powell and Rice. There are some works on Powell and Rice, although uneven, and they are not very critical. However, *Colin Powell and Condoleezza Rice: Foreign Policy, Race, and the New American Century* is one of the first serious attempts to place their views, policy positions, speeches, interviews, and their overall approach to U.S. foreign policy and international affairs within the parameters of international relations and domestic politics by a leading political science scholar. By examining the intersection of race, gender, politics, and hegemony this work moves way beyond the traditional scope of the international relations framework. By problematizing the intersection of race, gender, and politics, Clarence Lusane opens critical new spaces of inquiry long ignored by scholars of U.S. foreign policy and international relations.

Does racial identity as well as racial perceptions on the domestic and international level help shape the consumption of the new paradigm in U.S. foreign policy as presented by Powell and Rice?

How does their racial identity disturb or interrupt conventional notions about the role of race in international affairs?

Given the long history of African American participation in foreign affairs, in what ways do Powell's and Rice's views converge or deviate from other influential African Americans (W.E.B. Du Bois, Shirley Graham Du Bois, Paul Robeson, and Ralph Bunche)?

What is the political relationship among race, contemporary U.S. foreign policy, and global security in the post–September 11 era?

By posing such questions—as well as providing answers—Lusane liberates international relations and U.S. foreign policy from its staid and rigid approach that ignores or downplays race and its intersectional consequences. By doing so, he provides a fresh angle from which to examine U.S. foreign affairs, international relations, and the crucial role of African Americans in international affairs. This work is a critical as well as a serious examination of the reconfiguration of U.S. national security strategy and the commonly referred to "war against terrorism." Against the backdrop of Bush's newly emerging security paradigm, pivotal foreign policy adventures are analyzed that include: the World Conference against Racism 2001; the attacks of September 11, 2001; the invasion of Afghanistan (2001) and Iraq (2003); the ouster of Jean-Bertrand Aristide in Haiti (2004); and Bush's foreign policy toward Africa, Latin America, and the Caribbean—to name only a few.

Lusane meticulously locates Powell and Rice shifts and transformations as foreign policy thinkers within the historical and ideological evolution of the Republican Party. He draws a high resolution picture of Powell and Rice within the larger context of black Republican activism. Powell and Rice, as two of the most visible and powerful black Republicans, are considered oddities. First, neither has been elected to political office. Second, unlike some black Republicans, they became Republicans late in their political lives. Third, both use race strategically and symbolically when it is convenient or necessary. Fourth, both use the raw narrative power and moral underpinnings of the civil rights movement, albeit differently, in their official discourse. However, it is Powell more that Rice, who has drawn a clear distinction between himself and the Republican Party. Powell is pro-choice, believes in a person's right to bear arms, but posits some form of gun control, and supports affirmative action. It is argued that as players in the administration, Powell's views were considered more centrist or moderate while Rice was further to the Right. Powell, moreover, appears to be more race conscious than Rice as he generally acknowledges that his achievements can be attributed to affirmative action.

Lusane accurately points out that within the broad trajectory of the Republican Party, the black moderate Republican view, such as Powell and others, has increasingly been drowned out by a more aggressive, vocal, and influential current lead by far right elements. This dominant right leaning faction, sometimes referred to as the neo-conservatives, would emerge in George W. Bush's administration as the main architects of U.S. foreign policy and international relations. According to the neo-conservatives, the United States is and remains unchallenged in its military, political, and economic power; and, the main strategic priority should, therefore, be to preserve and extend its advantageous position well into the future. Additionally, the unilateral use of force with or without the consent of U.S. traditional allies, multi-lateral institutions, and without regard to domestic and world opinion is a view common among neo-conservatives.

Along these lines, the United States has clashed with its traditional allies and the global civil society over Iraq; it has provided a rather novel if not untenable interpretation of the Geneva Accords by refusing to acknowledge prisoners of war; it has demonstrated unmitigated contempt toward the United Nations and the European Union—only using the UN when it fits its needs; it has unsigned an international human rights treaty (the Rome Treaty that established the International Criminal Court), and cut bilateral agreements with other countries stipulating that under no circumstances should U.S. soldiers be delivered to any body investigating war crimes; it has also allegedly practiced rendition—kidnapping and arresting a suspect in one country and taking him to another for interrogation, torture, and detention; and it has been widely alleged, but not yet proven, that the United States has secret American detention centers in Eastern Europe. This is U.S. exceptionalism taken to new levels.

It is argued that Powell would find his views more and more isolated as Rice continued her hard shift to the Far Right. It would be the views of the neo-conservatives—after years of being on the fringe—that emerges as the most contentious, controversial, and divisive aspects of U.S. foreign policy and international relations. Their views, which only ten years ago, were considered untenable, unworkable, and inconsistent with post–World War II U.S. foreign policy would now find expression. As Richard Holbrook opined, the neo-conservatives' views were "a radical break with 55 years of bipartisan tradition in U.S. foreign policy" (Barry and Lobe 2002).

Lusane astutely points out that strength should not be equated with legitimacy. Using political scientist Randolph Persaud's concept of "primitive hegemony," it is argued that Bush's foreign policy team believes that "strength is more important than legitimacy." Powell and Rice would now play key roles in the execution of the neo-conservative game plan. The supreme irony is that Powell and Rice entered the administration as realists. As protégés of Brent Scrowcroft's realist thinking, they would now be constricted to the neo-conservative's ideological straitjacket. The question is: How will Powell, the moderate centrist, and Rice, the unreconstructed realist, navigate the treacherous terrain of neo-conservative foreign policy? It is against this backdrop that this book deconstructs with laser-like precision the broader policy objectives of neo-conservative paradigms with Powell and Rice at the center.

References

Barry, Tom, and Jim Lobe. "The Men Who Stole the Show." *Foreign Policy in Focus*, October 2002.

Bonilla-Silva, Eduardo. "Rethinking Racism: Towards a Structural Interpretation." *American Sociological Review* 62 (June 1996): 465–480.

Crenshaw, Kimbele, ed. *Critical Race Theory that formed the Movement*. New York: New York University Press, 1995.

Delgado, Richard. *Critical Race Theory: An Introduction*. New York: New York University Press, 2001.

Dudziak, Mary L. *Cold War Civil Rights: Race and the Image of American Democracy*. Princeton: Princeton University Press, 2000.

Horne, Gerald. *Black and Red: W.E.B. Du Bois and the Afro-American Response to the Cold War*. Albany: SUNY Press, 1986.

———. *Communist Front? The Civil Rights Congress, 1946–1956*. London and Toronto: Associated University Press, 1988.

Isaacs, Harold. "Race and Color in World Affairs." *Foreign Affairs* 28 (January 1969): 235–250.

Krenn, Michael. *The African Voice in U.S. Foreign Policy since World War II*. New York: Garland Publishing, 1988.

———. *Black Diplomacy: African Americans and the State Department, 1945–1969*. Armonk, NY: M.E. Sharpe, 1999.

Persaud, Randolph B. "Shades of American Hegemony: The Primitive, the Enlightened, and the Benevolent." *Connecticut Journal of International Law* (spring 2004).

Plummer, Brenda Gayle, ed. *Window on Freedom: Race, Civil Rights, and Foreign Affairs, 1945–1988*. Chapel Hill: University of North Carolina Press, 2003.

Von Eschen, Penny. *Race against Empire: Black Americans and Anticolonialism, 1937–1957*. Ithaca, NY: Cornell University Press, 1997.

Kwame Dixon
Distinguished Visiting Professor of Black Studies
DePauw University, Indiana.

Acknowledgments

As always there are so many individuals and institutions to thank for their invaluable assistance, comments, views, and sacrifices to turn an idea into the book you are reading. I began this project while living and working in London from 2001 to 2003. Critical intellectual and political support and friendship were given by my co-worker/friends at The 1990 Trust, the UK's most effective anti-racist human rights organization. Much thanks to Karen Chouhan, Lee Jasper, Lydia Brathwaite, Haven Lutaaya, Audrey Adams, and everyone else. My other indispensable London "advisors" and "consultants" included Rubina Asfar, Etienne Bryan, Makeda Coaston, Barbara Cohen, Alpa Kapasi, Azra Khan, Rhon Reynolds, Albert Rose, Donna St. Hill, Amina Sidikhoya, Veena Vasista, Simon Wooley, and Patrick Yu. For most of the time I lived in London, I also had the good fortune to know and borrow ideas directly from one of the most perceptive and insightful journalists of our times, Gary Young of the *Guardian* newspaper.

In addition, there were the other refugees from Bush's America who were there at the time who also contributed ideas, beer, and pub hopping to this project. Thanks to Catrell Brown, Sunita Patel, Aisha Tyrus, and Natalie Williams.

A wide number of friends and colleagues in other parts of Europe were also requisite. This includes Michael Simmons (Hungary), Kwame Dixon (Spain), Aranka Kellerman (the Netherlands), Filamena Henrique (Portugal), Nicola Laure al Samari (Germany), Dimitria Clayton (Germany), Sheila Mysorekar (Germany), the Black German Initiative (ISD), Debbie Robinson (Switzerland), Bashy Quraishy (Denmark), and the rest of the ENAR folks, Brima Conte (France), and Anatasia Tsoukala (France).

As always, my colleagues in the School of International Service at the American University remain critical sources of scholarship, insights, and general support. Thanks and much appreciation to Phil Brenner, Carol Gallaher, Lou Goodman, Nanette Levinson, Randolph Persaud, and Cathy Schneider. My graduate and undergraduate assistants were also very crucial in making this book happen. They conducted research, read and edited the manuscript, wrote letters, and hung in there. Thanks to Helen McClure, Kristin Rawls, and Jim Bredemus.

There were countless folks who sent articles to me, told me stories, shared ideas, and were just friends at the right time. This includes Karen Jefferson, James Steele, Cheryl Hanna, Cecelie Counts, Sylvia Hill, Geoffrey Jacques, James Early, Karin Stanford, Mark Harrison, Melvin Lewis, Nathalie Thandiwe, Daryl Harris, Bill Fletcher, and Carleen and Walter Watson. My apologies for anyone that I omitted.

Many of the topics and ideas in this book were road tested. Venues included the Institute for Policy Studies (thanks John, Karen, Phyllis, and everyone), National Conference of Black Political Scientists, and my jazz conspirators in the Listening Group and at our Tuesday night jams (Aisha, Barry, Munier, Joe, Tariq, Michael, Tom, Askia, Fred, Wilmer, Foodhead, Mike, Howard, Willard, and everybody).

This book began with an unsolicited email from Jim Lance, then an editor at Praeger, about another subject he wanted me to write about. However, very quickly Jim and I decided on doing this book, and he became its champion. I cannot thank Jim enough for his determination and tireless efforts to turn rough ideas into finished work and to argue the importance of this work in the face of initial opposition. He is truly a warrior.

I also must give a deep thanks to my extremely patient editor Hilary Claggett and my extremely meticulous copyeditor Arlene Belzer.

My summer in Ghana working on this book was facilitated appreciatively by O. T., the best guide ever.

In a project of this type there are always people to thank whose contribution is much more personal and all-encompassing than anything else. This has been especially true of my close friends and family in Detroit and New Jersey. Although they shared ideas and gave meaningful feedback, more important was their daily presence in my life and helping to keep it normal in the face of deadlines, writing blocks, and real-life events. Special and unqualified thanks and much love to James Steele, Ayo Heinegg, and my cousin Noelle Lusane.

Finally, I want to give heartfelt recognition to Zezeh, who actually had absolutely nothing to do with this book but everything to do with my happiness at waking up each morning. It must be said.

Introduction

> I'm in the refrigerator.... I'm in the ice box.... They've got me put
> way and they'll pull me out like a carton of milk when they need me,
> and then put me back.
>
> Colin Powell[1]

Colin Powell and Condoleezza Rice were the first two appointments announced
by George W. Bush after officially being declared the winner in the controversial 2000 presidential election. In fact, the first four announcements by Bush
were two blacks (Powell and Rice), one Hispanic (Alberto R. Gonzales as White
House counsel) and one other woman (Karen P. Hughes as counselor to the
president). These strategically timed announcements were proffered, in part, to
blunt criticisms of racial and gender exclusion long associated with the Republican Party.[2]

Coming on the heels of one of the most contentious elections in U.S.
history—buoyed by the widespread conviction among African Americans that
the disenfranchisement of black votes in Florida were the key to Bush's victory—
the nominations were drenched in racial and political irony. Although Bush
studiously evaded the issue of race in his remarks surrounding the nominations,
few were unaware that Powell was about to become the first black secretary of
state and Rice the first black woman (and first woman) national security advisor.
Explicitness being unnecessary, race was put on the shelf by the president.
Powell, on the other hand, did raise the issue directly. He stated that he believed
news reports would note that he was to become the first African American
secretary of state.

And I'm glad they will say that, and I want it repeated. I want it repeated because I hope it will give inspiration to young African-Americans coming along—but beyond that, all young Americans coming along—that no matter where you began in this society with hard work and with dedication and with the opportunities that are presented by this society, there are no limitations on you. And I also want to pay tribute to so many people who helped me reach this position in life: African-Americans who came before me who never could have risen to this position because the conditions weren't there and we had to fight to change those conditions.[3]

Rice would also, for the moment, take race off the shelf. In her very brief remarks, she stated, "If I may close with just a personal note, this is an extraordinary time for America because our values are being affirmed, and it's important to always remember what those values are at home. And I grew up in Birmingham, Ala. I did not go to integrated schools until I was in 10th grade and we moved to Denver, Colorado."[4]

The nexus of racial advancement and the Bush administration's highly managed image of U.S. foreign policy objectives would echo, sometimes softly, sometimes loudly, during Powell's and Rice's tenures. Both Powell and Rice linked their success to the view that great progress had been made in overcoming the nation's fractious racial past, and they were living proof of it. Leapfrogging another black Republican appointment from a political generation back—Supreme Court Justice Clarence Thomas—they would become the highest ranking black U.S. government officials ever. This also meant that they would become two of the most powerful and influential figures in international politics.

The shelving and unshelving of race, or rather its strategic employment, would characterize not only Powell, Rice, and the Bush administration's racial perspective on a range of issues, but also shape its domestic and international policies. It was not only Powell who was put on the shelf except when needed to make a political point, but the entire panorama of issues related to civil rights, equal opportunity, racial equality, and global racism. More than any other president in the post–World War II era, the Bush administration engaged in what political writer and activist James Steele terms appropriately "deracialized racism."[5] As he notes, by ignoring the issue of race and cultivating a constituency that allowed it to do so, the "Republican Party does not have serious internal racial dynamics to manage. . . . It can simply advance platitudes, accuse the Democratic Party of taking blacks for granted, while attempting to take African Americans and Latinos for a ride."[6] George W. Bush and those in his administration responsible for addressing issues of inclusion and bigotry embraced the position that except for a few individual cases and a few individual miscreants racism had been overcome effectively barely worthy of presidential discussion or attention. As detailed in chapter 3, Bush rarely mentions terms such as "civil rights," "equal rights," "diversity," or "discrimination," and when he does it is usually not related to addressing racism or any substantial initiatives from his administration.

Given the history of the United States, the appointment of two black Americans to the highest level of U.S. foreign policy making would be significant under normal circumstances. Their tenure has taken place under circumstances that were far from normal. Already engaged in a repositioning of U.S. global relations, Bush's response to the terrorist's attacks of September 11 accelerated the speed by which the administration would attempt to preserve and expand its radical program of unchallengeable hegemony. September 11 was a turning point, not because it focused the United States and the world on terrorism, but it provided the near perfect storm justification for all future foreign policy (and many domestic) initiatives whether they had to do directly with terrorism or not. Within the context of the events of September 11, the reconfiguration of the U.S. national security strategy and the wars in Afghanistan and Iraq, assessing the ideological and political roles of Powell and Rice is made more complicated by the intersection of race, politics, and hegemonic assertion. It is argued here that racial identity and racial perceptions on both the domestic and global levels shaped the consumption of this new paradigm in U.S. foreign policy as presented by Powell and Rice through the creation of a racialized regime of representation. This framework of representation, as expressed across many spaces, ideologies, and experiences, is the subject of this book and interrogated throughout.

This work critically examines the roles that Powell and Rice played in the construction of U.S. foreign policy under the George W. Bush administration and how their racial identity disturbs conventional and widespread notions about the role of race in international relations. Neither Powell nor Rice consciously allowed their racial identity to substantially influence or characterize their participation in the defense and projection of U.S. hegemony although they would both use their racial identity and experiences in key circumstances to argue and defend Bush administration policies. In this sense, they occasionally practiced what could be called strategic racial affinity, that is, bringing race off the shelf when useful. Despite their reluctance to be seen as racial figures, from a number of publics their race was significant in the consumption of U.S. foreign (and sometimes domestic) policy. Among the publics concerned with these questions were:

- The **Republican Party** for whom the trope of racial inclusion and upward mobility, projected to the party's moderates, helps mask substantive policy that attacks affirmative action and other core issues important to the black community and other racial minorities

- The **U.S. state**, in the immediate form of the Bush administration, that needs to project a post-racism image of U.S. society as constitutive of its marketing of U.S. hegemony

- The **U.S. black community** for whom the issue of racial representation still animates much of black political discourse and activity although there is little consensus on what that representation should be or what it is suppose to achieve

- The **U.S. white community** including both liberals, who have been cautious in criticizing Powell and Rice because of fear of being labeled racists, and conservatives, who use them to argue that color blind society has arrived, and, any criticism of the two (by white and black liberals) is probably racist

- The **international black community**, that is, in Africa and throughout the African Diaspora, that has in various ways also felt representational issues, particularly regarding Powell, who is of Jamaican heritage, that conflicts with their nearly unanimous rejection of U.S. foreign policy, and that has also been challenged to rethink long held views about the progressive or even radical political character of U.S. black communities

- **Multi-racial and multi-ethnic states** that have minority representation issues to address who have identified Powell and Rice as patriotic models of accommodation and achievement to be applauded and emulated

The disappointment that some black Americans feel toward Powell and naked anger at Rice—deemed a "race traitor" by a major black website and a prominent black academic—reflects a nod to the complicated and often untenable politics of racial representation, a politics effectively exploited by the Bush administration.[7] The racial hope by some that Powell or Rice would be "loyal" to the race led to unreal expectations. In fact, Powell and Rice have been remarkably consistent in their views and behavior on the nexus of their racial identity and their ideological stance. In addition to a certain level of racial shelving, Powell's passive-aggressive approach and Rice's hard-line loyalty were on display in the past administrations that they both served. That they accommodated themselves to the Bush post–September 11 agenda, indeed, helped develop it, is simply not surprising given their histories. Unlike many, I do not assume that (while having differences) Powell was an outsider politically and neither does he in terms of his public pronouncements about the Bush administration. He accepted, articulated, and promoted the fundamental assumptions of the Bush doctrine. Now that he is out of office, he may state otherwise, but this will constitute a direct conflict with clear public statements and authored articles he made during his tenure as secretary of state, as well as his political actions. He certainly expressed difference in terms of means, methods, and temperament in how to achieve Bush's objectives, but though important these differences were not a fundamental break with the paradigm of hegemony.

All of this is not to say that their race does not matter, for it does. Popular perceptions of their racial meaning(s)—what Stuart Hall perceptively calls "floating signifiers"—and the behavior that arises out of those perceptions provide insights into the workings and contours of contemporary race politics, the intersection of race with U.S. foreign policy, and the racial interests of a number of different publics as noted above.[8] These overlapping and interlinked processes raise a number of pertinent questions including:

- Are race and ethnicity no longer barriers to reaching the highest levels of strategic foreign policy making?

- Are Powell and Rice, ultimately, high-level functionaries operating within scopes in which they can agree but cannot fundamentally decide or did they substantially determine the direction of U.S. foreign policy?

- What is the political relationship between race, contemporary U.S. foreign policy, and global security in the post–September 11 era?

- How will the growing immigration of people of color impact on the construction and consumption of U.S. foreign policy?

- How can a progressive alternative to the current U.S. foreign policy be realized?

- Is there a black consensus on foreign policy and, if so, what are its dimensions, driving force(s), and stability?

This work locates Powell and Rice within the genealogy of the current national security strategy, and broader foreign policy shifts under George W. Bush, and argues that their racial location in the context of the construction of U.S. foreign policy is symbolic and serves to distract from the substantive part they play in the ongoing reconfiguration of U.S. global power. It specifically focuses on the role and representational significance of Powell and Rice in relation to the most critical revamping of the discourses and strategies of global politics in the last half century. The hegemonic objectives of the U.S. state and the global corporate, military, and ideological interests that it represents have spawned and sustained a more dangerous and callous world in which neo-liberal economic policies eviscerate all social safety nets, and neo-conservative foreign policy is conducted through military preponderance further devastating the lives of billions. The racio-class disparities that mark U.S. society are mirrored by the growing economic and social gaps that shape virtually every society in the international system. The ongoing many-headed social crises—AIDS, civil war, poverty, debt, fallout from natural disasters, fundamentalist extremism, and so on—engulfing much of the world with little relief in sight is neither incidental nor accidental. It is the collateral impact and ultimate consequence of the strategic thinking and planning that was able to take advantage of the disruptive shocks of September 11, but in an organic way having little to do with the resolution of those events. The Bush administration's war on terrorism is a bait-and-switch political operation that while calling for a global war on terrorism (and failing to address strategically or effectively the causes of contemporary global terrorism) has used the fear of the phenomena to bully through policies— foreign and domestic—that would have been difficult if not impossible to implement prior to September 11, 2001.

More than in any other period since World War II, the Bush administration is enacting what political scientist Randolph Persaud has termed "primitive hegemony."[9] He notes that among other features the principle that "strength is more important than legitimacy"[10] is perhaps the most salient. It is certainly no stretch to argue that in the current period, the United States has been willing to rebuff virtually the entire global community, from institutions and governments to popular opinion and millions of street protesters, in its quest to advance its agenda in the Middle East and beyond. Equally important has been Persaud's point that "primitive hegemony assumes its own national and cultural values are superior, and, in fact, universal."[11] As captured in post-2004 election statements by Bush and Rice, the United States intends to spread its notions of "freedom" and "liberty" around the world.[12] The righteousness of this effort is so self-evident, assumes Bush, that it deserves no debate.

Hegemony in Crisis

There is little debate among scholars that the United States emerged as a hegemon following the end of the Cold War. It was and remains unrivaled in its capacity to project military, political, and economic power anywhere on the globe. This preponderance of power is defended consciously and methodically and across the mainstream political spectrum of U.S. foreign policy strategists is a solid consensus that any rival to this configuration must be prevented.

However, maintaining global domination is easier said than done. The challenge to hegemony appears to be everywhere not the least driven by the Bush administration's military hubris and overextension and political arrogance. The instability in Afghanistan and Iraq, despite the direct military and political take-over of these states by tens of thousands of U.S. troops, is only a flash of a larger wildfire of resistance in the region and beyond. In spectacular fashion, the goal of dominating the Middle East is faltering. Afghanistan is not stable despite show elections with little political control outside of Kabul. Even the United States has been forced to acknowledge that "With an estimated 40 to 60 percent of its GDP attributed to narcotics...Afghanistan is on the verge of becoming a narcotics state."[13] Iraq's resistance shows no signs of degradation and is likely winning support each day the United States remains as occupiers. Even Powell, according to *Newsweek International*, grew to believe that the insurgents were winning the battle on the ground.[14] Elsewhere in the regions, avid U.S. support for repressive regimes in Saudi Arabia, Egypt, and elsewhere only enflames the Arab street and erodes any support from even the most democratic of forces. The gross imbalance shown by the United States in the Palestine-Israeli conflict furthers erodes its credibility and believability about a fair resolution.

Thousands of miles away, in Latin America, a new generation of progres-sive and leftist parties and movements is stirring. In Brazil, Uruguay, Chile, Bolivia, Argentina, and Venezuela, they have come to power and strongly ad-vocated for a fairer political and economic global justice. Even Mexico refused to go along with some U.S. proposals including opposing Bush's war in Iraq and the abhorrently unacceptable policies of the United States and Western-dominated World Trade Organization. Meanwhile, accommodationist pro-U.S. govern-ments in Colombia, Guatemala, and elsewhere have weak legitimacy and are surviving under the most tenuous of circumstances. And, of course, Cuba remains defiant despite the harshest policies of perhaps any administration toward the island since the Bay of Pigs invasion, policies made even more incongruous by the transformation of the U.S. base at Guantanamo into an edifice of violations against international law and human rights standards.

In Asia, North Korea and China have only grown as powers that seek to challenge the U.S. presence in the region. The "Iraq" solution has little capital against these two nuclear powers, yet the administration's approach has been belligerent and tactless in most issues related to Asia. China's influence is as-cending as Washington's wanes accelerated by Bush's often crude policy stands. India is also rising as both a regional power and a leader of the global South. While it is more or less an ally of the United States, its Hindu and Muslim populations are not naturally so and popular resistance to Bush's policies have been strong.

While virtually all states in Africa have had to lasso themselves to the United States out of economic necessity, it has not been uncontested terrain either. The

United States was criticized heavily in Africa for bowing out of the UN World Conference against Racism held in Durban, South Africa, in 2001, and a year later Powell was booed during his very brief appearance at the UN World Summit on Sustainable Development also held in South Africa. And to the surprise of many, in 2003, then UN Security Council members Angola, Cameroon, and Guinea, under a great deal of pressure, refused to support the United States and Great Britain when they sought a second Security Council resolution to go to war against Iraq.

And finally, fissure with Europe has short-term and long-term implications that bode badly for the United States. The resistance to the U.S.-British war in Iraq is unlikely to ease not only because there is little popular support anywhere in Europe for their Iraq policies, but also because European leaders simply do not and cannot bear the costs of a restructuring that brings them little benefit politically. In the broader sense, both the Americans and the Europeans recognize that the European Union (EU), while never likely to become a military rival, certainly has the potential to challenge the United States economically and politically as it continues to grow. In fact, the reluctance to engage in U.S.-driven military campaigns has the grand advantage of allowing European governments to benefit from a real "peace dividend" and to spend capital on social and economic development rather than squander it on military adventurism. Though it lacks the reach of the United States, the EU has begun to emerge as an alternative political center. Indeed, it is the only entity in the international system with the capacity to contest politically the United States. Despite the administration's post-2004 election belated effort at reconciliation, the divisions are deeply rooted and linked to long-term agendas that are at odds.

Finally, domestic consensus on hegemonic defense and maintenance is tentative and one economic depression from collapse. Although Bush won the 2004 election, and despite the spin of Karl Rove, the margin was closer than the administration desired and, in any case, more than 57 million people voted against Bush, very few of whom accept his victory graciously or passively. The administration's capacity to carry out domestic programs such as Social Security reform and permanent tax cuts are held hostage by the costs of its military adventures and the means by which it seeks to press its war on terrorism. In addition, the costs of Katrina and other hurricane disasters, made more extensive by the administration's ineptitude and negligence, are heavy. Many Republicans in Congress take the long view and are very reluctant, rhetoric notwithstanding, to be the instigators of what could be the largest economic catastrophe since the Great Depression. Neither did the election solve Bush's Iraq problems. Bush sought to argue that his winning the 2004 race demonstrated acquiescence for his actions in Iraq. However, polls taken after the election show that there was in fact a deterioration of support as events on the ground by determined insurgents continued to dominate reports on the war.[15]

Of Rice and Men

In addition to the issues of race, perceptions of Rice must also be seen through the lens of gender politics. As Laura Flanders points out in *Bushwomen*, "Republicans have made a concentrated effort to cultivate their own female fight force" to compete with the gender gap in national elections that favored Democrats.[16] Under Bush, the GOP strategy of wooing women away from the Democratic Party includes the projection of its high-profile female appointees to foster an image of gender inclusion that had been absent in previous Republican administrations. That these women opposed overwhelmingly many of the issues that are championed by the women's movement or simply desired by ordinary women, such as equal pay for equal work, does not concern the Karl Roves of the administration. The political use of gender by the Republicans included Rice who campaigned strongly among women for Bush in 2000, and more surreptitiously in 2004, the latter generating a mini-scandal given a tradition of cabinet members or high-level administration officials staying above the political fray. Rice's travel schedule, as noted by the *Washington Post* and *Los Angeles Times*, coincided with the election map of the Bush campaign.[17]

From another angle, gender is relevant in media and popular curiosity of understanding the dynamics of an African American female operating on an equal or superior basis within an environment dominated by highly privileged and self-entitled white men starting with Bush himself. The administration argues that, like race, gender bias was not and is not a factor in how Rice is treated or engaged. Rice herself essentially repeats this theme contending that she has not only been accepted on relatively equal terms with her white male counterparts, but that discussion of gender bias degrades her achievements. She is unequivocal that she should be evaluated solely on her merits sans gender considerations. Sexist incidents, such as when Israeli Prime Minister Ariel Sharon stated that he could not concentrate during a meeting with her because he was staring at her legs, are dismissed as trivial and passing.[18] While little-to-no attention was paid to the physical characteristics of her predecessor Madeleine Albright, Rice's dress size, exercise routine, clothing selections, and even her walk are regularly commented on by journalists and columnists alike. These themes continued even after her elevation to secretary of state. Within several weeks of her assuming her new role, the *Washington Post* ran three extensive articles that focused on her attire (complete with pictures of her legs in long stylish black boots), her love of football, and food tastes, all in the *Style* section of the newspaper.[19] In describing Rice's clothing persona, on her first trip abroad as secretary of state, the *Washington Post* writer Robin Givhan wrote, "Rice brought her full self to the world stage—and that included her sexuality. It was not overt or inappropriate. If it was distracting, it is only because it is so rare."[20] The eroticizing and sexualization of Rice elicited only minor rebuttals, but demonstrated that her tenure will not be race or gender neutral despite her best wishes.

In God and Bush We Trust

Though given minor attention in most writings about Rice's relationship with Bush, perhaps the strongest connection between the two is not ideological or political, but religious. The born-again Bush mobilized millions of evangelical Christians in his 2000 and 2004 elections including large swaths of African Americans. Their presence has also been felt in the administration from policy initiatives, through issues such as same-sex marriage, abortion, and stem cell research, as well as being given plum positions such as attorney general under the first term of John Ashcroft.

Rice has stated on numerous occasions how her strong religious beliefs inform the moral dimensions of the policies that she articulates and defends as does Bush. Her father, John Rice, was a Presbyterian pastor, and church attendance and prayer were organic to the family's daily routines. She said of the president, "I love the fact that family means so much to him, and I love the fact that God means so much to him."[21]

It is practically an eleventh commandment for evangelicals that Bush is in the White House through divine intervention. Reverends Billy Graham, Jerry Falwell, and countless others have often repeated this act of faith. Indeed, Bush himself seems to carry that belief according to Stephen Mansfield's *The Faith of George W. Bush*, a study on the role of religion and faith in virtually every decision that Bush makes including political and policy ones.[22] Rice's deep religious faith and her loyalty to Bush, and their well-known tendency of frequently praying together indicates that she too does not necessarily separate religious mission from political mission.

Structure of Book

Chapter 1 traces the history of black American efforts to influence U.S. foreign policy from both inside and outside of government. Within a narrow scope of interests, a black foreign policy consensus has been forged in different periods and black leaders articulated that consensus to a domestic and international audience. The chapter also examines the efforts of those who have had official responsibilities representing U.S. foreign concerns who were part of the U.S. foreign service more generally, or black legislators in Congress who focused on foreign policy such as Reps. Donald Payne, Ron Dellums, and Charles Rangel among others. Powell and Rice are placed in this pantheon of activity as paradoxically extensions of it and deviations from it.

Chapter 2 revisits the experiences of blacks in the Republican Party, particularly regarding the discourses related to the ability of black party members to leverage policy considerations concerning both domestic and foreign policy. Though disenfranchised by both parties following the end of Reconstruction, the transition of loyalty from Republican to Democrat by the overwhelming majority of blacks was in part shaped by foreign policy issues.

Chapter 3 focuses on contemporary discourses and strategies that deal with race and racism and how they have impacted U.S. domestic and global politics and policies in this era. A broad overview is given of the status of race relations in the United States under Bush and how that shapes perceptions of Powell and Rice. The 2001 UN World Conference on Racism is explored as a case study on the intersection of race and Bush's foreign policy including the direct involvement of Powell and Rice in the decisions surrounding the U.S. posture toward the conference. Bush's record on race issues is also examined.

Chapter 4 places Colin Powell and Condoleezza Rice firmly within the framework of the emerging U.S. security paradigm that stresses U.S. military, economic, and political domination and the imperative of protecting that supremacy. The new strategy redefines international relations and U.S. relationships to international institutions such as the United Nations, NATO, and the European Union. Both Powell and Rice, albeit with different roles, involvement, and commitment to the new direction, are embedded in the U.S. strategic circles guiding this development. In the main, their race is put on the shelf though a substantial discourse on the impact of the new strategy on multi-culturalism, ethnic relations, global race relations, and social group integration has been and is being held within the highest echelons of foreign policy circles.

Chapter 5 looks at the application of the Bush doctrine in practice and the roles that Powell and Rice played in its implementation. The focus here is on the war in Iraq and their role in it.

Chapters 6 and 7 examine George W. Bush's foreign policy toward regions with large black populations and areas where the black American community has expressed its most concern. This is not to exclude the interests of people of African descent who live in Europe, Asia, the Pacific islands and the Middle East, but their issues have not been embraced substantially or even recognized in the practice of U.S. black politics. This chapter analyzes Bush policies toward Africa and the Americas.

Chapter 8 looks at the legacy (thus far) of Powell and Rice. Powell left the administration after its first term, and Rice was promoted to secretary of state. It is doubtful that either one will remain out of the public eye. The profile of both Powell and Rice, hyper already in the aftermath of September 11, is cemented in the eyes of the domestic and global communities as unprecedented black images. What are the long-term implications of this repositioning of black Americans? What does it mean for the aims of empire? What will be Powell and Rice's legacies? What are the prospects for their political futures? Where are the progressive black American voices in international politics? How active will African Americans become in regional and international political, policy, and legal bodies, as well as with international non-governmental organizations (NGOs) in the Americas, Africa, Europe, and Asia? How can international concerns link with issues such as gender equality, democratization, environmental health, and economic development?

One

A Commonality of Circumstances: Black Americans and U.S. Foreign Policy

[T]hrough an identification with the exploited peoples of the world . . . the Negro has placed his problems in a new and larger frame of reference and related them to world forces.

Horace R. Cayton, February 27, 1943[1]

There was a time when the rest of the world looked at black America and saw dissidence. . . . Black America is now presenting a radically different face to the world. Today, they offer the developing world the official policy of one of the most reactionary US administrations in recent times.

Gary Younge, Journalist for the *London Guardian*, November 23, 2002[2]

What accounts for the transformation in how some in the global community perceive the foreign policy politics of black America? Does this new perception reflect a collapse of the general and historic consensus by leading activists and scholars in black America regarding U.S. foreign policy or is it a misreading? While there are a number of variables contributing to this development, it is difficult to escape the conclusion that a central factor shaping much of the world's view of black America is the ubiquitous images of former and current Secretaries of State Colin Powell and Condoleezza Rice. For many around the world, it appears that a progressive black American foreign policy agenda and consensus, which has existed for centuries, has eroded if not disappeared altogether. It has been replaced, it seems, or at least been contested, by an acquiescence to the politics of hegemony.

In fact, the consensus continues to exist. Researchers Fran Scott and Abdulah Osman argue that group consciousness, among other factors, is the key element in determining whether racial or ethnic groups are engaged in political action and the efficaciousness of that engagement.[3] This group consciousness has a direct bearing on how black Americans read and analyze U.S. foreign policy, specifically as it relates to Africa, according to Scott and Osman, but can be extended to include the Caribbean, Latin America, and other venues of black communities.[4] Black Americans have recognized historically the collective state of their discriminated status within the United States, and it is this status that fostered identification not only with each other but also with similar conditions faced by Africans in their common historic homeland and other people of African descent. The authors refer to this linkage as a "commonality of circumstances."[5] In fact, this framework goes a long way in explaining black American support for a wide range of struggles and campaigns in much of the developing and developed worlds. As Cayton notes above, to a significant degree black Americans identified with those around the world who were being exploited by an amalgam of politics—U.S. foreign policies, in particular, but not exclusively—to which they opposed. It was understood that the configuration of power in the United States, whereas blacks and other racial minorities were at the bottom and whites were on top, was being visited upon the rest of the world. Unfortunately, it is not difficult to find congruence between the long-term, persistent, social and economic disparities between whites and people of color in the United States, on the one hand and people of African descent in other parts of the world as well as other people of color, on the other. From Brazil and Colombia to France, Britain, and Canada and elsewhere, African-descended peoples are among those on the bottom rungs of the social ladder.

The solidarity that black America has generally expressed with subjugated communities had, until recently, meant that for most of the rest of the world, black Americans as a whole were perceived to be progressive politically and in unity with those who oppose the anti-democratic and unjust dimensions of U.S. foreign and military policies. In 2006, however, as UK journalist Gary Younge has pointed out, the global consensus that black American politics is opposed inherently to mainstream U.S. foreign policies has degraded considerably if not completely in the post–September 11 period. While there are other factors to take into account, it is to a great degree the pervasive images of Powell and Rice that have challenged the view of the international community regarding the historic consensus among black activists, policy-makers, and scholars to resist U.S. hegemony.

This turn of affairs has generated fierce political and ideological debate within the black American community, a debate generally unknown outside of the United States. Ideological warfare has broken out over the significance and relevance of Powell and Rice to race politics as well as to U.S. foreign policy and to what degree their status in U.S. politics should be celebrated or reviled. In addition to Powell and Rice, a small number of black conservatives who endorse Bush's policies, and are financed and promoted by wealthy white conservatives, also have been given media prominence fostering a false image of seemly equally legitimate voices emanating from across a wider political spectrum in the black community.

Yet, according to polls, large majority sectors of the black community have expressed intense disagreement with central and peripheral elements of George W. Bush's foreign policies—the war on terror, the Iraq war, aid to Africa, intervention in Haiti—and, for many, this is linked to a feeling of a sense of betrayal by Powell and Rice regarding their roles in the construction and implementation of those initiatives. This collective rejection of Bush's policies underscores the fact that a commonality of circumstance, though weakened, still generates a consensus among black Americans on key dimensions of foreign policy. The resistance has been expressed by the increasing presence and participation of black Americans in international forums and institutions, and from black scholars who focus on the international arena. Thus there remains a continuity of sorts between the long history of politically progressive black American concern and involvement in international affairs and the contemporary struggle against Bush's efforts.

Until fairly recently, much of the engagement of black Americans in foreign policy took place outside of (and usually in opposition to) the official auspices of the State Department and other governmental bodies tasked with addressing foreign policy. Those activities were overwhelmingly, though not totally, concentrated on issues related to Africa and the Caribbean or circumstances that involved significant numbers of people of African descent. When black Americans began to join the Foreign Service in significant numbers, were appointed to important foreign policy positions, and were elected to Congress in sufficient numbers, it was assumed by many that they would, in part, represent the somewhat broad consensus established in the black community on international issues.

Pressure politics on the state by a wide array of black social, political, and ideological movements—Pan-Africanist, Socialist, Communist, Social Democratic, and Liberal—have defined and shaped that consensus despite internal differences on long-term goals (reform or revolution) and short-term strategies (lobby and/or protest). A high degree of unity on what political demands to call for have created a black foreign policy doctrine that has focused on human rights, anti-racism, political and civil rights, democracy, anti-colonialism, economic fairness, and social justice. In recent years, concerns about environmental discrimination, women's rights, and indigenous rights have also become more central. Accompanying this broad spectrum of demands has been an extensive range of strategies including lobbying public officials, grass-roots demonstrations, conferences, legal maneuvers, petitions, testimony before national and international bodies, media campaigns, education campaigns, non-violent demonstrations, and coalition-building among others. At its essence, this subterfuge process of foreign policy construction has been a counter-hegemonic movement that has melded domestic objectives rooted in principles of equality, justice, and human rights with an international vision.

It is important to draw a distinction, though not too fine, between efforts by the black American community to internationalize its domestic struggle and engagement with issues that function externally to the United States but in which the U.S. state has played or could play a decisive or determinant role. A number of scholars, including Azza Salama Layton, Carol Anderson, Penny M. Von Eschen, and Brenda Gayle Plummer among others, have documented carefully the efforts in the mid-twentieth century to take the situation of black Americans to an international stage, particularly the United Nations.[6] The petitions submitted by Du Bois and the NAACP in 1947 (*An Appeal to the World*), and the Civil Rights Congress in 1951 (*We Charge Genocide*) to the United Nations were examples of the effort to bring the issues of black America to a world audience. That strategy has continued up to the present period as in the efforts by black Americans to make presentations before international political and policy bodies, such as the UN Committee on Human Rights and participation at the 2001 UN World Conference against Racism in Durban, South Africa (see chapter 3).

The principal concerns here, however, are the attempts by black Americans, inside and outside of official state channels, to effect U.S. foreign policies overall as they impact on other societies and peoples around the world. This level of engagement has often stunned U.S. policy-makers and political elites—for example, when Martin Luther King, Jr., came out against the Vietnam War in 1967 or the emergence of the Free South Africa Movement in 1984—who view foreign policy as outside the mandate of the civil rights movement or black political concerns. These politics represent a very different level of consciousness and political activism than traditional civil rights demands but are not necessarily counter to them. Indeed, Anderson has shown that the call for international human rights that included rights for black Americans was the core demand of the civil rights movement in the years immediately after World War II. As noted, the distinction is not always clean as a situational linkage has often been part of the articulation of solidarity and concern.

Black Americans Inside America's Foreign Policy Establishment

> I don't believe we can have world peace until America has an "integrated" foreign policy.[7]
>
> Martin Luther King, Jr.

On September 15, 1789, Congress passed an act that formally established the Department of State whose mission was to oversee a wide range of functions related to the foreign affairs of the new U.S. government. Notwithstanding a number of presidential diplomatic appointments, the department would remain virtually all white until 1925 when Clifton R. Wharton joined the Foreign Service.

There were blacks officially involved in U.S. foreign affairs prior to Wharton outside of the State Department. Early black American diplomats included William A. Leidesdorff, who was appointed as vice consul to Yerba Buena (now San Francisco) in October 1845. He served in that capacity until July 1846. Under the Ulysses Grant administration, another black American diplomat was Ebenezer Don Carlos Bassett who served as minister resident and consul general in Haiti (1869–1877), the highest ranking position possible until the introduction of "ambassadors" in 1893. He was also of Native American descent from the Pequot tribe, which also made him the first Indian diplomat. Haiti, along with Liberia, would continue to be the two nations where both Republican (and later Democratic) presidents would appoint black Americans to represent the United States. Black leader Frederick Douglass was appointed to the position held by Bassett by President Benjamin Harris from 1889 to 1891.

These earlier appointments were driven by a number of considerations. In part, they were paybacks to the black community for its long loyalty to the Republican Party of the era. Douglass had worked hard to elect each of the post–Civil War Republican presidents though he was never given a cabinet level or other significant position as a result of his faithfulness.[8] There was little doubt that race played a blatant role in these appointments. Second, they also occurred before Jim Crow was completely consolidated. Douglass died in 1895, the year emergent conservative black leader Booker T. Washington gave his (in)famous "Atlanta Compromise" speech and a year before the *Plessy v. Ferguson* Supreme Court decision that legalized "separate but equal" policies in the nation. In his last years, Douglass had campaigned aggressively to stem the tide of Jim Crowism by lobbying with national Republican Party officials but with little success.

Third, black appointments to Haiti and Liberia did not threaten U.S. foreign policy interests, which at the time were consolidation of power in the Western hemisphere, gaining influence in Europe and other regions, and U.S. business and corporate expansion. These objectives were not challenged by making black diplomatic appointments. Indeed, their symbolic meaning aided in the projection of U.S. international growth as they served as icons for the argument that the United States represented a democratic state more inclusive and more benevolent than the European powers that dominated the world stage during this period. Bringing race off the shelf was useful in this sense. Haiti, the first independent black nation outside of Africa, and Liberia, the state founded officially in 1847 by free African Americans and white Americans officials of the American Colonization Society, were both dictatorially run by corrupt and repressive regimes. U.S. policy was to prop up those regimes and black diplomats did not change that stance.[9]

Black Americans have also risen to the rank of ambassador, the first being Edward R. Dudley who became ambassador to Liberia in 1949 during the Harry Truman administration. Truman did not appoint any other black American ambassadors while Eisenhower selected three (two to Liberia and one to Guinea).[10] In 1965, Lyndon Johnson chose the first black woman ambassador, Patricia Roberts Harris, who was appointed ambassador to Luxembourg.

Researcher Michael L. Krenn argues that there were salient and conflicting racial factors involved in the appointment (or lack of appointments) of black ambassadors during the Jim Crow and civil rights eras. On the one hand, posting a black ambassador to an African or Caribbean nation could be interpreted by those nations that they were considered second class because, given the second-class status of black Americans, these appointments were likely crass tokenism and those ambassadors powerless to assist the nations to which they had been assigned. For other nations, sending a black ambassador was seen as an insult and diminution of political favor for similar reasons.[11] These attitudes placed a limit on the rise and appointment of black ambassadors. In addition, during the Cold War era, J. Edgar Hoover's FBI, conservatives at the State Department, and officials in all of the different administrations were uncomfortable with the strong relationship, ideological and political, between black America and the developing world. The path of least resistance, rather than having to gauge and monitor the level of loyalty that black Americans brought to the department, was simply to not appoint any.

In 1925, a year after the Rogers Act established the Foreign Service as a "merit" system rather than one of patronage, racial ground was broken at the State Department when Clifton R. Wharton joined the Foreign Service later becoming the first African American Foreign Service officer to become chief of a diplomatic mission when he was appointed minister to Romania on February 5, 1958. According to the State Department website, "he was the first of his race to be chief of a diplomatic mission to a European country. He served in Romania until October 21, 1960. He then served as Ambassador to Norway from April 18, 1961 to September 4, 1964."[12] For Wharton, it was a lonely era. According to Krenn, "between 1924 and 1949, only five African Americans became Foreign Service officers."[13] They and the few black staffers or technicians were assigned, as in the past, to either Haiti or Liberia. In 1973 during the Nixon administration, Wharton's son, Clifton R. Wharton, Jr., would follow in his father's diplomatic footsteps eventually becoming for eights months the Deputy Secretary of State, the second highest position at the department.

The diplomacy track, for the most part, was not only white, but also male. Very few women were allowed to reach the higher levels of either the Foreign Service or other areas of the diplomatic core. As noted above, the first black woman to become an ambassador was Patricia Roberts Harris in 1965. Harris would later become the first black woman cabinet member when she was appointed to first head up the Department of Housing and Urban Development and later the Department of Health, Education, and Welfare.

The most controversial high-level black diplomatic appointment prior to Powell and Rice was the Carter selection of civil rights leader Andrew Young to ambassadorship to the United Nations in 1977. Young, who viewed himself as a politician rather than as a diplomat, was the first black person, first minister, and youngest to received that position. Though well traveled as a civil rights leader and U.S. representative in Congress, he did not have any formal diplomatic experience or training. He stated in an interview, "A diplomat, in the traditional sense, is instructed by his government to maintain the status quo. A politician is generating activity, hoping to produce change, trying to make things happen in a positive way for his country. I find that the State Department trains people not to take chances, to do the safe thing for their careers."[14] These remarks and others, as well as Young's political style would create tensions between him and the State Department. However, Young was in an enviable position because he was close to Carter and also maintained close ties to the civil rights leaders and black congressmembers, which initially gave him political cover and protection.

During Young's tenure, he was able to bring attention to issues related to Africa. Independence for Namibia and the end of Apartheid in South Africa were among his top concerns that reflected the views and foreign policy priorities of most black Americans as well. His perspectives on these issues were not necessarily radical, and, in fact, were much in line with prevailing contemporary conservative solutions to the problems of the developing world. In 1977, after being in office only a few short months, Young told a group of South African business leaders,

I hear a lot of talk about revolution around the world. There are many, many ideologues that promise a transfer of power from one group to another, and yet as I have traveled around this world the places where I see the hungry being fed, the places where I see the naked being clothed, the places where I see the sick being healed are places where there happens to be a free market system. Where there's no ideology at all of change. And yet, in fact, in those free market countries more social change, more revolution is in fact taking place.[15]

His free market moderating approach was similar to the centrist approach to civil rights that distinguished Young from Martin Luther King, Jr., or other more progressive civil rights leaders. Along these lines, he was reluctant to back sanctions against Namibia or South Africa although that was the preferred strategy of many, if not most anti-Apartheid activists across the political spectrum. Even Colin Powell would write that he thought sanctions could be a "useful weapon."[16]

Like Powell, Young would make a number of impolitic statements that were inconsistent with the administration's position on several issues. In early 1977, he found himself on the defensive for stating that Cuba was a "stabilizing" factor in Angola during a time when official U.S. policy backed the anti-communist forces, Angolan and South African, that the Cubans were fighting. In July 1978, in an interview with *Le Matin*, he stated, "there are hundreds, perhaps thousands of political prisoners in the United States."[17] Both these remarks, for which he would apologize profusely, and Young's general blunt style branded him as somewhat a renegade and preceded the incident that would lead to his brunt dismissal. In August 1979, the story broke that Young had met secretly with the UN representative of the Palestine Liberation Organization (PLO). He was not only in trouble for not informing the administration about the meeting that had taken place on July 26, 1979, but also initially gave misleading information about how the meeting came about, first stating that it had been an accidental encounter and then revealing that it had been pre-arranged. The meeting clearly violated the Carter administration's agreement with Israel that there would be no unscheduled U.S. meetings with the PLO. Young's resignation quickly followed the revelations.

In this instance, Young's overtures to the PLO reflected a strong sentiment in the black community, among activists and elites alike, that U.S. policy in the Middle East should be more balanced in tone and approach. Black leaders and organizations, including the Southern Christian Leadership Conference (SCLC) and Operation PUSH as well as several members of the Congressional Black Caucus, called for human rights for the Palestinians and the right of self-determination.

The ultimate lesson from this episode was crystal clear: black State Department staffers and ambassadors implement rather than make policy decisions. Young may or may not have believed consciously that in addition to his own personal political objectives he was carrying out the policy preferences of the black community, but, in any case, he was not in sync with the administration. While there may be leeway regarding the particular means in which policy is carried out, fundamental strategic decisions and policy objectives are established at the very top of the political pyramid.

Young was succeeded by his deputy for Security Council Affairs, Donald McHenry, who is also African American. McHenry was a career diplomat and more than qualified for the position, yet his appointment could also be seen in part as mollification for the black community in the wake of the Young disaster. McHenry, however, was not linked to the civil rights establishment or black community organizations in an organic way as was Young. His tenure as ambassador, with a few minor snafus, was relatively traditional and certainly straightforward in representing the Carter administration's policies. A number of researchers conclude that in a substantive way, Young (and by extrapolation, McHenry) had little to no impact on U.S. policies toward Africa.[18]

However, the Carter period is seen as a "great watershed" for black Americans in the Foreign Service.[19] Carter named fifteen black ambassadors who were dispatched not only to sub-Saharan Africa and the Caribbean, but also to Romania, the former East Germany, Algeria, and Malaysia. In addition, Secretary of State Cyrus Vance ordered a study on diversity at the State Department that concluded, in part, that the department was an "elitist, self-satisfied, walled-in barony populated by smug white males, an old-boy system in which women and minorities cannot possibly hope to be treated with equity in promotions and senior level responsibilities."[20]

During the Reagan and first Bush administrations, black Americans actually lost ground in terms of appointments in the Foreign Service and ambassadorships. The number of black ambassadors fell precipitously from fifteen to five who were sent to outposts such as Mauritius, the Seychelles, and Sierra Leone. Reagan's focus on the Soviet "evil empire," manifest in his anti-communist surrogate wars in Africa and Latin America underscored the long-held view by conservatives that one had to be exceptionally nationalistic and patriotic to represent the United States and that perhaps black Americans (as well as Hispanics, Jews, and other racial and ethnic groups) were not demonstrably so. Reagan did find a few black Americans who were willing to defend his policies such as Alan Keyes who served as assistant secretary of state for international organizations. Keyes had also previously been on the staff of the National Security Council and been ambassador to the UN Economic and Social Council. Powell, of course, would also join the Reagan administration as national security advisor among other appointments. George H. W. Bush maintained Powell later promoting him to head of the Joint Chief of Staffs, and added Rice via her sponsor National Security Advisor Brent Scowcroft. Under Bush's Secretary of State George Schultz, there was very little growth in the number of black staffers or appointments to substantial foreign policy positions.

Nor did circumstances improve significantly during the Clinton years. Susan Rice, an articulate and forceful diplomat and scholar, was assistant secretary of state for African affairs and ran interference for Clinton on African policy. She developed close though sometimes contentious ties with many of the NGOs and black community groups involved with African issues. Clinton also appointed, for a short period, Rev. Jesse Jackson to be his special envoy for the president and secretary of state for the promotion of democracy in Africa. This appointment gave Jackson official status to represent Clinton in several matters regarding issues across the continent. In that capacity, Jackson met with Nelson Mandela, then president of South Africa, Kenya's president Arap Moi, and Zambia's president Frederick Chiluba. While this position gave Jackson a diplomatic legitimacy he had been accused of lacking when he intervened (successfully) in conflict situations in the Middle East and elsewhere, it also put him at odds on several occasions with many of the progressive activists who had disagreements with some of Clinton's African policies. Many activists as well as some black policy-makers had sharp disagreement with Clinton's proposed "Africa Growth and Opportunity Act," a key piece of legislation aimed at providing economic assistance to certain countries in Africa but which many felt locked those countries into an unfavorable economic relationship with the United States while failing to address more fundamental issues facing the continent such as crushing debt.[21] There were also tensions between Jackson and some in the African policy community concerning how to deal with Nigeria as it underwent regime changes. In May 1994, Clinton also appointed former Congressional Black Caucus (CBC) member and then president of the United Negro College Fund Bill Gray to be his special advisor and secretary of state on Haiti to address work on the return of Bertrand Aristide to the presidency of Haiti after being overthrown in September 1991.

While the Jackson and Gray appointments were celebrated by some, Clinton was also being criticized for, first, using special envoys for short-term solutions to problems that were long standing and required fundamental changes in U.S. polices. Overall, the administration dragged its feet on issues such as debt relief and increased foreign aid to Africa and only moved on Haiti after a dramatic hunger strike by TransAfrica's executive director Randall Robinson and pressure from the Congressional Black Caucus and other black and human rights organizations. Second, these appointments only brought into sharp relief the dismal record of the State Department and Foreign Service in the hiring of blacks and other racial and ethnic minorities.

By the time Young was appointed ambassador to the United Nations, though small, the number of blacks in the Foreign Service had expanded to the point where black former and current Foreign Service officers formed a group that began to meet regularly. In 1973, the Thursday Luncheon Group, as it became known, was created by two black Foreign Service officers, William B. Davis and

Roburt A. Dumas.[22] The organization pushed for affirmative action, better postings, and it raised more than $2 million for fellowships to bring more people of color into the Foreign Service. By the end of the 1990s, it would have over 200 members and begin to receive recognition from State Department officials. In 1998, the group was addressed by then Secretary of State Madeleine Albright who noted that "only 2.7 percent of all Foreign Service Officers are black."[23] She was the first secretary of state to speak to the group, but would not be the last. When Colin Powell rose to the position, he also spoke before the group.[24] Other groups would emerge as well including the Association of Black American Ambassadors,[25] which was founded in 1983, and the International Association of Black Professionals in International Affairs (BPIA) established in 1989.[26]

Powell sought to increase the number of blacks in the Foreign Service during his tenure. In 2001, when he became secretary of state, blacks constituted about 5.34 percent of the Foreign Service personnel.[27] In collaboration with Howard University, Powell managed to secure a $1 million grant from Congress that was given to Howard University's Ralph J. Bunche International Affairs Center (IAC) to prepare blacks and other minorities for careers as diplomats. The IAC was established in 1993 as a premier research and scholars' center on the Howard campus. The grant created the Charles B. Rangel International Affairs Fellowship Program that provides funding for graduate students who are seeking Masters in the field of International Relations or a related study. Rangel, a prominent black member of Congress who has focused on U.S. foreign policy while in office, was the catalyst in securing the funding. Under the program, students do an initial internship in Congress and a second internship abroad at a U.S. embassy.

Powell clearly was proud of this achievement and framed it, in part, in racial terms. In expressing his racial pride and linking it to his immigrant background, he stated, "In having been in senior positions in government over the years, having been privileged to be an African American who served as national security advisor, as deputy national security advisor, as first black chairman of the Joint Chiefs of Staff, first black secretary of state, it's just terrific to be able to walk into a room somewhere, in Africa, Russia, in Asia, in Europe, and you know they're looking at you. It's always a source of inspiration and joy to see people look at me and through me see my country and see what promise my country offers to all people who come to these shores looking for a better life."[28]

While Powell acknowledges his black American roots, and clearly engaged in race conscious initiatives as secretary of state, his (and Rice's) tenures have represented a significant break from those who preceded him. First, until relatively recently, race was a clear, conscious, and present factor in the constitution of the State Department and the Foreign Service. Whether it was struggling against the individual or institutionalized racial bigotry inside the State Department, attempting to influence policies that specifically affected other black people or other people of color, or negotiating segregated or discriminatory spaces in the nation's capital in their private lives, race was never an afterthought or incidental. Addressing the vicissitudes of racial discrimination could not be limited to solely increasing the number of blacks in the Foreign Service without a transformation in the broader policy arena. Second, these individuals were willing to challenge the policies and politics that marginalized the interests of the black community either domestically or globally. This was expressed not only in individual ways, but also through collective action in the form of various organizations and campaigns. There is no indication that either Powell or Rice participated in any of the black American foreign policy organizations or networks. Finally, many of these individuals were connected organically to the political and social movements and issues that animated the black community. They publicly expressed a sense of responsibility regarding representing, to the degree possible and to the degree identifiable, a black consensus on foreign policy, and conversely, the black community viewed them as representative of its issues. While clearly this was not universal, the political arc among blacks in foreign policy positions bent toward the consensus. In the end, there were severe limits on the capacity of those who officially represented the United States to advance the consensus. Few were in a position to have anything but minor impact on policy. Most important, fundamental decisions on policy are derived from sites of political power, not from bureaucracies. The fight to advance a progressive black foreign policy consensus would be left to a long, continual, and insistent struggle by the black community outside of official government channels. In this regard, one of the most important individuals, who operated inside and outside the U.S. government, and was one of the world's top, if not the top, diplomat for many years, but whose legacy is relatively buried from contemporary audiences is Ralph Bunche.

A Bunche of Diplomacy

> Peace, to have meaning for many who have known only suffering in both peace and war, must be translated into bread or rice, shelter, health, and education, as well as freedom and human dignity—a steadily better life. If peace is to be secure, long-suffering and long-starved, forgotten peoples of the world, the underprivileged and the undernourished, must begin to realize without delay the promise of a new day and a new life.
>
> Ralph Bunche, Nobel Lecture, December 11, 1950

Ralph J. Bunche, one of only two black Americans to win the Nobel Peace Prize—Martin Luther King, Jr., being the other—was one of the most pivotal American figures in international diplomacy in the twentieth century. Yet, Bunche has received little contemporary acknowledgment and study for his stellar and remarkable achievements in international affairs. His tenure with both the U.S. government and the United Nations occurred during crucial periods in international politics where the highest level of diplomacy was needed to address the critical issues facing the global community. The fact that Bunche is largely unknown says a great deal about the perception of the intersection of race and international affairs. With a few important exceptions, neither the black political community, as a whole, nor those in the field of International Relations, in general, give Bunche the kind of critical inquiry that he deserves. His life and significance have been best captured in the works of Charles Henry, Brian Urquhart, and other scholars who have recognized not only Bunche's diplomatic genius but also where those talents met at the intersection of race and global politics.[29]

The United Nations, which has been a central character in the Bush political drama, was shaped and formed to a significant degree during its formative years by Bunche. Long before Powell's discomposed February 2003 speech, Bunche's extraordinary diplomatic endowments echoed through the UN's chambers. Long before Rice negotiated deals with world leaders, Bunche met with heads of states and political movements on a regular basis. While Powell and Rice represented perhaps the most aggressive U.S. administration in living memory, Bunche always carried a mandate for peace.

Bunche, of course, matured under very different circumstances. In February 1934, he became the first African American to receive his doctorate from Harvard University's Government and International Relations department writing a dissertation that analyzed French colonialism. The dissertation, titled "French Administration in Togoland and Dahomey," won the Toppan prize for best dissertation in political science at Harvard that year. While working on his doctorate, he established the Political Science Department at Howard University and taught there until 1941. During this period, some of the nation's most eminent black scholars were teaching at Howard including Sterling Brown, E. Franklin Frazier, Kelly Miller, Alain Locke, Charles Wesley, and Percy Julian among others, who Bunche engaged in political and ideological discourse. These were intellectually productive years for Bunche. He would play a key role in the research project commissioned by the Carnegie Corporation and led by Swedish scholar Gunnar Myrdal that would result in the groundbreaking study published as the two-volume *An American Dilemma*.[30] This work would echo the arguments and scholarship that black intellectuals such as W.E.B. Du Bois, E. Franklin Frazer, and others had been producing for at least a generation.

Bunche's politics were also undergoing dramatic changes. While he had considered himself a Marxist or a Socialist during his early years, he had clearly become more moderate in his work and in his political activities. Whether he was preparing consciously for his career as a diplomat or more likely expressing the political distance that often befell academics, he had clearly toned down his leftist ideologically fervor. While he had been active with radical organizations such as the National Negro Congress and Brotherhood of Sleeping Car Porters, he was now more likely to be found engaged in academic exchanges with scholars representing a spectrum of political viewpoints.

The significant turning point would come in 1941 when Bunche took a leave of absence to work in the Office of Coordination of Information (OCI), which was located in the Library of Congress and a part of the U.S. Foreign Service. The OCI engaged in intelligence work and gathered intelligence for the war effort. According to the Central Intelligence Agency (CIA) website,

> The office of the Coordinator of Information constituted the nation's first peacetime, non-departmental intelligence organization. President Roosevelt authorized it to . . . collect and analyze all information and data, which may bear upon national security: to correlate such information and data, and to make such information and data available to the President and to such departments and officials of the Government as the President may determine; and to carry out, when requested by the President, such supplementary activities as may facilitate the securing of information important for national security not now available to the Government.[31]

In 1942, the OCI became the Office of Strategic Service (OSS), the chief U.S. espionage agency during the war and the precursor to the Central Intelligence Agency that was formally established in 1947 by the National Security Act.

Bunche advanced in these operations and eventually became head of the Africa section. In January 1944, switching to the State Department, he was first appointed to the Near East and Africa section and later to the International Security Organization section. Like Powell and Rice, Bunche was being placed in critical national security positions. At this point Bunche was not only representing U.S. strategic interests in global politics but also helping to develop them. He has written very little about this period in his political career and what personal conflicts he might have had in fashioning the politics of a state he had criticized previously and hoped to transform radically. Given the important positions he had achieved in the OCI/OSS and then at the State Department, it was natural that he became part of the U.S. team involved in the development of the United Nations. Recognizing the conservative character of the U.S. delegation, Bunche worked behind the scenes with W.E.B. Du Bois and the National Association for the Advancement of Colored People (NAACP) leadership to push, unsuccessfully as it turned out, for a progressive trusteeship plan to be included in the founding charter. The Truman administration and other Western powers blocked any progressive initiative that would move forward the process of decolonialization. In relation to other black Americans who were trying to influence the nature and politics of the new organization, Bunche encountered conflict with his former leftist associates from the National Negro Congress, who viewed him as essentially gone over to the enemy camp.

Bunche's days with the State Department were coming to a close. In December 1946, he joined the UN Secretariat as head of the Trusteeship Division. He would never again represent the United States in international affairs. In 1948, Bunche was courted by the Truman administration and offered the position of assistant secretary of state, and later President John Kennedy wanted to consider him for secretary of state. He refused both offers because did not want to leave the work he was doing at the United Nations, and he also did not want to live in segregated Washington, D.C.

He would go on and have a stellar career as a diplomat representing the United Nations, winning the Nobel Peace Prize in 1950 for the exceptional work he did in bringing a settlement to the wars in the Middle East. After the chief negotiator Count Folke Bernadotte was assassinated, with Bunche surviving by arriving late to the meeting where the killing took place, he obtained armistice agreements between Israel and several Arab states including Egypt, Lebanon, Syria, and Jordan. Bunche went on to hold several posts including becoming under secretary general in 1955 and was viewed by many as virtually running the United Nations during that time. Bunche also established the UN's peacekeeping functions and operations.

Not being content with his demanding involvement in global issues, Bunche joined several civil rights demonstrations, including the historic 1963 March on Washington, and he strongly supported the civil rights agenda. Ironically, he was critical initially of Martin Luther King, Jr.'s agitation against the Vietnam War, believing that it hurt the civil rights efforts and that the two movements "have too little in common in any case."[32] King shot back that he acted out of his religious beliefs and moral consciousness and that drove him to oppose oppression and injustice everywhere, and that he was disturbed by Bunche's narrow position on the issue.

Outside the (Foreign Policy) Box

While Bunche toggled back and forth between officially representing the United States and being an official of the United Nations, there were many other black Americans who struggled to transform U.S. policy from the outside dating back to well over two centuries. These black "citizen diplomats," as Karin Stanford termed them, were able to have a palatable though usually small impact on U.S. foreign policy decisions.[33] She defines citizen diplomacy as "the diplomatic efforts of private citizens in the international arena for the purposes of achieving a specific objective or accomplishing constituency goals. One of the most distinctive features of this type of diplomacy is that it operates outside of the existing national foreign policymaking system and may not be supportive of official policy."[34] Stanford's analysis appropriately identifies the labors by black Americans, individually and collectively, to intervene and redirect U.S. foreign policy via non-standard channels. Most critical is the belief by citizen diplomats that they represent a clear and identifiable constituency whose goals they seek to achieve.

Black efforts at influencing U.S. foreign policy took on many forms from lobbying and demonstrating to participation in international strategy conferences and even wars. Beyond the long-standing solidarity with African freedom movements, black Americans in the nineteenth and twentieth centuries gave support to anti-colonial and democratic struggles in Cuba, Spain, and elsewhere in contradistinction to stated U.S. foreign policy.[35] African Americans were part of the 2,800 volunteers of the Abraham Lincoln Brigade that fought on the side of the anti-fascists during the Spanish civil war in the mid-1930s. The brigade, ironically, was the first racially integrated military unit in U.S. history and had black officers.

A wide range of strategies have been employed to win foreign policy concessions including political conferences. In 1900, in London, Trinidadian lawyer Henry Sylvester Williams, convened the first Pan-African Conference that was attended by W.E.B. Du Bois. Picking up on Williams's example, from 1919 to 1994, Du Bois organized or inspired a series of gatherings known as the Pan-African Congresses (PACs) that were held to bring together blacks from the United States, other parts of the Diaspora, and from Africa itself.

Du Bois was the driving force behind the first four congresses held in 1919, 1921, 1923, and 1927, all located in Europe. The fifth gathering was held in 1945 in Manchester, England, and although Du Bois was in attendance, it was brought together and dominated by a number of African activists whose focus was again on African independence. In attendance were leading activists such as Kwame Nkrumah, who would become president of Ghana, and Jomo Kenyatta, who would rise to head an independent Kenya. In 1974, the Sixth PAC was held in Tanzania, the first to be held in Africa, under very different circumstances than the previous gatherings. Nearly all of the nations of the continent (and in the Caribbean) were "independent," which created the political dilemma of determining who actually should be given official representation to attend: governments or the (black) movements in opposition to them. When the decision was made to accommodate the former, a number of prominent activists and scholars criticized the decision and did not attend (e.g., radical historian and activist Walter Rodney and Caribbean intellectual and global scholar C.L.R. James). Nevertheless, several thousands attended including hundreds from the United States. In 1994, a Seventh PAC was held in Uganda, but only achieved sparse participation.

The emergence of African, Caribbean, and Asian states from direct colonialism would be new opportunities for black American participation in international politics, such as the Bandung Conference. Officially titled the Afro-Asian Summit, it was held in Bandung, Indonesia, from April 18–25, 1955, and was arguably the signature moment of the collective expression of the developing world's resistance to Western and Eastern global power. As writer Richard Wright noted, "The despised, the insulted, the hurt, the dispossessed—in short, the underdogs of the human race were meeting."[36] The event brought together leaders of twenty-three Asian and six African nations to address "racialism and colonialism."[37] This historic gathering sought to not only place on a world stage a critical discourse and critique of the manner in which their nations and peoples had been exploited, but also to declare independence from the ideologies and political machinations of the Western European powers and its allies, and the Soviet Union as well. Leaders of these nations rejected the notion that they would be pawns or cannon fodder in the Cold War.

There were a number of black Americans in attendance including Rep. Adam Clayton Powell; Margaret Cartwright, the first black reporter assigned to the United Nations; as well as writer and ex-patriot Richard Wright. They were able to hear and engage the likes of Prime Minister Jawaharlal Nehru of India, Prime Minister Kwame Nkrumah of the Gold Coast (which later became Ghana), President Gamal Abdel Nasser of Egypt, Premier Chou En Lai of China, and Prime Minister Ho Chi Minh of Vietnam. Another black journalist, Carl Rowan as a correspondent for the *Minneapolis Tribune*, attended the conference with a somewhat dubious relationship with the CIA and U.S. State Department.[38] Though unable to attend for various reasons, activist Paul Robeson, scholar W.E.B. Du Bois, and NAACP leader Roy Wilkins all sent messages of solidarity.

Concerns about U.S. policy toward Africa would continue to grow. During the 1960s, the issue of African independence and liberation became rallying calls for the black power movement in the United States. Pan-Africanist perspectives led many to push for stronger U.S. actions to end Apartheid in southern Africa, as well as Portuguese colonial rule in Angola, Mozambique, Cape Verde, and Guinea Bissau. The African Liberation Support Committee emerged in the early 1970s as an articulation of a more leftist black U.S. politics in solidarity with the armed liberation movements in Africa. It sought to influence U.S. policy through demonstrations, education, and direct aid to the movements on the continent rather than through traditional lobbying activities or mainstream political strategies. One of the most important collective expressions of black foreign policy influence related to Africa occurred on Thanksgivings Eve 1984. The Free South Africa movement grew out of protests initiated by TransAfrica's Randall Robinson, U.S. Civil Rights commissioner Mary Francis Berry, Congressman Walter Fauntroy, and Georgetown University law professor Eleanor Holmes Norton who sat down with the South African ambassador at its embassy in Washington, D.C., and as pre-planned, when the forty minute discussion was over, they announced that they would not be leaving unless two demands were met: freedom for all political prisoners in South Africa and an immediately beginning to dismantle the Apartheid system. For more than a year, thousands would volunteer to be arrested outside of the embassy in Washington while others protested and were arrested at South African consulates around the country. In addition to Robinson's TransAfrica, other organizations had been working for years educating countless numbers around the country about the oppression and racist conditions faced by blacks, Asians, and Coloureds in South Africa. This included the Southern Africa Support Project, American Committee on Africa, Washington Office on Africa, Southern Africa Project of the Lawyer's Committee for Civil Rights, American Friends Service Committee, Interfaith Center on Corporate Responsibility, Coalition of Black Trade Unionists, and many local groups.

As Sylvia Hill, one of the organizers noted, "[O]ne should never underestimate the power of symbolic protests to create a political climate for political change . . . even though protests create a political climate, the organizers must have the organizational infrastructure to respond politically to a legislative agenda and cracks in the power elite" to bring about transformation.[39] By involving policy-makers, including moderate Republicans in this instance, as well as grass-roots organizations, a tidal wave of political resistance pushed the Reagan policy of constructive engagement into history's dustbin. On October 2, 1986, two years after the protest began, Congress passed the Comprehensive Anti-Apartheid Act of 1986 over Reagan's veto, his first and most significant foreign policy defeat.

In a tactic that would be repeated over the years, the Reagan administration employed a number of black Americans to defend its African policies. Then assistant secretary of state Alan Keyes, Lincoln Institute for Research and Education president Jay Parker, and consultant Marcus Dawkins among others were mobilized to challenge the black (and broader) consensus that U.S. policies toward South Africa were flawed and against the interests of the majority of the South African people. The administration also persuaded conservative black business groups, churches, and colleges to host its anti-communist allies, such as the murderous UNITA out of Angola, on tours to black communities in the United States. These visits were protested and generally failed to sway black communities to the administration's side.

Is There a Black Consensus on Bush's Foreign Policy?

The sense of betrayal regarding the positions of Powell and Rice begs the question of whether there is a consensus among black Americans on what should constitute the goals and principles of U.S. foreign policy. The most consistent opposition to Bush's foreign policy doctrine within the United States has come from the black American community. From his war on terror to his war with Iraq to his policies toward Africa, Bush has been resoundingly criticized by black policy-makers, scholars, and activist organizations. This opposition was expressed most dramatically when the only member of Congress who voted against H.J. Resolution 64, the vote giving Bush the authority to wage war in the immediate days following the September 11 attacks was Rep. Barbara Lee (D–CA), who is African American. Reflecting the distrust and caution that many other African Americans would express, she stated,

> We must not rush to judgment. Far too many innocent people have already died. Our country is in mourning. If we rush to launch a counter-attack, we run too great a risk that women, children, and other non-combatants will be caught in the crossfire. Nor can we let our justified anger over these outrageous acts by vicious murderers inflame prejudice against all Arab Americans, Muslims, Southeast Asians, or any other people because of their race, religion, or ethnicity. Finally, we must be careful not to embark on an open-ended war with neither an exit strategy nor a focused target.[40]

Her remarks generated numerous death threats and, for a time, around the clock police protection. Many of the criticisms that were raised against Lee, on talk radio and directly to her office, were racist to the core. For the most part, the Congressional Black Caucus and the congressionally independent Congressional Black Caucus Foundation (CBCF) have been sharply critical of the Bush administration. In a document issued in late fall 2004, the CBCF's Center for Policy Analysis and Research took Bush to task on a number of foreign policy issues. It charged that his Iraq policy is flawed and "that even by U.S. Intelligence [*sic*] estimates, the best-case future scenario in Iraq is bleak with no clear exit strategy."[41] In the broader sense, it stated, "Unfortunately, under President Bush the U.S. now has strained relations with major European allies and the United Nations as a direct result of its (semi) unilateral aggression in Iraq and exclusion from the bidding process in post-war Iraq."[42] The report was also critical of the administration's policies toward Afghanistan and addressing the global HIV/AIDS pandemic.[43] Perhaps most notable, in terms of foreign policy, is what is not addressed. There is no discussion of Haiti, Colombia, the International Criminal Court, World Trade Organization, Israel-Palestine conflict, aid and trade with Africa, environmental concerns, or the war on terrorism. It is doubtful that there is any consensus on these issues among the forty plus members of the CBC. It is also likely that a unified CBC position on foreign policy will become more difficult as more conservative black members join Congress. As the website "The Black Commentator" points out, a number of black congressmembers have backed Bush on some of his most controversial bills including bankruptcy law reform and changes in the estate tax. The CBC did not take—could not take—a unified position on these bills, and about a quarter of the caucus voted with the Republican majority.[44]

The CBC has staked out a number of positions on other foreign policy concerns. For instance, it called for the resignation of Donald Rumsfeld after one of his brusque and insensitive statements regarding the Iraq war. The CBC wrote in a press release, "Last week, while addressing American troops in Kuwait, Secretary Rumsfeld stated that, 'you go to war with the Army you have, not the Army you might want or wish to have.' This statement of reckless disregard for the safety of U.S. troops who put their lives on the line every day to protect our country is another example of why it is past time for Mr. Rumsfeld to go."[45]

Individual black congressmembers and national leaders, from Revs. Al Sharpton and Jesse Jackson to the heads of the NAACP and TransAfrica, also spoke out strongly against Bush's foreign policy initiatives. In 2002, Black Voices for Peace (BVFP), a grass-roots activist organization, was formed specifically to oppose the drive to war with Iraq. As did other organizations, it condemned the terrorist attacks but linked them to broader policy issues. It stated, "BVFP strongly condemns the 9/11 attacks and the murder of innocent civilians by any individual or group. At the same time, we believe that the best defenses against terrorism in all forms are policies which promote and respect human rights and disarmament. BVFP therefore opposes the Bush administration's policies of war, violence, and threats against other nations in response to the attacks."[46]

These sentiments were in sync with the views of the majority of black Americans. Like other Americans, the initial response to the September 11 attacks showed a great deal of support for Bush by African Americans; an almost unbelievable 94 percent thought Bush's handling of the attacks were "excellent, good or fair" according to a poll by Zogby International conducted on September 20, 2001.[47] Less than a year later, support for Bush had fallen precipitously with only 14.8 percent of black Americans rating his performance as excellent.[48]

A 2003 Harris poll, conducted for *Time* and CNN just before the U.S. invasion was launched, revealed the racial divide that emerged around Bush's foreign policy aggressions. When asked "Do you think the U.S. should or should not use military action involving ground troops to attempt to remove Saddam Hussein from power in Iraq?" only 34 percent of blacks said yes compared to 57 percent of whites.[49] In a July 2004 poll by BET/CBS, a question was asked about whether the Iraq war was worth the costs. For Americans overall, 36 percent said yes while 59 percent said no. Among African Americans, only 8 percent said yes while 90 percent said no. Even among military families in the black community, that is, individuals either themselves or with an immediate family member in the military, there was overwhelming opposition with 86 percent saying it was not worth it. More than one-third, 36 percent, of blacks surveyed stated they were a military family compared to 21 percent of those in the survey generally.[50] The same poll found that when asked to name the most important national African American leader, Jesse Jackson was at the top of the list (21%) followed by Powell (13%). Rice was the only woman mentioned by respondents, and she garnered only 2 percent in the ranking.

Black opposition was conditioned on a number of factors. First, black antagonism toward Bush was fervent only subsiding momentarily in the immediate aftermath of the September 11 attacks, but then rising up dramatically to previous levels of hostility and rejection. The memory of the 2000 election and black disenfranchisement would not go away. Bush's refusal to speak before groups such as the NAACP or meet seriously with the Congressional Black Caucus only reinforced perceptions that he simply was unconcerned about the issues that faced the black community.

Black leaders opposed the war not only in the United States, but in forums around the world. Reverend Jesse Jackson spoke out often against the war and appeared at the massive anti-war rally held in London on February 15, 2003, the day when tens of millions protested around the world. He stated,

Why are we here today? Because we choose coexistence over co-annihilation. Because we choose brains over bombs and brute force. To stop the cycle of terrorism before it spreads. To stop a war before it starts. . . . I spoke at both of the massive antiwar rallies in the United States, last October and just last month in Washington, D.C. And I was invited to speak in New York, where there will be a huge rally later today. But I decided that London was the decisive link in the chain of events leading to war. Tony Blair's support for a war on Iraq, and England's place in the war coalition is literally the difference between majority support and majority opposition in the United States. As England goes, so goes the peace. And as the people of England go, so should go your Prime Minister. This is a democracy, after all.[51]

TransAfrica executive director Bill Fletcher, Jr., pulled no punches in criticizing the war. He stated,

The Bush administration has brazenly decided upon a course of action that breaks international law by adopting a perverse notion of preemptive war. The notion of a preemptive assault as applied by this administration in a situation where there has been no evidence of a threat to the United States or to Iraq's neighbors is aggressive and dangerous. It places the United States on a collision course with most of the rest of the world. Instead of political analysis, the Bush administration is advancing fortune-telling, that is, predicting what a certain leader might do in the future if they obtain certain weapons. Using that "logic" this planet could annihilate itself in a never-ending search for potential threats.[52]

The Black Radical Congress (BRC), a network of leftist and progressive activists and scholars, issued a number of statements condemning the war and also mobilized its base to participate in anti-war activities. Calling the invasion "criminal" and "illegal," the BRC "opposes the war against the Iraqi people and call on all black, brown, red, yellow, and white people (in short, the majority of the peoples of the world) to oppose this war. The attempts to use religion to divide the non Islamic peoples of the USA from the peoples of the Islamic faith must be opposed. . . . Above all, this war continues the traditions of racial genocide of the US military."[53]

Black journalists have also spoken out forcefully against the war. "The Black Commentator" has published numerous articles identifying the racist dimensions of the war and linking the invasion with other concerns of the black community such as Haiti and U.S. policy toward Africa. It has been especially critical of the roles played by Rice and Powell in Bush's imperialist project. Chastising Rice for her statement about the U.S. determination to spread its definition of "democracy," the website states, "In both Haiti and Iraq, many thousands have been slaughtered in pursuit of Condoleezza Rice's 'organizing principle'—a policy that the Bush men fantasize will prevail for the remainder of the century."[54]

One dimension of black protest appears to be emanating from young people who are opting out of going into the U.S. military. The so-called poverty draft (i.e., the recruitment of poor and working-class youth into the military with financial and education incentives that are otherwise available to middle- and upper-class youth), has long drawn in young black people with promises of post-military service benefits. In 2005, it was reported that U.S. military recruitment targets were not being met, and a significant drop-off in young blacks was notable. A U.S. military with a black presence that had been as high as 30 percent following the Vietnam War was down to about 14 percent. There was little doubt by army recruiters that the Iraq war was a major reason why young blacks—where polls showed only 36 percent support for the war compared to 61 percent for young whites—were refusing to enlist.[55]

Yet, both in the United States and globally, black voices of opposition were drowned by the ubiquitous images of Powell and Rice as unapologetic supporters and mangers of the Bush doctrine. While some U.S. black activists were calling Powell and Rice turncoats, "Uncle Toms," and worse, they were being praised by some world leaders because of the positions they achieved and the (erroneous) perception that they arose out of poverty to do so. In October 2001, in his speech to the Labour Party conference, Prime Minister Tony Blair of the UK stated, "America has its faults as a society, as we have ours. But I think of the Union of America born out of the defeat of slavery. I think of its Constitution, with its inalienable rights granted to every citizen still a model for the world. I think of a black man, born in poverty, who became chief of their armed forces and is now secretary of state Colin Powell and I wonder frankly whether such a thing could have happened here."[56] Powell, who was not born into the lair of abject poverty that Blair sought to evoke, was exemplified as a bootstrap hero and the objective symbol of a multi-cultural Britain. Within a year, Blair would appoint the UK's first black cabinet minister, Paul Boateng, who became the chief secretary to the Treasury Department and one of the strongest supporters of Blair's highly unpopular decision to back the United States against Iraq. In 2003, Blair appointed his second black cabinet minister, Valerie Amos, to the position of secretary of international development, replacing the volatile and combative Clair Short who resigned over her opposition to the UK's involvement in the war in Iraq. Prior to her appointment, Amos had been sent to visit and un-successfully lobby several African countries that sat on the UN Security Council during the time the United States and Britain were seeking a second UN res-olution in support of the war against Iraq. Amos was later removed from this position. Boateng and Amos were both criticized heavily in the UK's black press for their support of the Iraq positions of Bush and Blair.

Foreign Policy and Race

Black foreign policy views and praxis are directly linked to the history and status of blacks in U.S. society. The effort to influence public policy, whether foreign or domestic, has been as the center of the black politics as it has tried to negotiate for social justice and racial equality with a resistant American political system. In real terms, for most, this has meant choosing between two or three major political parties as imperfect conduits of the goals and objectives of a black political agenda. For at least the last four decades that vehicle has been the Democratic Party.

Thus observers of black politics can be forgiven for assuming that black "firsts" in the higher echelons of U.S. foreign policy would emerge during a Democratic administration. Under Clinton, the first black secretary of com-merce (Ron Brown) and first black Secretary of Veteran Affairs (Jesse Brown) were appointed. And for his first year in office, Clinton kept Powell as his head of the Joint Chiefs of Staff. These appointments have strained the commonality of circumstances, but have generally been celebrated by the black community as a sign of racial, if not political, progress. Yet, none of these positions were at the core of U.S. foreign policy construction, or more important, critical to the ideological campaigns necessary to win domestic support for the U.S. interna-tional agenda.

Ever since the Dixiecraticization of the Republican Party and its infamous southern strategy of wooing whites from the old Confederacy, it was difficult to see any black American penetrating the high-end policy and political circles that were off-limits to even most prominent white politicos. However, a confluence of opportunism on the party of modern-day black Republicans and the party's strategists have broken color barriers that only a short while ago seemed burly and permanent.

Two

This Is Not Your Father's Republican Party:
Powell, Rice, and the GOP

> Stagolee shot Billy,
> Oh he shot that boy so fas'
> That the bullet came through him,
> And broke my window glass
> *The Ballad of Stagolee*

It turned out not to be such a merry Christmas for Billy Lyons who was shot on Christmas day in 1895 by Lee "Stack Lee" Shelton. He died around 4 A.M. the next morning. That incident, which occurred in the Chestnut Valley section of St. Louis, has been immortalized in hundreds of version of the song, "Stagolee." Many versions of the song allude to a fight between these two black men over a white Stetson hat (partly true) or a gambling dispute (not true). No version of the song, however, details the political context of the quarrel, or the fact that Shelton was a Democrat and Lyons a Republican.

In 1895—the year black leader Booker T. Washington delivered his infamous "Atlanta Compromise" speech, where he argued that African Americans should not directly politically challenge racism—St. Louis was a battleground over black political allegiance. Both the Republican Party and the Democratic Party were attempting fiercely to win over black voters and activists. Although the black community, as elsewhere, had given their loyalty to the Republican Party in the period after slavery, that support had diminished significantly by the mid-1880s as the Republican Party broke promises and failed to deliver any significant benefits to its African American base. As one black Republican leader stated, "The Republican party has secured black voter allegiance by falsely depicting itself as the sole instrument of black emancipation, while in reality Democrats and blacks also had helped to win the Civil War."[1] This anger translated into many blacks defecting to the Democratic Party, which held their first convention in St. Louis in spring 1895.

Shelton and Lyons were both caught up in this political whirlwind. To win recruits, the Democrats used hustlers, bar owners, con men, and pimps, such as Lee Shelton, to reach out to and, when necessary, bribe black voters. Lyons, on the other hand, was the brother-in-law of Henry Bridgewater, one of the most prominent black Republicans in the state. Though not much is known about Lyons, it is very likely that he was involved in Republican Party politics. According to researcher Cecil Brown, Shelton and Lyons were having a political argument that preceded the hat grabbing incident that would lead to the latter's murder.[2]

While battles between black Republicans and black Democrats have been somewhat less violent in the modern era, animosity between the two is perhaps no less intense. Since the Reagan era, a very different type of black Republican has emerged that has very little resonance with those blacks who traditionally identified themselves as supporters of the Republican Party but whose focus was on the betterment of the black community. Unlike many contemporary black Republicans, they did not distance themselves from the interests of the black community or adopt positions contrary to a wide consensus among black Americans on a variety of concerns.

Among organized contemporary black Republicans, there appears to be little debate or engaged discourse on the direction of the Republican Party and its significance to black America. It is assumed without contestation that the Democratic Party has taken blacks for granted, encouraged political dependency, fostered racial division, and the only legitimate alternative is the Republican Party. The biggest crime, according to these self-identified black Republicans, is that the Democratic Party sees blacks only a group and not as individuals. This is the ideological linchpin, they argue, because in the histography in which they travel the United States was built upon, grew, and prospered, and will survive due to each and every person expressing their individual capacities, talents, and determination unfettered by notions of collectivities. The American meritocracy is the exceptionalism that separates the United States from every other nation. Without too much modification, Powell and Rice embrace this framework.

Yet, Powell and Rice do not always fit comfortably into the modern black Republican paradigm. While clearly the most successful of contemporary black Republicans, their focus on foreign policy, and their positions on several issues that depart from conservative orthodoxy diminishes their ideological usefulness in the battle for the political hearts and minds of black America. Black Republicans are overwhelmingly concerned with domestic policies and therefore have found it difficult to use their best weapons, the "star power" of Powell and Rice, in their battles with black liberals. Powell's support for a woman's right to choose and affirmative action; Rice's claim that she is "mildly pro-choice" and her ambiguous (and sometimes) changing position on affirmative action; and their reluctant to launch broadsides against the civil rights movement and its leaders make utilization of their prominence in wooing black voters difficult for ideologues who have built careers in harsh opposition to any form of affirmative action, abortion, or government intervention generally.

While it has become commonplace to argue that political labels no longer matter—liberal vs. conservative, Republican vs. Democrat vs. Independent—and that political interests make strange alliances, ideological postures among Republican Party leaders have actually hardened in recent years as the extremist wing of the party has gained influence, and, in terms of the White House and much of Congress, real power. This includes hardline Christian evangelicals, far right political ideologues, nativists, neo-conservatives as well as the traditionally most reactionary wing of capital and the corporate sector. While Powell has situated himself deliberately in the moderate camp, Rice has swung both ways. Most other premier black Republicans have tended to line up with the party's far right wing. There is little evidence of a struggle between moderate black Republicans and those further to the right as the moderates, black or otherwise, are being increasingly marginalized altogether. These categories are critical to understanding the state of the party's current black politics and those who expound them. For the most part, the Republican strategists do not foresee a black realignment of any significance in the immediate or near future. In their wisest moments, they recognize that black anger or frustration with the Democratic Party is because it is moving closer to Republican politics, not in the other direction. Thus, in practical terms, Republican black political discourse is aimed at moderate white Republicans and independents that are hesitant to align with policies that appear racially insensitive or unreasonable. The party, therefore, in seeking political advantage on the issue of race must not only mythologize its present racial narrative but reconstruct its past one as well.

A Counter-History

> You see, I believe in my heart that the Republican party, the party of Lincoln and Frederick Douglass, is not complete without the perspective and support and contribution of African Americans.
>
> George Bush, July 23, 2004[3]

According to Republican Party racial orthodoxy, it is common—indeed necessary—to cite the party lineage of Abraham Lincoln and black leader Frederick Douglass. The two are often cited together because the objective is to associate Lincoln and the Republican Party with the black freedom struggle and imply that the two were one and the same. The purpose is to evoke an affinity with the party that was in power when the slaves were freed and then pushed through radical legislation attacking racial discrimination that led to the brief, but critical Reconstruction era. While the link between Lincoln and the current party of George W. Bush is farcical, the story of a party committed to black liberation in the antebellum and post-antebellum periods is imaginative as well. Despite modern claims to it being the hub of the anti-slavery movement, Lincoln's moderate wing of the party had resisted fighting the Civil War explicitly on the grounds of abolition and black emancipation. As James Steele points out:

> First, Lincoln was unwilling to move outside of the national mood and in the early months of the war there was not a national consensus on emancipation. Second, emancipation raised the question of citizenship rights for the ex-slaves.... Third, a fairly substantial stratum of the North's population had a financial and commercial stake in slavery. Fourth, proslavery sentiment was strong among Union army officers.... Fifth, many Northern Democrats, former Whigs, and conservative Republican businessmen cited the daunting and material costs of the war to urge "peace at any cost."[4]

In the end, left with little choice in order to hold the union together and the need to suppress the rebelling southern states, Lincoln and the party's interests coincided with black objectives of emancipation. By the time he delivered the November 19, 1863, Gettysburg Address, Lincoln recognized and courageously stated that the nation had "unfinished business" and had to deal with the "great task remaining before us."[5] In retelling this history, the contemporary Republican Party has turned a necessity into a virtue and erased the important differences that existed not only between the Republican Party and the Democratic Party, but also between conservative Republicans and their liberal/radical opponents within the party. Black Republicans of the era fell solidly into the latter camp as they took on the challenges and opportunities offered by the Reconstruction period following the end of the Civil War.

Reconstruction was actually two eras: presidential Reconstruction (1865–1867) and congressional or radical Reconstruction (1867–1877). In the first period, which includes the period before Lincoln was assassinated on April 14, 1865, the 13th Amendment, which abolished slavery, was passed and the Bureau for Refugees, Freedmen and Abandoned Lands (known as the Freedmen's Bureau) was established. However, under Lincoln's successor Andrew Johnson little was done to enforce and expand the rights of blacks. In fact, Johnson became increasingly aggressive against the freedom march of blacks including tolerance of restrictive Black Codes being passed in the South and vetoing the Civil Rights Act of 1866, which was overridden by Congress. In 1867, he vetoed three Reconstruction acts that were all again overridden by Congress. Johnson also sought to deny reauthorization of the Freedmen's Bureau. In the second period, progressive congressional Republicans rebelled against the retrenchment of Johnson and passed the 14th Amendment, which gave citizenship to the ex-slaves, and the 15th Amendment, which guaranteed blacks voting rights. Led by Congressman Thaddeus Stevens of Pennsylvania, radicals in Congress called for full rights for blacks.

In this era, 17 blacks were elected to Congress, including Hiram Revels (R–MS) and Blanche K. Bruce (R–MS) to the U.S. Senate, and over 2,000 to local and state offices—all Republicans. While little real long-term economic and social equality was gained, the tremendous leap from slavery to citizenship was an empowering time for black Americans. In their new positions blacks were able to embrace rapidly the few opportunities for political and economic advancement mostly through collective and community efforts. As black Republican political leaders, ironically, the policies advocated by these new politicians served to benefit not only blacks, but also the white working class, the poor, and other excluded groups in society for the first time in U.S. history. The period was one of the most democratic in the country's history.

What is generally erased from the popular version as presented by contemporary Republican spokespeople is that the period came to an end due to the willingness of the conservative Republican Party leadership of the time to trade off black rights for political gain. The Hayes-Tilden Compromise grew out of the battle over disenfranchisement of the black vote and the efforts by southern capital to secure greater appropriations from the federal government. Repressing the black vote and addressing the interests of southern capital were allied because freed blacks were becoming the newest and most exploited sector of southern labor. The 1876 presidential election was thrown in turmoil when Republicans challenged the initial Electoral College and popular vote victory of Democrat Samuel J. Tilden over Republican Rutherford B. Hayes. By challenging and dismissing the votes in Louisiana, South Carolina, and Florida, Tilden's 203–166 Electoral College margin over Hayes shifted to 185–184 for Hayes. The election was thrown to Congress and the Republicans eventually reached a compromise with southern Democrats, who could swing the vote, which gave Hayes the presidency in exchange for removing what was left of the token force of federal troops that protected blacks, increased funding for internal improvements, and a free-for-all land grab. Many troops had already been pulled out, and "black codes" that were reintroducing segregation were increasing, so in one sense the compromise had little real impact on the trajectory of race relations. However, it symbolized the formal retreat by government (Republican) on security and protection of black rights. This bargain between the parties fed white working-class racial prejudices but also served the financial, banking, industrial, and agricultural interests of southern and northern capitalists whom the parties represented. The destruction of Reconstruction also stifled a growing political resistance that embodied class identities as well as racial ones.

In fact, both conservative Republicans and Democrats wanted an end to the era of radical Reconstruction.[6] The retreat on black freedom by the elite political class of both Republicans and Democrats began before the compromise but rapidly consolidated after it. By 1901, there was not a single black in Congress, and virtually all of the political gains at the local and state levels were gone as well except in the all-black western towns. It would take about thirty years and the beginning of a political shift before another black—Oscar S. DePriest (D–IL)—would serve in Congress.

By the time Stagolee shot Billy, Reconstruction had been dead for nearly twenty years with more setbacks and retrenchment to come. In 1896, a year later, the infamous *Plessey v. Ferguson* case was decided in the U.S. Supreme Court that made "separate but equal" legal and completed the destruction of post–Civil War black advancement. In effect, both major parties reached an agreement that black rights were sacrificial. Southern Democrats sought successfully to reestablish white supremacy in the region. Northern Democrats were willing for the sake of party unity to acquiesce to its southern wing. Conservative and moderate Republicans were also willing to tolerate white racism, and, therefore, did not come to the defense of their black constituents. And radical and progressive Republicans were marginal and unable to influence the direction of the party in terms of a progressive agenda on black rights. Above all, the long-standing interests of the northern corporate and financial sectors upon which the Republican Party was founded were no longer threaten by the southern agrarian economy and although the latter still maintained clout in Congress, its dominance of the U.S. economy was broken. From the vantage point of the Republican Party and its objectives, there was nothing to gain by advocating or championing black voting and civil rights. Indeed, there was a great deal to lose: white support. Economic interests aside, the end of the nineteenth century was also an era in which race "science" and eugenics were cited as proving the inferiority of blacks and others who were not white, therefore, justifying their unequal treatment.

The betrayal by both political parties of black interests is the one consistent factor during this period. Blacks continue to participate predominantly in the Republican Party up through the mid-twentieth century because primarily most blacks still lived in the South where Democratic Party resistance to black rights was most acute and the Republicans, for their own political reasons, technically allowed blacks to join the party and gave symbolic reference to civil rights and anti-lynching politics at national conventions. They were the only game in town, a point raised by Condoleezza Rice in explaining her father John's decision to join the GOP in Alabama during the 1950s. It should be noted, however, that during this era the Republican Party did very little to defend or expand black voting rights. This configuration of power would only begin to change when black migration to the North between the two wars generated a renewed contestation for the black vote coupled with benefits gained from the Roosevelt era social programs that were necessary to starve off the collapse of the failing capitalist economy. The emergence of a Keynesian welfare state was urgent and indispensable but had also had the additional advantage that it raised the social and economic life of the poor and working people inclusive of millions of blacks beginning a shift away from the Republican Party.

The increasing conservative tenor of the Republican Party, from Eisenhower to Nixon, pushed many blacks toward the Democratic Party. Just as the earlier Republican Party's stand against slavery had been a catalyst for a political shakeup, an anti-segregationist wing of the Democratic Party became more vocal, and, in 1948, following a strong anti–Jim Crow speech by Minnesota senator Hubert Humphrey, then South Carolina governor Strom Thurmond led a walkout of Dixiecrats who would eventually find their home in the Republican Party. Lyndon Johnson's "war on poverty" and "Great Society" programs had much of the same pull effect as did Roosevelt's redistributive projects a generation earlier. These concrete benefits were much more salient than the oft-noted symbolic phone call made by JFK to Coretta Scott King in 1960 to console her about Martin Luther King, Jr., who was in jail at the time. While it did convey to many blacks that Kennedy was sensitive to the civil rights struggle, it was not enough to qualitatively transform black party allegiance. This pivotal event occurred when Kennedy was running for president against Richard Nixon.[7] Nixon still won 32 percent of the black vote in a losing cause.[8]

Eight years of Democratic presidents, Democratic dominance in Congress, and a growing social uprising by blacks, women, young people, peace activists, and others, led to a revolution in strategy by the Republican Party. The party that Rice and Powell celebrate as looking at them as individuals concluded in the late sixties that it could be successful in national elections if it consciously and methodically went after the white southern vote, thus was born the infamous "southern strategy."[9] The overt and covert themes of the new strategy included opposition to the Civil Rights Act (1964) and the Voting Rights Act (1965), and championing "states' rights," and "law and order," the latter two very thinly veiled expressions of racial coding. Nixon would perfect the strategy in 1968 by winning all of the southern states—states that went to war against the Republican Party—and many non-southern states who still viewed him as a moderate of sorts. The strategy would reach its apogee with the coming of Reagan. He opened his campaign at the Neshoba County Fair near Philadelphia, Mississippi, a city only known for being the site of the murder of three civil rights workers (Michael Schwerner, James Chaney, and Andrew Goodman) in 1964, delivering a speech that defended "states' rights." While he only devoted a small part of the speech to states' rights, the symbolism was glaring, especially since it was revealed that he had initially planned to open his campaign with a speech before the National Urban League. Throughout all of his campaigning in the South, Reagan's strategy was unambiguous: consolidate the white southern vote by making it clear that his administration would stand strong against any expansion of civil rights and indeed would roll back the clock as far as possible on these issues.

By this time, the shift of the Republican Party to the political Right and the near obliteration of its moderate faction were complete. Even more so, the most visible black Republicans since the Reagan era, including elected officials, scholars, businesspeople, and moral and ideological activists, have dedicated themselves to destroying the legacy and gains of past progressive black social movements that did indeed include black Republicans as well as black Democrats, independents, and radicals.

Becoming Republican: Powell and Rice Join the GOP

Powell and Rice are evolved Republicans. They officially and, it can be argued, ideologically became Republicans rather late in their political lives. However, like religious and political converts everywhere, once they crossed the line there was no coming back and intense loyalty has become an ingrained and automatic characteristic. Unlike a number of black Republicans who either joined the party when they were college students or even younger and became conscious politically, or join for opportunistic economic reasons and profited personally from their association with the party, Powell and Rice marinated for many years before completely surrendering to the call. Both admit that they are not natural Republicans and still hold views that are markedly different from the conservative orthodoxy that defines the contemporary iteration of the party. While Powell appears to have come to an ideological rest as a party centrist, Rice continues to move further to the right the longer the Bush administration goes on.

Rice and Powell entered the party through different professional doors and family histories. According to Rice, the Republican Party represents both inclusion, that is, her father's story, and strength, that is, her story. She famously stated at the 2000 Republican National Convention, "My father joined our party because the Democrats in Jim Crow Alabama of 1952 would not register him to vote. The Republicans did. I want you to know—I want you to know that my father has never forgotten that day, and neither have I. I joined the party for different reasons. I found a party that sees me as an individual, not as part of a group. I found a party that puts family first. I found a party that has love of liberty at its core, and I found a party that believes that peace begins with strength."[10] To the cheers of thousands, Rice rewrote the history of party politics in Alabama and her father's own political leanings. First, both parties supported and defended Jim Crow in Alabama and throughout the South, despite momentary or peripheral breeches, countering her implication that the state's Republican Party was not only not racist, but also enlightened.

Second, her father's political actions in both Birmingham and later when the family moved to Denver indicate a more complicated political figure than his daughter presented. There certainly were hesitations on the part of many in Birmingham's black middle class, including the Rices, who retreated from or even criticized the tactics and activities of the civil rights movement in the 1950s. John Rice, though certainly not a leader of the movement, did support it and was involved in black resistance to white terror such as patrolling and protecting a black neighborhood from racist invaders.

Even Rice's own political travels are not the straight line that many Republicans would love to believe. She has said she voted Democratic when she was young in the 1970s and, even after switching parties because she did not agree with Carter's response to the Soviet invasion of Afghanistan in 1980, she served as a foreign policy advisor for liberal Gary Hart's campaign in 1984 to unseat Reagan, hardly the politics of a hardcore Republican conservative. Three years later she came to the attention of Ford's former national security advisor Brent Scowcroft and when Scowcroft resumed that post under the first Bush, she was asked to join his office. She has never stated why she preferred Hart over Reagan, however, as opportunities were proffered through her connections with high-powered Republicans, and as she morphed from academic to political appointee, Rice became more and more conservative in her views eventually forswearing any liberal tendencies and notions.

While the first George Bush's foreign policy team was dominated by moderate realists, a political posture that Rice once articulated, the second Bush rejected those views and gave free rein to the neo-conservatives in his administration who reflected his ideological leanings. Her new convictions seemed less opportunistic and more the responses of an apostle who had no doubts about the conversion and the need to defend doctrine. As she had done in her academic career, Rice demonstrated no dissonance in her loyalty to Bush, his administration, and the Republican Party.

Powell's Republican journey was a bit different. His military career embodied a number of Washington posts that facilitated his climb to general. Because Republicans dominated the White House in the 1970s and 1980s, Powell's political ties were more closely forged with the GOP. However, he also served Democrats thus building bipartisan alliances. Just as he often functioned as the reluctant secretary of state, Powell's tenure in the Republican Party has been stop-and-go from the beginning. Courted by both parties in the mid-1990s when he was the non-partisan chairman of the Joint Chiefs of Staff, his affinity for the Republican Party grew more obvious after he left the Clinton administration in 1993. A concerted move to draft Powell as a candidate in the Republican race for the presidency let Powell tease the nation for months before he finally announced in November 1995 that he would not join the race. While publicly the Republicans floated the "Powell for President" balloon as high as possible, there was trepidation from the conservative and increasingly dominate wing of the party about Powell's politics and where he stood on the issues of the day. This was an era of ascendancy for Newt Gingrich, Tom Delay, and other conservatives in Congress. Building the mythology that the Republican Party core would nominate a black moderate as their candidate had great public relations and ideological value, but had little basis in reality given the hold on the party that the hardliners had seized. Even Powell recognized this contradiction. He stated, "my moderate social views would clash violently with the very conservative and active right wing of the Republican Party, which dominated the primary process."[11]

On November 8, 1995, in a move that took few by surprise, Powell announced that he would not run for the presidency, but also declared his decision to join the Republican Party. He would explain this decision at the press conference stating, "I will continue to speak out forcefully in the future on the issues of the day. . . . I will do so as a member of the Republican Party, and try to assist the party in broadening its appeal. I believe I can help the party of Lincoln move once again close to the spirit of Lincoln. I will give my talent and energy to charitable and educational activities. I will also try to find ways for me to help heal the racial divides that still exist within our society."[12] Evoking Lincoln was necessary of course as Powell sought to rationalize joining a party whose record on race was abysmal.

His differences with the party, on the surface, would appear pretty severe. He has expressed his revulsion at the infamous "Willie Horton" campaign advertisement developed by the late Republican strategist Lee Atwater. He viewed the ad as "racist" and a "political cheap shot."[13] By his own admission, he is pro-choice though he advocates abstinence, adoption, and contraception as first options. He believes in a person's right to bear arms, but argues for some forms of gun control. A fourth intolerable position is his support for affirmation action—"without quotas"—that he believes is still needed. He wrote, "I identified myself as a fiscal conservative, but a moderate on social issues. I was clearly out of step with the prevailing social views of the very conservative, activist wing of the Republican Party, although probably very much in step with the mainstream."[14]

Despite these reservations, he announced his formal entry into the party the year after Gingrich and his radical Republicans won the House of Representatives and let loose the "Contract with America" agenda that restructured and reformed that body in the most conservative manner in living memory and set public policy on a right-wing course. What many called the "Contract on America" was an extremist assault on public policies that were viewed as gratuitous and even destructive concessions to liberals, minorities, women, labor, human rights organizations, and environmental groups. While Powell hinted at his reluctance to join the Gingrich coup, he also did not speak out forcefully against it. More so, he did not explain how his membership in the increasingly shrinking and marginalized moderate wing of the party was going to make a difference. Between the time he joined in 1995 and was selected to enter the Bush II administration, there is little evidence that Powell fought to bring the party "close to the spirit of Lincoln" as he saw it other than what he did as personal services outside of the party.

Yet, despite their high profiles and commitment to the party, neither Powell nor Rice dominate or reflect contemporary black Republican political styles and activism. That slack is carried by an array of faux organizations, political appointees, and media-built individuals with financial and political backing by the Far Right and elite political interests. It is at the far end of the political spectrum where black Republican leaders dwell.

Bought and Souless: Contemporary Black Republicans

> Supporting segregation need not be racist. One can believe in segregation and believe in equality of the races.
>
> Ward Connerly[15]

The most notable fact about activist black Republicans during the George W. Bush era is their political and social distance from the black community and its concerns, although their careers are fundamentally constructed on the soft sands of their black racial identity. In other words, their political value to the Republican Party is based on the very factor that they reject. While perhaps one could make a similar case regarding the Democratic Party and its relationship with the black community, the politics of black Republicans exhibit little overlap with the expressed interests and concerns of the black community. As individuals and organizations, their agenda has more or less merged with the most conservative ideologues of the party. They echo the party's stalwarts who argue that anti-black racism has virtually disappeared and, in any instance, does not account for persistent black poverty and other long-term disparities. That is attributed to faults of those internal to the black community and the inability of the black community under its current liberal leadership to get its own house in order. Government intervention programs, such as the loathed affirmative action, minority set-asides, or job training and education programs specifically aimed at minorities, not only are unnecessary, but also actually cause more harm than good to blacks. They offer as an alternative strategy a renewed entrepreneurial spirit of self-help (although they are not opposed to government-sponsored education vouchers and faith-based initiative funding), and the embrace of market capitalism. For many black Republican activists, there is also a strong link with Christian fundamentalism, which drives their opposition to abortion, gay rights, gay marriage, and stem cell research and other cultural issues. There is little intellectual debate among them, and they more often than not simply echo the most pedestrian bromides from the political Right.

As a whole, Bush era black Republicans not only lack politically independent ideas, but also are economically enslaved to their conservative benefactors. Black Republicans (and black conservative groups who dishonestly claim non-partisanship) are almost universally funded by a small set of white conservative organizations, think tanks, and research institutions. Much of the funding for these groups, if not all for some, is from right-wing foundations such as Castle Rock Foundation, John M. Olin Foundation, Lynde and Harry Bradley Foundation, and Hoover Institution.[16] These are the bedrocks funders for the political right in the United States. They have financed anti–affirmative action campaigns, attacks on liberal policy-makers, anti-abortion organizations, and the whole litany of conservative Republican causes.

Underlying these political molestations is an ideological framework that seeks to rollback the progressive policy initiatives, particularly those that emerged out of the 1960s, which are viewed as aberrations in U.S. social history that has bequeathed a liberal legacy in public life that must be reversed. Individual liberties, that is, the right to be a bigot, overreaching court decisions, states' rights, and family values are foundational themes of this ideology that have been embraced by black conservatives. While Powell may reach back to Lincoln, most contemporary prominent black Republicans find their ideological roots in Ronald Reagan.

Organizations

At its 1972 national convention in Miami, the Republican National Committee formally established the National Black Republican Council (NBRC). In part, this was the Republican Party's insincere response to a politically mobilized black community that fought for substantial changes in distributive public policy regarding race and poverty. Nixon himself would embrace the notion of "black power" by which he meant some version of black capitalism. However, the NBRC seems to have disappeared possessing no website or, as far as can be determined, a stable national office. In any case, it was stillborn never having the capacity or perhaps even the will to challenge the party's racial politics and policy agenda. At the national level, the most visible black Republican organization is the African American Republican Leadership Council (AARLC) whose stated purpose is "to break the liberal democrat stranglehold over Black America."[17] Touting the values of Reaganism, the AARLC seems averse to actually promoting black American Republican leadership given that thirteen of its fifteen-member advisory board are white including high-powered hard-line conservatives such as Gary Bauer, Sean Hannity, Grover Norquist, and Paul Weyrich. Much of the material on the website seems to be concerned with continuing the legacy of Reagan while ignoring the issues that black Americans consistently state are most important to them. The organization is very specific about the types of black Americans it seeks. According to the website, "AARLC is the only nationwide conservative Republican organization dedicated to elect [sic] Reaganite pro-growth economic security African American Republicans to local, state and the federal government."[18]

Rice and Powell are pictured on the website (as well as Reagan and George W. Bush), but they are not given any prominence or special attention. Much of the information consists of news stories from conservative websites covering both domestic and international news. In other words, the ideological warfare that AARLC claims it wants to engage in with black liberals appears pretty muted. Its statements on social security, national defense, fiscal policy, and education are more sound bites than arguments. Though it boasts branches in Baltimore, Baton Rouge, Chicago, Mississippi, and Seattle, there is little information on the actual work of the organization.

Another black Republican organization is the National Leadership Network of Black Conservatives, also known as Project 21. One of the most prominent black conservative groups, Project 21 is a subsidiary of the National Center for Public Policy Research. The NCPPR was formed to support Reagan's covert wars in Central America during the 1980s and other conservative policies of his administration. As it notes on its website, it is "an initiative of the National Center for Public Policy Research to promote the views of African-Americans whose entrepreneurial spirit, dedication to family and commitment to individual responsibility has not traditionally been echoed by the nation's civil rights establishment."[19] The NCPPR is a major conservative think tank born in the Reagan era and maintains a strong base with evangelical Christians. It promotes a hard line on defense policies as well as on most other issues.

Project 21 has commented on a number of foreign policy concerns. In a press release issued by Project 21, it cheered the efforts of the Bush administration, Powell in particular, regarding the crisis situation in Darfur, Sudan.[20] The press release consisted mostly of statements by Project 21 members such as Kevin Martin who stated, "I applaud President Bush and Secretary Powell for taking a leadership role in this attempt to end what I call pure ethnic cleansing in the Darfur region of Sudan." While noting the overall deaths that have occurred, Project 21 seemed to focus in particular on the welfare of Sudanese Christians who were being targeted by government-backed militias. Project 21 and other conservatives failed to note that when Powell declared that genocide was occurring in Darfur, a declaration that in the past initiated (theoretically) immediate international intervention, the Bush administration did nothing.

Project 21 also weighed in on the Iraq war again targeting liberal black activists. It denounced Rev. Jesse Jackson as a virtual traitor for raising criticisms about the war. Again, it cited whom it called African American leaders who were outraged by Jackson's statements calling the U.S. invasion a "crime against humanity." Michael King of Atlanta stated, "Jesse Jackson's motives have never been as transparent as they were with these statements. If anyone needs to apologize, it's him. He indulges his fantasies and delusions of grandeur by calling for Bush's impeachment and calling for United Nations action against us. But blacks are beginning to see the truth—that Jackson's bluster is exactly that: all smoke and no substance." This and other statements, for the most part, read like White House press releases containing little substantial critique or salience. In any case, Project 21 leaders were out of sync with the overwhelming opinion of the black community that Bush's war was wrong, unjustified, built on false claims, and murderous.[21]

Another foreign policy issue that afforded Project 21 with an opportunity to blast liberal black leaders was the crisis in Haiti. The Brotherhood Organization for a New Destiny, headed up by Project 21 member Rev. Jesse Lee Peterson, sent a letter to Rep. Joel Hefley (R–CO), chair of the U.S. House of Representatives'

Committee on Standards of Official Conduct asking for a formal investigation of the relationship of the Congressional Black Caucus to deposed Haitian president Jean-Bertrand Aristide. The April 1, 2004, letter was supported by Project 21. Implying a traitorous relationship, the letter stated, "We are seriously concerned about the inflammatory language and tone of [the CBC's] accusations. By misinterpreting the truth about what happened in the last few hours before [former Haitian president] Aristide left office, these lawmakers are inciting hatred, suspicion and possibly violence towards the White House, State Department officials and the new administration in Haiti."[22]

It is notable that in each instance, Project 21 counts on its blackness as a legitimizing factor in being able to raise criticisms against liberal and progressive black leaders, policy-makers, and activists. While they abhor racial identities, they are tactical enough to attempt to use their in-group identity to raise issues that cannot be raised so comfortably by white conservatives. Yet, their surrender to racializing their identities undercuts their very argument since their views are so in contradiction with prevailing stances by black Americans. Arguments are not put forth from the well-developed conservative paradigm but rather from the shaky edges of accusations, demagoguery, and bluff.

Black America Political Action Committee (BAMPAC) was founded in 1994 and is led by Alan Keyes. It focuses, like other black conservatives, on abortion, economic self-help, moral values, and limited government. As a "registered unaffiliated non-partisan Political Action Committee," it supports candidates who "are committed to supporting our common sense approach to public policy and politics; promoting Social Security reform, improving public education, expanding economic opportunities to historically disadvantaged sectors in America, vigorously promoting equality for all Americans, protecting the sanctity of human life and restoring moral values and the importance of the family in our communities."[23] The organization claims that it is among the "top 25 PACs in the country, with over 137,000 donors," and that in 2003, it had revenues over $1.6 million.[24]

While not as vitriolic as Project 21 or some other black conservatives, in the end BAMPAC's agenda blends well with the objectives of the Bush administration, which is featured prominently in BAMPAC's materials. Keyes is well known as a combative political foe of black liberals. And although most of the donations made to BAMPAC are unitemized, it is likely that it comes from a white conservative constituency that has funded much of the black conservative movement. A similar relationship exists between the Black Alliance for Educational Options, the aforementioned African American Republican Leadership Council, Alternative Black Speakers Program, American Civil Rights Initiative, and Lincoln Institute, the best known of the conservative black groups.

Individuals

A strategy of modern Republicanism, dating back to Reagan, is to locate extremely conservative racial or ethnic minorities and help them win elected office, or give them prominent appointments or nominations for high offices. The objective is to display visual racial diversity while maintaining ideological lockstep. George W. Bush has followed in this tradition and a number of individual black elected Republicans have been given national prominence by the Republican Party. Although none have been elected with much black support, they feed the illusion of inclusion sought by Bush. This includes individuals such as Secretary of State Ken Blackwell of Ohio, who played a central role in Bush's victory in that pivotal state in the 2004 presidential election. He served not only as secretary of state, which made him the state's chief elections officer, but also co-chair of the Committee to Re-elect George Bush in Ohio.

Prior to the 1980s, Blackwell had been a member of the Democratic Party and the Charter Party of Cincinnati where he had served as a council member and mayor. He finally landed in the Republican Party's far right corner and garnered several positions under George H. W. Bush including deputy secretary in the Department of Housing and Urban Development, and ambassador to the United Nations Commission on Human Rights, and then appointments by Ohio Republican governor George Voinovich. George W. Bush tasked Blackwell to lead the U.S. delegation to the preparatory meetings for the UN World Conference Against Racism where it played a disruptive and sabotaging role. Though he would never be mistaken for a human rights activist, Blackwell has managed to be involved with a number of (conservative) human rights groups. This includes his past or present board membership with the Physicians for Human Rights and the Congressional Human Rights Foundation, and a scholar-in-residence at the Urban Morgan Institute for Human Rights at the University of Cincinnati's College of Law, and associations with the International League for Human Rights and the National Council of the Lawyers Committee for Human Rights. In the 2004 Ohio election, Blackwell not only supported a measure to ban same-sex marriages, which served to mobilize the Republican conservative base including blacks, but also was the only prominent Republican to want to include additional opposition to civil unions, domestic partnerships, and attacked other rights and anti-discrimination policies for homosexuals that have been enacted in most other states. That he was ever appointed to positions having to do with human rights and racial justice is a travesty. He has decided to run for governor of Ohio in the 2006 election.

An equally enthusiastic partisan can be found in Lt. Gov. Michael Steele of Maryland. Steele reached a national audience when he gave a rabid speech at the

2004 Republican National Convention attacking Democrats. He is on the executive committee of the National Republican Committee and former state chairman of the Maryland Republican Party. Prior to his election as lieutenant governor, he was the first black chairman of the Prince George's County Republican Party and then the first chairman of the Maryland Republican Party. He was a monk for about two-and-a-half years but left before he took his vows. From there he went to law school and became a corporate lawyer specializing in securities. As of this writing, Steele is considering a run for the U.S. Senate in Maryland in 2007 setting up a potential challenge to ex-congressman and former president of the NAACP Kweisi Mfume in 2007, who is running as a Democrat.

In 2004, the racially cynical nature of contemporary Republican black politics was on display in Illinois when the party decided to support as a candidate for the U.S. Senate long-time Republican gadfly Alan Keyes to challenge Democrat Barack Obama, the aforementioned black state senator who had won the primary and was virtually assured of a November victory. Although Keyes did not and had never lived in Illinois, and had accused Hilary Clinton previously of being a carpetbagger when she ran for the Senate in New York State, he and the Republican Party demonstrated no hesitation in attempting to racialize the contest and essentially offer white voters a black alternative to Obama. Keyes's platform consisted of opposition to gay marriage and other conservative causes. Lacking any legitimacy, political base, or popularity whatsoever he was trounced in the election wining only 27 percent to Obama's 70 percent.

The most infamously successful of the black Republican activists has been Ward Connerly. The former aide to then California assembly member and future governor Pete Wilson built his connections with Republicans into a million dollar consulting business. In 1993, Connerly was appointed to the University of California's Board of Regents, where he made it his mission to attack affirmative action, not only in education but also across the spectrum. He established his American Civil Rights Institute, with massive funding from the Lynde and Harry Bradley Foundation, Hickory Foundation, John M. Olin Foundation, William Donner Foundation, and Sarah Scaife Foundation among others, the elite of the conservative foundations. From that perch, he launched Proposition 209, which sought to eliminate affirmative action in the state. Known as the "California Civil Rights Initiative," and drafted by two California State University professors Glynn Custred and Tom Wood, the initiative was passed on a ballot. In 2003, Connerly launched Proposition 54, the "Racial Privacy Initiative," which sought to bar the state from collecting racial data. It was opposed by not only civil rights groups, labor unions, and community groups, but even Arnold Schwarzenegger who was running for governor in a special election. The initiative was soundly defeated with about 64 percent of the state voting against it.

While a number of Bush's white nominations to the federal judiciary have been just as unqualified, it is somewhat stunning the sheer gall he has displayed in some of his black judicial choices. He nominated, for example, Janice Brown for the DC Appeals Court. She is an extremist in every meaningful sense of the word. Using tactics similar to those employed in placing Clarence Thomas on the U.S. Supreme Court and Condoleezza Rice as secretary of state, Republicans highlight her background of being born into southern segregation and rising to serve on the California Supreme Court, a self-help narrative meant to reinforce a paradigm of government disengagement and personal responsibility. In an April 2000 speech, Brown stated, "Where government moves in, community retreats, civil society disintegrates and our ability to control our own destiny atrophies.... The result is a debased, debauched culture which finds moral depravity entertaining and virtue contemptible."[25] She does not just oppose affirmative action and abortion rights, but vigorously so. Roosevelt's New Deal was referred to as "the triumph of our socialist revolution."[26]

No Integrity Left Behind

The closeness of black Republicans to the Bush White House was revealed in a scandal that erupted in early January 2005. *USA Today* broke the story that Armstrong Williams, one of the nation's most visible black Republican commentators, had been paid $241,000 to promote the administration's "No Child Left Behind" (NCLB) program, specifically to the black community. In his newspaper columns, on the radio, and on several television programs including his own he praised and pushed the NCLB law without disclosing that he was being paid to do so. According to the *Washington Post*, the contract not only obliged him to run advertisements on his show but also to "regularly comment on NCLB during the course of his broadcasts" and to encourage other producers to "periodically address NCLB" in a positive light as well.[27]

The arrangement stipulated that the Ketchum public relations firm hired by the Education Department would "arrange for Williams to regularly comment on NCLB during the course of his broadcasts" and that "Secretary Paige and other department officials shall have the option of appearing from time to time as studio guests" and that "Williams shall utilize his long-term working relationships with 'America's Black Forum'... to encourage the producers to periodically address the No Child Left Behind Act." Ketchum is the same agency hired to do the fake news videos for the Department of Health and Human

Services about its Medicare prescription drug plan, which were determined to be in violation of the 1998 Appropriations Bill in May 2004. Section 628 of the law prohibits the use of appropriated funds for publicity or propaganda purposes within the United States.

Williams begrudgingly acknowledged that he had used, in his words, "bad judgment," and attributed his mistake to a lack of training in journalism. When he was asked about his violation of the well-known code of ethics that journalists abide by, or the Public Relations Society of America's [PRSA] Code of Ethics that prohibits "lying by omission," he gave the equivalent of Butterfly McQueen's famous quote in "Gone With the Wind" and stated, "I don't know anything about these kinds of documents."[28] The PRSA guidelines state that publicists should, "Avoid actions and circumstances that may appear to compromise good business judgment or create a conflict or potential conflict between personal and professional interests . . . [publicists should] Disclose promptly any existing or potential conflict of interest to affected clients or organizations."

His mea culpa only went so far however. He stated defiantly, apparently clueless to the seriousness of the accusations being made or the damage to his reputation, that "I have no intention of giving any money back. They got what they paid for—and they got it cheaply. I'm in a business. This is how I earn a living, I sell advertising."[29] Williams offered an apology of sorts. He wrote,

> In 2003, I agreed to run a paid ad on my syndicated television show, promoting the Department of Education's No Child Left Behind Act. I subsequently used my column space to support that legislation. This represents an obvious conflict of interests. People have used this conflict of interests to portray my column as being paid for by the Bush Administration. Nothing could be further from the truth. At the same time, I understand that I exercised bad judgment in running paid advertising for an issue that I frequently write about in my column.[30]

It was not only Williams's column that had been paid for by his Republican benefactors but his entire career.

He first became known nationally during the Clarence Thomas Supreme Court confirmation hearings when he defended Thomas vigorously in the media. He had once worked for Thomas when he headed up the Equal Employment Opportunity Commission. Williams parlayed his few moments in the media spotlight into a feeble public relations career including a radio show, short-lived television show, "On the Right Side," and a syndicated news column. Although he had no training as a journalist, scholar, or professional publicist, his novelty as an outspoken black Republican and his ties to the conservative establishment propelled him forward. As a loyal aide to Sen. Strom Thurmond, the segregationist who lead the Dixiecrats from the Democrat Party to the Republican Party in 1948, Williams glued himself to the right wing of the party at an early age. He saw no contradiction in working for a staunch defender of white power who had secretly fathered a black daughter, Essie Mae Washington-Williams, a secret he shared with Williams. He was also mentored by the late Republican strategist Lee Atwater.[31]

Black Republican Women and the Growing Security State

While the black Republican media landscape has been dominated by men, there are a number of black women Republicans who are protégés of Rice, and who are becoming prominent in U.S. foreign policy and international affairs circles. If the idea that black Americans would adopt the conservative foreign policies of George W. Bush and the neo-conservatives seemed anathema to black progressives, it is probably even more of a tremor to blacks and feminists that black women would embrace and promote such policies. However, the second Bush administration has demonstrated time and time again that race, ethnicity, and gender are trumped by ideology. For these black women, their racial and gendered experiences traveling in venues that have been exclusively white, male, and upper class have been mostly veiled, and it is unlikely that they will address these issues in any public manner.

Kiron K. Skinner has emerged as a scholar and strong proponent of Ronald Reagan's vision and ideology. Skinner is an assistant professor of history and political science at Carnegie Mellon and a research fellow at the Hoover Institution at Stanford University where Rice taught and served as provost. She formerly conducted research for then Secretary of State George Schultz's memoir. She also worked with Rice on her book *Germany Unified and Europe Transformed: A Study in Statecraft* as a researcher and is collaborating with her on a book about the end of the Cold War. Skinner has built her reputation as one of the pre-eminent Reagan scholars in the country. She has edited or co-edited five books of his writings: *Reagan, In His Own Hand: The Writings of Ronald Reagan that Reveal His Revolutionary Vision for America*; *Stories in His Own Hand: The Everyday Wisdom of Ronald Reagan*; *Reagan: A Life in Letters*; *Reagan's Path to Victory: The Shaping of Ronald Reagan's Vision: Selected Writings*; and *Reagan In His Own Voice*. She has also written for the conservative *National Interest* on whose board sit a number of prominent conservatives including former Secretary of State Henry Kissinger; scholars Francis Fukuyama, Daniel Pipes, and Samuel Huntington; journalist Charles Krauthammer, and former Bush official Richard Perle.

In her undoubting admiration for Reagan, his extensive polarizing record on race is ignored or rationalized. During his early political years he opposed open housing legislation in California, the Civil Rights Act of 1964, and the Voting Rights Act of 1965. During his run for president he judicially used racially coded language ("welfare queens" and "states' rights") and reinvigorated the southern strategy. As president, he resisted the extension of the Civil Rights Act, attempted to win tax exemption for the racially discriminating Bob Jones University, accorded support to Apartheid in South Africa, and honored Nazi soldiers in Germany. It is well documented that the social and economic gap between black and Latino Americans and white Americans (as well as between lower income and upper income Americans) grew under Reagan, reversing gains that had been made under Presidents Johnson, Nixon, Ford, and Carter. Throughout his entire political career, he exhibited a long history of racial insensitivity at best and raw bigotry at worse.

Skinner not only ignores this part of Reagan's character, but also actively defends him. Reagan was roundly criticized for not condemning the endorsement of his campaign by the racist, far right John Birch Society when he first ran for governor of California. Skinner accepted his excuse about the "free speech" rights of the John Birch Society as his cover—although he had launched an all out assault against the free speech rights of liberals and student activists when he was elected to the governorship—viewing it as an admirable stand on principal.[32] Skinner also conveniently ignored Reagan's delay in condemning his endorsement by the Ku Klux Klan during the 1980 race.[33] She took the same position of respecting "principal" on Reagan's decision to visit the German Nazi cemetery at Bitburg.

Beyond the academic world, Skinner has been appointed to the Defense Policy Board Advisory Committee (DPB). The bipartisan board advises the secretary of defense on matters related to defense policy. Under George W. Bush and Defense Secretary Donald Rumsfeld, the DPB has been dominated by neoconservatives and influential in policy battles over Afghanistan and Iraq. She also sits on the boards of the Atlantic Council of the United States, a conservative foreign policy think tank, and the World Affairs Council of Pittsburgh, a nonpartisan organization active around international affairs.

Another protégé of Rice's is Jendayi Frazier current U.S. ambassador to South Africa. She attended Stanford, studying under Rice, and later worked with her at the National Security Council as senior director for African affairs. When Rice testified before her combative hearings regarding her nomination as secretary of state, Frazier sat behind her as a show of support and perhaps to send a not-so-subtle message that the all-white and nearly all-male Senate Judiciary Committee was confronting issues of race and gender as well as politics.

Summary

Contemporary black Republicans have one main purpose: obfuscate and deflect attention from the persistent and deeply rooted racial disparities that characterize U.S. society. The black-white social and economic divide is impossible to ignore and uncomfortable to address by a Republican Party that holds political power across the board, therefore, deflection, remains the strategy of choice. Significantly, this is a strategy aimed at white America.

Moderate black Republican views, those that Powell wants to associate himself with, are muted and have little currency among party leaders. Surveys indicate that even among black Republicans, in general there is support for redistributive social programs that would address the social and economic gap. And clearly some black support for the Republican Party is borne out of frustration with the limits of the Democratic Party. However, there is little room for moderate views on race and other issues in the current era.

It was reported that one of Reagan's greatest personal disappointments is that he was seen widely as racially insensitive. He found it difficult to believe that his stories of having a black friend in college and a father who opposed segregated theaters were not enough to eliminate black enmity toward him. In Reagan's mind, there was a severe disconnect between the policies he advocated and implemented and their impact on racial progress and his view that individual relationships were all that counted when it came to racial equality.

George W. Bush has had a similar dissonance. His appointments of Powell, Rice, and other minorities, and his promotion of an "ownership society" are his conceptual limits in terms of race relations. That his policies as president have done little to address the racial divide is obscure to him. The high media visibility of conservative black Republicans, along with the presence of Powell and Rice, has reinforced his administration's and his own view that race—up until the Katrina disaster—does not matter any more.

Three

Turkeys in the Stew: Race and Representation in the Era of George W. Bush

A few carefully bred turkeys, the occasional Colin Powell, or Condoleezza Rice...are given absolution and a pass to Frying Pan Park. The remaining millions lose their jobs, are evicted from their homes, have their water and electricity connections cut, and die of AIDS. Basically they're for the pot. Who can say that turkeys are against Thanksgiving? They participate in it!

> Writer Arundhati Roy, commenting on the annual presidential ritual of freeing one turkey at the expense of millions more[1]

Racial Realism in Contemporary America

While a famous black writer famously referred to Bill Clinton as America's first "black president," according to a poll by CBS-BET, only 11 percent of black Americans believed that George W. Bush has "soul."[2] The soul that Bush is perceived to be lacking is the alienation that his administration has generated with the black community due to its poor record on civil rights, his military and political assaults on the international system, and his personal inability or unwillingness to address the nation and the world's continuing racial disparities and other problems related to discrimination and social exclusion.

If one were only to listen to the speeches of George W. Bush, it would not be hard to conclude that racial discrimination in the United States is about as urgent as an increase in jaywalking or widespread shoplifting. When he is not evading the issue altogether, he speaks in clichés and sound bites that expose his marginal/tangential interest in the issue. As a draft report by the U.S. Commission on Civil Rights stated, "President Bush seldom speaks about civil rights, and when he does, it is to carry out official duties, not to promote initiatives or plans for improving opportunity."[3] This is not surprising given his record in Texas as governor on civil rights, a record long on injustice and disregard. That he came to power as a result of the disenfranchisement of Florida voters, disproportionately black, was an appropriate foreshadowing of his first term.

Bush came into the White House in a period when public commitment by policy-makers to racial equality and racial justice were in retreat. Since the 1980s, public policy and public discourse have been dominated by what an important study on race termed the "racial realists," whose views are coterminous with that of the Bush administration and, more broadly, conservative America.[4] The racial realists argue that racism is a phenomenon of the past; to the degree that racial disparities exist, it is not due to racism but to cultural, social, and perhaps even genetic flaws in racial minorities themselves; and civil rights leaders are more responsible for perpetuating racial division than white institutional or structural racism.[5] For the racial realists, including Bush, racism is "motivated, crude, explicitly supremacist, and typically expressed as individual bias."[6]

In the post–civil rights movement era, racial realism appears to be not only logical but also progressive and modern. Legal segregation is over. High-profile minorities exist in every field and occupation. Public discourse on race is intolerant of racist slurs and insults. Indeed, the only reason race remains an issue is due to the continual harping by civil rights leaders who use the issue to justify their existence. The racial realists argue that as far as public policy is concerned, there is no need for any new legislation nor, as conservative columnist George Will contends, even a commission to monitor civil rights compliance—even if that commission is dominated by conservatives.[7]

The racial realist theorists include academics such as Stephen and Abigail Thernstrom, Dinesh D'Souza, and Shelby Steele; and journalists such as Jim Sleeper and Tamar Jacoby whose writings have had a direct influence on public policy from welfare reform to affirmative action. Since the Republican revolution in Congress, much of their work has been cited in developing social policy on Capitol Hill. They have also gained influence since Bush came into office. In December 2004, after the forced early resignation of then–U.S. Civil Rights Commission chair Mary Francis Berry, Abigail Thernstrom, a member of the commission, was elevated to vice chairperson.

Individually, the racial travels of Powell and Rice represent very different narratives in the American black saga. Powell's is one of black Caribbean immigrants and the struggle for a multiple kind of integration in New York City. Rice's story embodies the contradictions of pre-1960s black southern middle-class lifestyles and political choices, as well as subsequently being raised in her teen years in overwhelmingly white Colorado, as far from the politics and culture of the deep South as possible.

Powell and Rice have a serendipitous personal linkage. In a way, Birmingham, Alabama, is a gateway to the racial perceptions of both Powell and Rice. She grew up in the city, and it is a salient point of reference that she uses often in explaining who she is (and what it has to do with her views on racial progress in the United States). In terms of Powell, Birmingham was the home of Alma Johnson, whom Powell married there on August 24, 1962. The Johnsons and the Rices were stellar representatives of Birmingham's relatively small but critical black middle class. Both families were engaged in the field of education. In 1944, Alma's father, Robert, became principal of Parker High School that had been the only high school for blacks in the city. Alma's uncle became principal of the second black high school in the city, Ullman High. Condoleezza's father, John Wesley Rice, was a guidance counselor at Ullman.[8] Though much older, Alma knew Condoleezza when she was a small child. For the northern urbanized Powells, Alabama and the South in general, in the early 1960s, represented racial backwardness at its worse. Powell's parents initially hesitated about going to the wedding and joked about being lynched. Unlike for most blacks in the North, the South was alien turf to the immigrant Powells known only through its notorious reputation as a cauldron of racism.

While many of the stories involving race in Powell's and Rice's lives have been told many times, more often than not they have been constructed in ways that speak of rags-to-riches or up-from-oppression mobility fables rather than provide insight on the multivariate means by which different racial constructions occur and how they are reinforced socially and politically in spite of individual resistance. These stories in their conservative incarnations have legitimated the arguments of the racial realists and served the political interests of a party that desires to break the hold that the Democratic Party has on the black vote without making fundamental changes in their policy objectives and rationalizations. They certainly would like to produce or reproduce large quantities of Powells and Rices, that is, black Americans who are high achievers and who deny, for the most part, that their achievements had anything to do with challenges to racial power relations or hard won government intervention, and who remain mostly silent on America's race problems.

Despite their affiliation and leadership roles in the Bush administration, Powell and Rice have remained popular figures in some sectors of the black community. Unlike many black conservatives, who seem to be clinical cases of self-loathing, Powell and Rice both speak of being black in positive terms. Although neither wants to be seen through a racial lens, they do not reject black identities or blackness in the disturbing manner of Clarence Thomas or Ward

Connerly, both of whom seem to speak of their racial being with shame and embarrassment.

Despite these important differences with other black Republicans, who focus on domestic issues, Powell and Rice unite with them on many other points of what can be called the black conservative racial orthodoxy. First, they deny the harms of collective discrimination as an ongoing phenomenon. This fits in with Rice's views of individualization, that is, racism is practiced by individuals and can be resolved by individual acts of resistance. Although less arrogant than Rice, Powell is in essential agreement with this thesis. This argument assumes that the end of de jure racism eliminated any role that the state had in the perpetuation or defense of racial discrimination.

Second, they also deny that they are beneficiaries of collective struggle. While they note the importance of the civil right movement, its fundamental goals and benefits are distorted and manipulated. Their critique here is nuanced. Black struggles are melted into a broad American narrative of ongoing democratization that denies any notion of white collective responsibility for the nation's horrible racial past. Individual merit is privileged over indirect group struggle.

Third, it is argued that real discrimination is buried in the past. To the degree racial prejudice is acknowledged to still exist, it is not institutional but individual, and it is not significant and no social strategy is needed, just individual boldness. Stories of Rice's resistance to racist teachers or to store clerks are never linked to the institutions that placed these individuals in their positions, likely defended their behavior, and continued to reproduce discrimination despite Rice's "heroic" intervention. Powell's views on the military also seem to echo these sentiments. While acknowledging the legacies of racism, some of which he experienced, he essentially sees a success story in which a system of racism in the military has disappeared. Indeed, Powell would ask, "How could an institution that selected a second generation black immigrant to be its chief be racist?" This question, for Powell, answers itself.

And fourth, under no circumstances is the notion of reparations or compensation to be considered. Opponents of these remedies argue that contemporary Western societies and whites as individuals played no role in past discrimination and should not have to pay for the misdeeds of their ancestors. They argue that the victories of the civil rights era and other legal changes have created a more or less even playing field and that everyone now begins with the same opportunities and chances. Remedies such as reparations would only punish innocent whites and reward undeserving blacks.

The paradigm of the racial realists has been challenged not only in the United States but also increasingly around the globe. As racial and ethnic minorities in other states demonstrate more agency in seeking social justice and inclusion, they have offered alternative critiques as to the nature and contours of their racial states. The international struggle against racism in all of its myriad forms was on full display only eight months into the Bush administration at the UN World Conference against Racism, Racial Discrimination, Xenophobia, and Related Intolerance (WCAR) in Durban, South Africa, from August 31–September 8, 2001. The twenty-first century began not only with a new U.S. administration determined to remap the international political system, but also with a global community that sought to place the issue of racism at the center of a world stage.

The World Conference against Bush

Powell and Rice would play major roles in the key political decisions regarding U.S. official participation in the WCAR. As a case study in Bush era diplomacy, it is an instructive point of departure demonstrating not only some critical differences between Powell and Rice and how they tactically seek (or not) to balance the issue of racial justice and U.S. strategic interests, but also the difference in their balance of power within the administration during its first term.

UN conferences reflect the general strengths and weaknesses of the United Nations itself. While the coming together of the global community is or should be a case of the sum being greater and more progressive than the parts, the politics of national sovereignty often reigns. Most states in the international system, including the United States, have signed and ratified many of the UN legal instruments regarding human rights and anti-discrimination, yet few would agree that those documents have been enforced broadly. Racism and xenophobia, in particular as related to minority populations and immigrants, have been ignored by most states in their domestic policies regardless of their stated commitment to equality and inclusion. An already limited mandate for the United Nations was weakened even more with the fall of the Soviet Union and its role balancing the political initiatives of the West. By the time Bush entered office, the posture of the United States was either to dominate the body or simply ignore it. Neo-conservatives in the administration, including John Bolton (who Bush selected to be U.S. ambassador to the United Nations), felt that the United Nations was anti–United States and perhaps not needed at all. Unlike most UN activities, however, the WCAR could not be disregarded by the United States, in part, because of its resonance among U.S. communities of color. The WCAR process actually involved two conferences: a gathering of non-governmental organizations (NGOs) at an "NGO Forum" that produced its own "Declaration" and "Program of Action," followed by a conference of governments in which some NGOs would be allowed to attend that would also produce a set of official documents.

The process involving U.S. official participation in the WCAR began during the Clinton administration. Though skittish about some of the themes and politics emerging around the conference, the Clinton administration was involved in the preparatory gatherings and was poised to attend. Though it is not possible to state definitively that the U.S. government under an Al Gore administration would not have concluded that what was perceived as unacceptable attacks on Israel—the main pretense used by the Bush administration—meant that it should bow out, at the practical level, at least, the Democrats were engaged. After the 2000 election, Secretary of State–designate Powell was briefed by UN officials, staff from the State Department and other agencies, and by NGOs about the conference and apparently was enthused initially about attending. Indications from those earlier meetings were that Powell likely would attend the conference. Yet, it was clear early on that the Bush administration was looking for an escape hatch, not only because it did not want to address the issue of racism, but also more broadly the conference conflicted with the administration's goal of marginalizing the United Nations.

National Security Advisor Rice, reflecting the general tone of the new administration, was alarmed about the WCAR from day one. According to the *New York Times*, she was critical particularly of the reparations proposal that called for Western governments to pay compensation for slavery and the slave trade, which was taking shape in a number of drafts of the official documents, a posture that a number of European governments were also taking.[9] She and Elliott Abrams, then with the National Security Council, were also concerned about drafts of statements regarding Israel, which they considered biased and that they argued singled out Israel for "practices of racial discrimination against the Palestinians."[10] What was really at stake beyond any untoward rhetoric was the Bush administration's alliance with Israel and its enmity toward PLO leader Yasser Arafat.

Meanwhile, there was overwhelming interest and participation by the black community and other U.S. communities of color as well as many whites in the WCAR process. This included attendance at preparatory conferences—known as "PrepComs"—in Geneva; Santiago, Chile; Strasbourg; Addis Abba, and elsewhere; organizing education forums; producing analytical documents; and eventually sending a large number of delegates to Durban numbering in the thousands. Participation was across the political and social spectrum including civil rights activists, youth groups, women's organizations, gay and lesbian groups, celebrities, and elected officials. As the administration showed increasing animosity toward the WCAR, Powell and Rice were both heavily criticized by not only black participants from the United States, but also from Africa and the Caribbean as well.

In August 2001, Bush issued a statement only three days before the governments' conference began declaring that the United States would not attend if the language regarding Israel (that argued that Israel practices racial discrimination against the Palestinians and Zionism was racism—a position that the United Nations had rescinded in December 1991 in Resolution 3379), did not change. It did not. In the end, Powell was force to accede to the position of Bush and Rice, and did not exercise the option of going and representing U.S. views on the struggle against racism as well as Israel, reparations, and other controversial topics. A small, low-level token U.S. delegation did attend and then, on September 3, dramatically walked out, along with the Israeli delegation, before the conference ended. It is important to note that Powell did not disagree publicly with the Bush administration's critique of the statements regarding Israel and reparations, but sought a different means of addressing those concerns that did not alienate the United States from its allies and the international community.

For the record, UN officials and others involved in planning and implementing the conference did speak out forcefully against expression of anti-Semitism that arose during the process and at the event and tried to be constructive in resolving the conflicts. Former president of Ireland Mary Robinson served as UN Commissioner for Human Rights and secretary-general of the conference. She presented draft language of the official documents that did not contain divisive language and declared that she would not allow discussion that equated Zionism with racism.[11] These efforts were dismissed by the Bush administration.

In the final analysis it did not matter that Powell's strategy of wanting to confront U.S. critics was defeated. It did not protect him from a wave of harsh criticism. In one infamous cartoon published by the South African newspaper, *The Sowetan*, Powell is seen looking forlorn standing in front of the White House as two black Americans are preparing to leave for the conference. They ask, "Coming, Uncle Tom?," and Powell replies in exaggerated black dialect, "De massa in de big house says I aint." The cartoon was blown up to poster size and tacked up around the conference site.[12] Official statements from black congressmembers were more sharply critical of Bush but did not single out Powell and Rice with the exception of Rep. John Conyers who stated, "There are two points about Colin. One, did he decide it was the right thing to do not to come here or was he ordered to do it? Now, it's much worse if he did this unilaterally on his own. . . . He's got an integrity problem now. If he can't come to a World Conference on racism, what can he do? This is minimal! We didn't tell him what to do at the WCAR, we just said come, we need an international presence, [of] the top African American in the current administration."[13] This growing skepticism would soon blossom into unmitigated disenchantment

Political cartoon by Jonathan Zapiro that appeared in the August 29, 2001, edition of the *Sowetan*. Reprinted with permission of the *Sowetan*.

with Powell and Rice by black congressmembers and other African American leaders.

For many attendees and observers, the WCAR was a decisive event in the struggle for racial justice. Global Rights Director Gay McDougall, who is a former member of the UN Committee for Elimination of Racial Discrimination, notes a number of important accomplishments that emerged out of the WCAR process. Speaking on behalf of the views of many participants, she writes:

- We grappled with the past in what I think is fair to call a historic discourse;

- We made an important statement about what racism looks like in the twenty-first century;

- We expanded the knowledge base about contemporary issues relating to racial discrimination;

- We re-affirmed some of humanity's most profound legal principles (equality and non-discrimination based on race), re-committed ourselves as a global community to them, and elaborated their meaning in this new era;

- We made plans for action around common ground;

- We identified the thorny issues around which there must be further dialogue, understanding, and struggle;

- We acknowledged the importance of civil society in the struggle against racism and gave birth to new global networks of civil society groups working to combat racism;

- We created a context that empowered a variety of victim groups.[14]

Despite the resistance from the United States and Israel, who also walked out of the conference after agreeing with the former that the drafted language in the official documents was "hateful," racism and the battle to eradicate it were put on the world stage.[15] Few who attended could not be overwhelmed by the breadth of issues and campaigns that the global community is confronting regarding racial discrimination and related intolerance. Many states, pushed and cajoled by NGOs, had for the first time been made to look in the mirror and see the Apartheid that exists within their own borders. The WCAR underscored that racism and cross-cutting forms of discrimination are a phenomenon that exists widespread in practically every country. For many U.S. participants, across racial lines, it was an initiation into the concerns of the Dalit of India, the Roma of Europe, the Afro-Latinos and indigenous peoples of the Americas, the Travellers of Ireland, the Ainu of Japan, and many other groups whose life-and-death issues never appear on the radar of U.S. media. Individuals who had survived modern-day slavery or genocidal attacks were given voice, dignity, and collective support. In forums, workshops, plenary sessions, presentation booths, and informal settings, issues regarding racism and intersecting discriminations from every conceivable angle were raised. Virtually all of these groups defined their issues not only in terms of racial discrimination but also as violations of human rights. Thus, the WCAR was an educational moment regarding human rights for the many black Americans who attended and those who could not but followed it closely.

A number of groups have, correctly, long called racism a violation of human rights.[16] In the international community, most scholars and activists promote a broad definition of human rights that covers not only race, ethnic, religious, gender and other discriminations, but also includes political, civil, economic, social, and cultural rights. The "family" of human rights instruments is seen to include the Universal Declaration on Human Rights, International Convention on the Elimination of All Forms of Racial Discrimination (ICERD), International Convention on the Elimination of All Forms of Discrimination Against

Women (CEDAW), International Covenant on Civil and Political Rights (ICCPR), and International Covenant on Economic, Social and Cultural Rights (ICESCR), Convention Against Torture and Other Cruel, Inhumane or Degrading Treatment or Punishment (CAT), and Convention on the Rights of the Child (CRC).[17] In all of these documents, the struggle against racism is noted.[18] The United States under both Republican and Democratic administrations either has not ratified these documents or did so with a large number of RUDS (Reservations, Understandings and Declarations) that effectively weakened the legislation to the point of impotence. Even with a clear legal understanding that international law has little impact on the decisions of U.S. courts and that the power of states' rights allows states to ignore these types of federal treaties, there are still efforts to further distance the United States from international norms. In 2004, a resolution was proposed in the U.S. House of Representatives, H. Res. 568, "Reaffirmation of American Independence Resolution," which explicitly sought to put on record that international law should not even have referral value in U.S. courts.[19]

The NGO Forum also produced a powerful "Declaration" and "Program of Action." The Declaration affirmed that "the Trans-Atlantic slave trade and the enslavement of Africans and African descendants" were crimes against humanity, called for reparations, condemned anti-Semitism, denounced the "Hidden apartheid" caste treatment of South Asia's 260 million Dalits, called for the recognition of the rights of the Kurds, acknowledged the situation of the Tibetan people, expressed solidarity with the self-determination struggles of indigenous peoples, rejected the occupation of the Palestinian territories, and deplored the treatment of Europe's Roma. These concerns were also linked to rights related to gender, disability, environment, religion, and labor.[20] There were also dozens of recommendations in the Program of Action for addressing these issues.[21]

The official Declaration and Program of Action adopted by the governments were much less radical, of course, but nevertheless made a number of groundbreaking statements and commitments. In the Declaration, it was agreed a global fight against racism, racial discrimination, xenophobia, and related intolerance are "a matter of priority for the international community."[22] It also acknowledged that the slave trade and slavery were "a crime against humanity and should always have been so."[23] States also committed themselves to developing national action plans to address racial discrimination and "to reinforce and implement preventive measures . . . with the aim of eliminating manifestations of racism, racial discrimination, xenophobia, and related intolerance."[24]

Within forty-eight hours of the official closing of the WCAR, terrorist strikes on the East Coast of the United States staggered the international community. With horrible ferocity, thousands were killed and injured in desperate suicide attacks by the al Qaeda terrorist network. The audacity and stunning nature of the aggressions witnessed an outpouring of sympathy and support for the United States unparallel in modern times. Unfortunately, the administration quickly eroded the wave of world support with its opportunistic overreaction (the civil liberties–bashing Patriot Act, establishment of extra-judicial incarceration at Guantanamo, the globally unpopular invasion of Iraq, the prisoner torture scandal, etc.) and actually brought into sharp focus the issues raised at the WCAR that the administration had chosen to dismiss. While in the early days of responding to the strikes, the administration admirably argued that Muslims as a whole should generally not be characterized or profiled as terrorists and not be attacked or persecuted, it would soon institute legislation and policies that essentially did such. The police and security targeting of Muslims and people from the Middle East overlapped, but did not completely coincide, with a race-oriented framework. The administration carried out and extended its policy of "extraordinary rendition" where people captured by the United States in the name of the war on terrorism are exported to brutal states, such as Egypt, Syria, and Pakistan, where torture is the norm.[25] Thousands of Arabs and Muslims, many American citizens, were arrested and held for months or years without charges.

WCAR and the September 11 attacks would both force a reexamination of the state of race relations in the United States. How would the call for patriotism and defending the homeland against radical Islamic fundamentalism mesh with the objectives of racial inclusion and equality? How serious are racial, ethnic, and religious differences inside the United States? Would the war on terror exacerbate religious tensions and be seen as disproportionately targeting non-Christians? Would gains made by racial and ethnic minorities inside the United States be compromised by racist reactions in the media, social life, and public policy to the attacks? Would having a black secretary of state and national security advisor mitigate, exploit, reflect, or obfuscate the opinions of the black community regarding the war on terror? In the rubble of the Twin Towers and the Pentagon, with the murdered and injured victims of the terrorist fanatics, lay these and other pivotal questions that would challenge the administration.

A Record of Neglect: The Bush Administration and U.S. Race Politics

Bush's race avoidance strategy was manifest during his tenure as governor of Texas from 1995 to 2000. He compiled a record on race issues that is disconcerting and woeful. While he claims that he appointed a diverse cabinet, his record regarding criminal justice, human rights, and other concerns demonstrate a harsh disregard for the interests of the state's racial and ethnic minority populations. In every instance, where he had an opportunity to demonstrate an enlighten view or create critically needed anti-discrimination policy regarding racial conflict and tensions, he choose ideology over doing the right thing.

On June 7, 1998, one of the most brutal racist murders in recent U.S. history took place near Jasper, Texas. A black man, James Byrd, Jr., was attacked by three white men, Lawrence Russell Brewer, John William King, and Shawn Allen Berry. Byrd's throat was slit, and then he was chained to the back of a pickup truck and dragged along three miles of road, his body literally coming to pieces. Despite the national and global infamy that this case brought, the only white politician in the state who came to his funeral was Sen. Kay Bailey Hutchinson. When the Texas legislature proposed a hate crime bill, named in Byrd's memory, then-Gov. George W. Bush vetoed the legislation ostensibly because he objected to the inclusion of gays and lesbians in the bill's coverage creating a two-for-one bigotry.

While governor of Texas, George W. Bush had the distinction of governing the state with the largest number of executions of any in the nation, which lead to him become the most executing governor in U.S. history. During his tenure, 152 executions occurred. Those of his defenders, who are embarrassed by his record, have argued that he was not responsible for the death penalty statues that were in place before he came into office, and as governor he had little authority to change the law. However, he opposed stridently any reforms including vetoing legislation that would have provided funding for legal assistance for the indigent and opposed legislation that would have banned executions for persons whose IQ was less than 65. Texas, under Bush, had the documented honor of being the state with the largest "number of death sentences upheld by Texas courts since 1990 for men whose lawyers slept during their trials: 3."[26] When Bush left office, there were 161 whites (36.2%), 180 blacks (40.4%), and 100 Latinos (22.5%) on death row.

As governor, Bush failed to address or remedy other egregious acts of racial discrimination that happened on his watch. During his tenure, approximately 10 percent of the African American residents in Tulia, Texas, were convicted of drug crimes and sent to prison solely on the basis of one white law enforcement officer's testimony. Although it was demonstrated there was absolutely no hard evidence against these citizens and appeals were made for clemency, the racialized war on drugs continued on for more than five years as these individuals fought their unfair convictions and incarcerations before being cleared. In January 2005, the officer, Tom Coleman, was determined to have committed extensive perjury, and the factually innocent residents were released from prison, although not pardoned. The defendants also won a $5 million lawsuit.[27] The pervasive racism in the Texas criminal justice system was ignored by Bush.

These incidents and his record overall foreshadowed his behavior as president. Rather than polarized on the issue of race as Reagan and his father did, Bush approaches the issue by omission, symbolism, and superficial gestures to dismiss race and racial discrimination as serious concerns in contemporary U.S. society. In 2003, when asked about his poor record on civil rights, Bush responded, "Let's see, there I was sitting around the table with foreign leaders, looking at Colin Powell and Condi Rice."[28] Then he just trailed off seemingly unable to elaborate any further. He embarrassingly equated having Powell and Rice in his administration as a civil rights agenda.

In early 2003, Sen. Trent Lott was sacrificed relatively quickly for saying at a December 2002 100th birthday celebration for Strom Thurmond that he voted for him happily after Thurmond stormed out of the Democratic National Convention (and party) in the 1948 and ran as a committed segregationist in the 1948 presidential race. The then-Senate majority leader went on to say, "We're proud of it. And if the rest of the country had followed our lead, we wouldn't have had all these problems over all these years, either."[29] The jettisoning of Lott, however, had more to do with the scandal's potential distraction from Bush's broader strategic and political interests than with seriously addressing the synergy between the politics of Lott and Thurmond and those of the Republican Party.

The Lott bludgeoning notwithstanding, racial disparities went unaddressed by the administration as it took a number of actions that actually furthered and undermined efforts to address racial discrimination and civil rights through public policy. In areas of the economy, health, education, housing, voting rights, and affirmative action in spite of overall advances in the last three decades, the disparities have remained and, in some instances, worsened. In addition, changes in the political composition of the U.S. Civil Rights Commission and Bush's nominees to the higher courts demonstrate that his words of a desire for racial harmony and racial progress are insouciant.

Reynolds Rap: U.S. Anti–Civil Rights Commission

For more than two decades, civil rights scholar and advocate Mary Francis Berry sat on the Civil Rights Commission, the last twelve years as its chairperson. She battled Republican and Democratic administrations over their reticence to recognize and enforce laws regarding civil rights violations. At the end of 2004, a month before their terms were up, she and vice chairperson Cruz Reynoso were abruptly fired by the Bush administration. Although Berry and Reynoso argued that their terms ended officially and legally on January 21, 2005, the White House not only stated that their terms finished on December 5, 2004, but already had named their replacements. The war between the commission and Bush had come to an end. The administration also replaced staff director Les Jin with Bush appointee Kenneth Marcus.

Since the Reagan era, the commission has been reduced to a paper-producing operation characterized by political in-fighting with little policy traction. The commission was established under the Civil Rights Act of 1957 and grew to be a valuable resource and advocate in the 1960s and 1970s. Then the Reagan team rolled into town, and the commission discovered it had a new front on which to fight. Unable to quash it, Reagan was able to stack the commission with as many anti–civil rights commissioners as he could legally get away with. Despite its internal warfare and outside critics, it still managed to produced some of the most revealing and important reports on the state of civil rights in the nation in the last quarter century. Led by Berry since 1992, the commission genuinely tried to meet its mission of investigating complaints, collecting data, issuing reports and recommendations to Congress and the White House, and, in general, defending civil rights across the board. Berry's tough posture meant not pulling the punches on issues such as electoral shenanigans, gay rights, and women's rights. Berry and other commissioners fought Carter and Clinton just as hard as they fought Reagan and both Bushes.

For its efforts, the commission was attacked consistently even by its own commissioners and underfunded by Congress. The mini-controversy over the exact time and date of Berry and Reynoso's final day at the commission obscured the more scandalous step taken by Bush to replace them with ideologues who for all intents and purposes are anti–civil rights at heart.

Berry was replaced by Gerald Reynolds as the new chairperson, and Abigail Thernstrom, already a commissioner, was elevated to vice chairperson. Both are well-known advocates of a "color-blind" rhetoric that is a sparsely covered feint regarding their real agenda of anti–affirmative action. Reynolds has referred to affirmative action as the "big lie."[30] Reynolds, long affiliated with such anti–affirmative action groups as Project 21, the Center for New Black Leadership, and the Center for Equal Opportunity, received a controversial recess appointment by Bush in 2001 to head up the Office of Civil Rights of the Education Department though he lacked any background in education. He was later appointed to a Justice Department post that did not need Senate confirmation. Like Bush, Reynolds disingenuously babbles that he is for diversity and race-neutral policies. Thernstrom, as noted above, is a key racial realist, and along with her husband Stephen Thernstrom, wrote *America in Black and White: One Nation Indivisible*, their overwrought treatise that argues that racism in America is a thing of the past except for a few black politicians and separatists who fan the flames of racial discord. According to the Thernstroms, it is the refusal to acknowledge black failure—rather than real racial discrimination—that is at the root of the social crisis in black communities, all of which is made worse by government intervention.

Bush has essentially put two individuals whose entire careers have been built on attacking government remedies toward discrimination in charge of a key government agency that addresses the issue. Reynolds and Thernstrom have been put in charge of an office whose statutory duty is to defend the very policies they have vigorously opposed.

Stopping the Clock

The 1990s witnessed an economic spurt in the United States combined with a more liberal administration that reversed a number of the negative social and economic trends that unfolded under Reagan and Bush I. The black community and other communities benefited from these reversals. Unfortunately, the forward motion stopped with the arrival of the Bush II administration.

As the study, *State of the Dream 2005*, notes, "The unemployment and income picture has gotten worse for people of color since 2000, eroding the progress made during the 1990s."[31] In concrete terms, this meant that while black unemployment had reached a historic low of 7.1 percent in 2000 when Bush was elected, it had risen to 9.9 percent or higher since January 2002. Latino unemployment saw a similar rise and fall. Discouraged workers and those imprisoned are not included in these figures. Black median income had risen from 55 percent of white's in 1988 to 65 percent of white's in 2000. After three years of Bush, it had dropped to 62 percent in 2003. In the starkest of manner, 300,000 black families fell below the poverty line during Bush's first term, a fact never uttered or addressed by the president or his administration.

The study further notes that, "The three major tax cuts from 2001 to 2004 widened the racial income divide by targeting high-income taxpayers, who are disproportionately white."[32]

Health care is another area where disparities have not been erased or even acknowledged by the Bush administration. Between 2002 and 2003, there was a 1.4 million increase in the number of people who became uninsured. More than 43 million are uninsured including 33 percent who are Hispanics, 27 percent who are Native Americans, 20 percent who are black Americans, 18 percent who are Asian Americans, and 10.6 percent who are whites.

In some other areas, during the Bush era, most notably the criminal justice system and access to democratic participation, circumstances have gotten significantly and qualitatively much worse. In particular, some of the criminal justice laws that appear neutral on the surface—such as the Three Strikes laws and laws that differ in punishments between crack cocaine and cocaine powder violations—have led to wide racial disproportionalities in the criminal justice system.[33] Of the over 2 million individuals in U.S. state and federal prisons, 832,400 (44%) are black Americans; Latinos constitute another 392,200 (19%) of this growing population.[34] The Justice Department estimates that at the current incarceration rates 32 percent of all African American males born in 2001 will spend some time in prison. In California, for "third strike" offenses where the punishment is life in prison without the possibility of parole, the incarceration rate for blacks is twelve times higher than that of whites (143 per 100,000 vs. 12 per 100,000 respectfully). Blacks constitute less than 7 percent of the state's population. Meanwhile, death row continues to be fully integrated. In spring 2004, according to the NAACP Legal Defense Fund, there were 1,591 whites (45.6%) on death row, 1,462 blacks (42.0%), 354 Latinos (10.2%), 40 Asians (1.2%), 39 Native Americans (1.1%) and 1 unknown.[35]

Linked with the increased number of black Americans being imprisoned is the egregious disenfranchisement in many states that ex-felons must suffer. In seven states—Alabama, Florida, Iowa, Kentucky, Mississippi, Nebraska, and Virginia—all ex-felons automatically lose their voting rights in some instances for life. In many other states, including Arizona, Delaware, Maryland, Nevada, Tennessee, Washington, and Wyoming, most ex-felons are disenfranchised permanently until they apply for clemency or through some other legal process to regain their right to vote, usually having to wait at least five years after they have completed their sentences. In all these states, the process for regaining voting rights is often arduous, arcane, and obstructionist. Only two states, Maine and Vermont, allow prisoners to vote. In most instances, those on parole and probation also cannot vote (or run for office or obtain professional licenses). As a result of the disenfranchisement laws, 1.4 million black men, about 13 percent of the black male adult population, have lost their voting rights; they constitute 36 percent of the 4.7 million disenfranchised by these statutes. In the Florida election in 2000, with a vote margin of only 537 that officially gave the state and the presidency to George W. Bush, more than 400,000 ex-felons were unable to vote including more than 200,000 black men. About 31 percent of the black men in the state are ineligible to vote.[36] Given the disproportionate number of blacks and Latinos in U.S. prisons, these circumstances undermine the hard won voting rights victories gained during the civil rights era. In the overwhelming majority of countries, not only are ex-felons allowed to vote after serving their sentences, but in many countries prisoners have the right and are even encouraged to vote such as the Czech Republic, Denmark, France, Israel, Japan, Kenya, the Netherlands, Norway, Peru, Poland, Romania, Sweden, and Zimbabwe.[37]

Bush, Rice, and Powell and the Politics of Affirmative Privilege

> Q: "Do you support the hiring and contracting preferences based on race and sex that are inherent in affirmative action programs?"
> Bush: "I support what I call 'affirmative access'—not quotas, not double standards, because those divide and balkanize, but access—a fair shot for everyone."[38]

Perhaps the best-known recipient of affirmative action in the country is George W. Bush. He attended elite schools—Phillips Academy in Andover, Massachusetts, Yale University, and Harvard Business School—always accumulating mediocre grades and little scholarship. He received business opportunities that most will never come see. While thousands of working-class boys and men were sent to Vietnam, Bush passed over many other applicants and was given a plum position in the National Guard, thus avoiding combat. And when he abused that opportunity, his denials notwithstanding, by disappearing for a year, he was unpunished. His reward for a getting by on a lifetime of advantage was the presidency. The "affirmative access" that Bush garnered was due to the prestige and influence derived from being the offspring of George Herbert Walker Bush and the grandson of Prescott Bush, influential alumni of Yale and political powerhouses. Class privilege is so embedded in the social structures of power it is nearly treasonous to question its existence let alone its inherent unfairness. Entitlement is assumed to the point of a natural way of being. Gender and race-based affirmation action flips the script. As an essential remedy for addressing past and present employment and education exclusion of women and people of color in the United States, it is under attack because it not only challenges class power, but also conflicts with the racial realist arguments of an equal playing field and the end of racism with the passage of civil rights laws.

Affirmative action remains the most divisive item on the racial justice agenda. To its chagrin, the Bush administration was forced to address the issue in 2003, and both Powell and Rice were drawn on to the battlefield. Despite all the heated debates over affirmative action, the Supreme Court had not made a critical decision on the use of affirmative action in higher education since the *Regents of the University of California v. Bakke* case of 1978.[39] In that case, the Court struck down the use of specific quotas, but stated importantly that race could be used among other factors in admission determination. Some lower court decisions in

Texas (*Hopwood*) and elsewhere had given body blows to the policy, and other Supreme Court decisions would weaken affirmative action programs even further, but the ability to use race as a variable in education, employment, and other areas remained legal. For the opponents of affirmative action, the battle was far from over and conservative groups, particularly the Center for Individual Rights, aggressively sought test cases that they hoped to bring back to the Court that would dismantle affirmative action once and for all. In 1997, they found their cases.

On October 14, 1997, Jennifer Gratz and Patrick Hamacher file a lawsuit in the U.S. District Court alleging that the University of Michigan gave unlawful preferences to minorities seeking undergraduate admission. Two months later, on December 3, Barbara Grutter filed a similar suit against the university's law school. Both cases were ruled class-action lawsuits.

Bush called the University of Michigan admissions program "clearly unconstitutional" and "fundamentally flawed," and the administration, at the last hour, submitted two amicus briefs against the school's admissions program.[40] Controversy arose when the *Washington Post* reported that Rice helped to persuade Bush to "publicly condemn race-conscious admissions policies" at the University of Michigan.[41] Some officials within the administration, who talked to the *Post* on the grounds of anonymity, considered Rice the prime mover and shaker behind the White House's hard line against the Michigan affirmative action programs. The Justice Department brief accused Michigan of "ignoring race-neutral alternatives and employing race-based policies that amount to racial quotas."[42] Bush attempted disingenuously some political cover by stating that he supported diversity.

Reportedly, Rice was livid. In defending herself against what she felt were charges that made Bush look bad and that racialized her and the issue, Rice wrote in response,

> When the President decided to submit an amicus brief, he asked for my view on how diversity can be best achieved on university campuses. I offered my view, drawing on my experience in academia and as provost of a major university. I agree with the President's position, which emphasizes the need for diversity and recognizes the continued legacy of racial prejudice, and the need to fight it. The President challenged universities to develop ways to diversify their populations fully. I believe that while race neutral means are preferable, it is appropriate to use race as one factor among others in achieving a diverse student body.[43]

Her statement, couched in appropriatedly conciliatory terms, attempted to both agree and disagree with Bush at one and the same time. Yet, she clearly stated that race could be a factor that contradicted Bush's implication that it should not. While there is little evidence that Bush "recognizes the continued legacy of racial prejudice, and the need to fight it," she apparently did. In another interview, she stated strongly that she agrees with affirmative action "if it does not lead to quotas and if people work hard at it to look at the total individual."[44] She does not, however, elaborate under what circumstances it is appropriate to use race as a factor. White House officials stated they saw no contradiction between Rice's position and Bush's because the president did not break his silence on the issue of whether race could or should ever be used as a factor in admissions. His silence, however, was widely seen as anti–affirmative action.

This highly unusual tête-à-tête was motivated by a number of concerns. First, the experiences with affirmative action that Rice cites as an academic and provost at Stanford University had been explosive. While Rice had acknowledged that she herself had been a beneficiary of affirmative action in coming to Stanford in 1981 as a Fellow in the Arms Control and Disarmament program, her tenure as provost was criticized by some black, Latino, women faculty, and some students as insensitive to their concerns and that she turned her back on the school's affirmative action policies.

One controversy was how far affirmative action should extend. Rice argued that while affirmative action in hiring was okay, it did not apply after that. Stanford University released minutes from a contentious 1998 faculty senate meeting in which Rice is quoted as saying, "I'm the chief academic officer now, and I am telling you that, in principle, I do not believe in, and in fact will not apply, affirmative action criteria at the time of tenure."[45] Her opponents, however, charged her with being unreasonable as she slashed and burned programs, services, staff, and faculty in achieving the goal of a balanced budget. The situation became so intense that at one point there were protests, a hunger strike, and even a Labor Department investigation after it received a 400-page complaint against her and the university alleging unfair treatment of minorities and women.[46]

What also made the Michigan case so intriguing politically was that Bush's other senior black official, Colin Powell, also opposed Bush's position on affirmative action. With Powell, there were no nuances and skirting the issue. Powell had stated during Bush's campaign that he hoped the University of Michigan would prevail in the case, and copies of his comments were actually being used by some University of Michigan officials to build support for their policies. In September 2000, in an interview with Detroit's WJR-AM, Powell stated that he thinks affirmative action "is still necessary" and "I will continue to speak out for it"; he continued stating, "There is a case now pending, of course, with the University of Michigan that I hope the university wins."[47]

Powell's long-term support for affirmative action also had another interesting connection with Rice. In 1996, as the fight grew over the California Civil Rights

Initiative (CCRI) (Proposition 209) that sought to outlaw affirmative action in the state, Powell was visited by Elaine Jones, then head of the NAACP Legal Defense Fund, and Connie Rice, an activist attorney and the cousin of Condoleezza Rice. They sought to have Powell use his stature to speak out publicly against the CCRI, which he did about six weeks later.[48] In a commencement speech at Maryland's Bowie State College, he stated, "There are those who rail against affirmative action. They rail against affirmative action preferences, while they have lived an entire life of preferences."[49] Bush had no comment on Powell's too-close-to-home remarks.

As governor and president, Bush advocated race-neutral admission policies, specifically the so-called "percentage plans" where a certain percentage of the top graduates of each school in the state is guaranteed admission to the state's best public universities. However, a wide range of studies from Harvard University and elsewhere concluded that the percentage plans, including the ones implemented by Bush in Texas and his brother Jeb in Florida, do not improve or maintain racial diversity as they claim, particularly at the state's most prestigious universities and colleges.[50]

On June 23, 2003, the Supreme Court announced its decision. The Court struck down the undergraduate admissions policies because it awarded points for underrepresented minorities solely on the basis of race, but it upheld the law school admission policy. Most important, it upheld the legal point that race could be used as a factor in admission's consideration. This was a victory for proponents of affirmative action though a cautious one. Bush attempted to spin the Court's decision toward his policy framework. He said in a statement, "I applaud the Supreme Court for recognizing the value of diversity. . . . I agree that we must look first to these race-neutral approaches to make campuses more welcoming to all students."[51] In fact, not only had the Court not supported Bush's race-neutral approach as he misleadingly stated, but Justices David Souter and Sandra Day O'Connor expressly criticized the percentage plans Bush favored.

Powell, Rice, and the Contours of Racial Identity

> There's an old saying. In the days of slavery, there were those slaves who lived on the plantation and there were those slaves that lived in the house. You got the privilege of living in the house if you served the master . . . exactly the way the master intended to have you serve him.
>
> Harry Belafonte on Colin Powell[52]

Questioning the racial sense of Powell and Rice was a popular pastime in the black community. Belafonte's remarks stunned many white supporters of Powell and generated a media swarm, but they reflected the views of many in the black community who believed that the two were "house slaves," unconcerned about other blacks. Neither spoke out on key domestic issues facing the black community and the civil rights community, other than the aforementioned affirmative action, and they were clearly on a different page from the overwhelming black majority on international concerns when it came to issues such as the Iraq war, the war on terror, and African policy. Most important, they were central players in an administration that was perceived widely to be anti-black.

In fact, Rice and Powell both spoke often about race. In general, Rice has been seen as less race conscious in her public life than Powell. Whereas Powell has often stated that his achievements can be attributed to everything from affirmative action to the efforts by those before him, for the most part, Rice's statements on race have been mostly allusions and restricted to her family and her upbringing in Alabama. However, Rice has used race carefully and tactically to make crucial political points. In discussing the war on terror, the hopes that she has for the country, and other issues, she has slipped the issue of race into the discourse.

Unlike many black conservatives, she has not excused or evaded the country's inglorious racial history. Before black and white audiences, she has underscored her identification with the history of oppression that black people have suffered. In 2003, she told the National Association of Black Journalists, "When the Founding Fathers said 'We the People,' they did not mean us. Our ancestors were considered three-fifths of a person."[53] She is referring to Article 1, Sec. 2.3 of the U.S. Constitution that states, "Representatives and direct taxes shall be apportioned among the several states which may include within this Union, according to their respective numbers, which shall be determined by adding to the whole number of free persons, including those bound to service for a term of years, and excluding Indians not taxed, three fifths of all other persons."

She has repeated a version of this statement on a number of occasions both in the United States and abroad.[54] The reference is used to make a larger point about the advances that have been made in racial harmony in the United States. As she told a London audience in June 2003, "Our own histories should remind us that the union of democratic principle and practice is always a work in progress. When the Founding Fathers said 'We the People,' they did not mean me. My ancestors were three-fifths of a man. But America has made enormous progress towards a multi-ethnic democracy."[55] She never elaborates on exactly how that progress is manifest or the limits of it given the glaring racial disparities that continue. It is one thing to be criticize the racism of the Founding Fathers; it is another to be critical of the contemporary state of U.S. race relations and identify the political forces responsible.

Rice not only refers to the constitutional status of black people but to the very institution of slavery itself. She neither excuses nor completely dismisses it as a foreclosed issue. At a press briefing on the eve of Bush's trip to Africa in 2003, she told a gathering of reporters, "Slavery was, of course, America's birth defect. We've been trying to deal with the consequences of it every [sic] since and to bring about reconciliation."[56] This is a fairly powerful statement in and of itself. Not only does she acknowledge the corrosive impact of slavery on American democracy but also notes that it has remained a struggle to bring resolution to the long-term divisions that arose out of slavery.

While she clearly has differences with many of the tenets of the civil rights movement and the harsh criticisms that civil rights leaders have of Bush, she surprisingly has been generous in her assessment of the contributions of the civil rights movement to U.S. democracy. She saw the civil right struggle as valuable but perhaps not in the manner that many in the movement did. She states, "The civil rights struggle was America's chance to resolve the contradictions inherent in its birth. And at its roots, it was a legal struggle, pitting the natural law that underpins our Constitution and Declaration of Independence against unjust laws on the books that fell far short of that ideal."[57] In that same talk, she gives a nod to a couple of the heroes of the civil rights era. Reflecting on Mississippi, she argues, "This message has particular resonance in Jackson, Mississippi a place that has been the site of so many key events in America's long-running struggle to define the meaning of justice. This is the city where the Tougaloo Nine and the Freedom Riders were arrested and where Medgar Evers was cut down by an assassin's bullet. It was a focal point of the Freedom Summer of 1964 and it was James Meredith's destination in his 1966 'March Against Fear.' "[58]

As is well known, a pivotal event of Rice's childhood was an act of violence that riveted the nation. Of the many horrible murders that occurred during the civil rights era, perhaps none was as stunning as that of the four young black girls— Addie Mae Collins, Denise McNair, Carole Robertson, and Cynthia Wesley— who died when a bomb exploded inside the Sixteenth Street Baptist Church on September 15, 1963, in Birmingham, Alabama.[59] Nearly two dozen others were injured including other young people. The bomb had been planted by the Ku Klux Klan, and it would take decades to obtain convictions for some of those involved including Robert Edward Chambliss in 1977, Thomas Blanton in 2001, and Bobby Frank Cherry in 2002. In the late 1950s and early 1960s, the activities of the KKK in the area were so violent that the city was known to civil rights activists as "Bombingham." According to the FBI, the bombing was done by a Klan splinter group known as the Cahaba Boys. In the riot and violence that occurred in the aftermath of the bomb blast, two young blacks, 16-year-old Johnny Robinson and 13-year-old Virgil Ware, were shot and killed by the police.

The Sixteenth Street Baptist Church was more than just a place of worship. Built in 1911, it was a revered institution in the black community and had become a meeting place for civil rights activists including the young preacher Martin Luther King, Jr., and other leaders such as Ralph Abernathy and Fred Shutterworth. Birmingham had become the frontline in the desegregation battles led by King and the Southern Christian Leadership Conference (SCLC), and other groups such as the Congress of Racial Equality (CORE) and the Student Nonviolent Coordinating Committee (SNCC). All that spring, demonstrations had been held in the city encountering unreserved resistance and brutality from Public Safety Commissioner Eugene "Bull" Connor. Despite an agreement eventually won by the civil rights activists from the Birmingham business community in May 1963, the violent assaults against the black community continued including explosions at SCLC headquarters and at King's brother's home.

At the time of the explosion, Condoleezza and her parents were attending church two miles away at the Westminster Presbyterian church. Rice recalls feeling a "sensation of something shaking" under her feet.[60] She was 8 years old at the time and she and her parents would later attend the funeral of Denise McNair, who had been a classmate of Rice. Understandably, this incident would follow Rice throughout her life, and she spoke of it both before and since joining the Bush administration. She told the National Association of Black Journalists, "Denise McNair and the others did not die in vain. They . . . helped reintroduce this nation to its founding ideals. And because of their sacrifice we are a better nation."[61]

After September 11, the story of the bombing took on a new significance. Now, Rice would link the violence of her childhood with the fight against terrorism. As she said on a number of occasions, "Growing up in Birmingham, I lived with the home-grown terrorism of that era. And I remember the bombing 40 years ago of the Sixteenth Baptist Church that took the lives of four young girls, including my friend, Denise McNair. Acts of terror are calculated to propel old fears into the next generation."[62] She would repeat this analogy on many occasions.

Powell's racial traumas came much later in life than Rice's. As a child, he more identified with his status as a second-generation immigrant than any racial identity. He essentially would grow to epitomize the difference between being an African American and a black American, the former being those of long descent in the United States and the latter those new or first-generation people of African descent. Powell has used the term "African American" to describe himself, but substantively he did not organically identify with African American cultural and social practices until mostly as an adult. As he states in his autobiography, he had "no such sense" of a racial identity growing up, in part, because he lived a multi-cultural existence surrounded by families that were Greek, Jewish, Polish, West Indian, Puerto Rican, and Italian.[63] He speaks to this issue extensively:

American blacks sometimes regard Americans of West Indian origin as up-pity and arrogant. The feeling, I imagine, grows out of an impressive record of accomplishment by West Indians. . . . West Indians had an opportunity to develop attitudes of independence, self-responsibility, and self-worth. They did not have their individual dignity beaten down for three hundred years, the fate of so many black American slaves and their descendants.[64]

These generalizations are somewhat problematic and were read by some as a distancing from African Americans. The relationship between immigration and race is much more complicated and nuanced than Powell allows. The relation-ship between African Americans and other black Americans is not only an in-ternal negotiation but also shaped by the politics and polices of the state and the majority population. Powell implies that choosing to identify as an immigrant eliminates or transforms one's racial categorization. He goes on to say that his parents came to the United States for the same reasons as other immigrants: to "seek better lives for themselves and their children." While true, that is not the end of the story, particularly in the Jim Crow era.[65] Although the Powells lived in the North, the racist attitudes of white superiority/black inferiority were national (and international) in scope.

It was only after he joined the army and was sent South that the racism that was normed for many African American began to become clear to him. He had a number of incidents—not being served in a restaurant, denied an award because he was black, warned about driving while black, and so forth—on and off the base that demonstrated that at least individual racism was very real and could affect his career and even his life.

He was also affected, at a distance, by the civil rights and black power movements. He speaks of his pain and that of other black soldiers at the assas-sination of Martin Luther King, Jr., in 1968. He stated that it reminded him that "racism still bedeviled America."[66] Like Rice, however, he did not participate in the civil rights movement directly or even follow it closely. Rice was much younger and was generally too young to really participate. For Powell, he had joined the army and spent the 1960s as a soldier. He was, of course, even more uncomfortable with the black power advocates. As he stated, "We heard the radical black voices—Stokely Carmichael, Eldridge Cleaver, and H. Rap Brown with his "Burn, baby burn!"—with uneasiness."[67] Although not completely de-void of or antagonistic to race consciousness, Rice and Powell are moderate at best on the issue. As their careers veered more and more toward an international focus, they would avoid having to address directly the state of black America altogether.

Four

What Color Is Hegemony?:
The U.S. New Security Paradigm

Cry "Havoc" and let slip the dogs of War.
William Shakespeare (*Julius Caesar*)

On September 11, 1990, President George H. W. Bush delivered a speech before a joint session of Congress. The occasion was to seek congressional approval for the war to remove Iraqi troops from Kuwait, which Iraq had invaded and occupied one month earlier. In that speech, Bush highlighted his meeting with then Soviet President Gorbachev and noted that they had reached a consensus on dispelling Saddam Hussein's military from Kuwait. For Bush, this meeting of minds signaled that the "new world order" that he was calling for was taking its first steps. He stated, "Clearly, no longer can a dictator count on East-West confrontation to stymie concerted United Nations action against aggression. A new partnership of nations has begun."[1] Eleven years to the date, a new world order led by another president—George W. Bush—would indeed be sparked with much darker and dire consequences than could ever be imagined.

September 11, 2001, for the neo-conservatives hovering in and around the second Bush administration, became the cry of havoc. The cataclysmic events of that morning allowed for the ready implementation of a radical redirection and rearticulation of U.S. foreign policy strategy that had been marinating for almost a decade. This remapping of the U.S. global imperative has direct and dire implications for the whole nation, including of course black Americans, and the global community. What is being called the "Bush doctrine," glaringly and frightfully on full throttle since that nodal date, was generated in the early 1990s by a coterie of neo-conservative think tanks, former government officials, and right-wing academics.[2]

While no blacks, or for that matter, any Americans of color, were central to this development, subsequent to that period, Colin Powell and Condoleezza Rice, were or have been at the center of the contemporary formation and execution of Bush's foreign policy, albeit with perhaps differing levels of commitment to the central themes of the emerging doctrine. As noted, it is not their views on domestic policies that have kept them in the public eye and shaped their careers but rather their participation and leadership in this political enterprise. Though both were part of previous administrations, it is the George W. Bush years that have shaped and focused their political standing. They both eventually became central to his inner circle of foreign policy leadership, the group that came to be known as the "Vulcans."[3]

The new strategy redefines U.S. international relations and U.S. relationships to international institutions such as the United Nations, NATO, and the European Union. Both Powell and Rice, albeit with different roles, involvement, and commitment to the new direction, are embedded in the U.S. strategic circles guiding this development. In this context, race is a relevant variable—brought off the shelf—due to a sustained and substantial discourse on the impact of the new strategy on multi-culturalism, ethnic relations, global race relations, and social group integration, a discourse that has been and is being held within the highest echelons of foreign policy circles. While their participation in, and differing interpretations of this process have received substantial examination, analysts have generally disavowed viewing their roles through a racial lens. However, the intersection of race and politics, their denials notwithstanding, is a critical element in grasping the full dimensions of the revived U.S. strategy of hegemonization.

The Rise of the Grand Strategists

> America has, and intends to keep, military strength beyond challenge.
> George W. Bush—West Point speech, June 2002[4]

The United States has emerged as a hegemonic power like no other in history. Its reach is truly global and it faces no real challengers at present or in the near future. It has the unique ability to project power and shape political, economic, cultural, and military affairs that affect nearly all of humanity. This is an unprecedented capability and how it will be used, for as long as it will last, has animated strategic thinking on the most monumental of scales. We have entered the era where grand power has come together with grand strategists.

There were several foundational works in the 1990s that foreshadowed the key dimensions of the "Bush doctrine." In February 1992, after the Gulf war and (unknowingly) soon to be on their way out of power, then Secretary of Defense Dick Cheney oversaw the development of a 46-page memo, titled, "Defense Planning Guidance" (DPG), put together by then undersecretary for policy Paul Wolfowitz.[5] Intended as an internal Pentagon document, it was leaked to the *Washington Post* and the *New York Times*. It generated considerable controversy for the boldness of its assertions on the post–Cold War foreign policy direction of the United States. As a special PBS's "Frontline" program noted, the key points from the draft were that the "number one objective of U.S. post–Cold War political and military strategy should be preventing the emergence of a rival superpower," and that, "If necessary, the United States must be prepared to take unilateral action."[6] These two elements, among others, are crucial features of the doctrine unfolded by George W. Bush in the months after September 11. After the row generated by the DPG document, President George H. W. Bush ordered a redraft that purged the sections mentioned above and ratcheted down its ideological rant, although it appears that no final version was ever authorized nor a full text reproduced.

In reporting on the document, the *Washington Post* contended that the last version, published in April 1992, also reflected the views of Colin Powell, who was chair of the Joint Chiefs of Staff at the time.[7] While it is clear that Powell supported the call for global dominance and ensuring that the U.S. military had enough resources to carry out its missions, it is not so certain that he united with the aims of unilateralism, isolationism, and reducing allies to role-players in the U.S. world game that the memo promoted.

In 1997, refusing to go away and with funding linked to the ultra-conservative Bradley Foundation, Cheney, Wolfowitz, *Weekly Standard* editor William Kristol and others, formed the Project for a New American Century (PNAC) with imposing ambitions and hegemonic purposes. PNAC, according to its website, "intends through issue briefs, research papers, advocacy journalism, conferences, and seminars, to explain what American world leadership entails. It will also strive to rally support for a vigorous and principled policy of American international involvement and to stimulate useful public debate on foreign policy and defense policy and America's role in the world."[8]

On January 26, 1998, a PNAC-led group of eighteen neo-conservatives wrote a letter to President Clinton advocating the military overthrow of Saddam Hussein. The letter stated, "The only acceptable strategy is one that eliminates the possibility that Iraq will be able to use or threaten to use weapons of mass destruction. In the near term, this means a willingness to undertake military action as diplomacy is clearly failing. In the long term, it means removing Saddam Hussein and his regime from power. That now needs to become the aim of American foreign policy."[9] A number of those individual would end up in the

Bush administration including Elliott Abrams, Richard Armitage, John Bolton, Richard Perle, Donald Rumsfeld, and Paul Wolfowitz.

The innocuous babble about stimulating a "useful public debate" hid much broader and grander intentions. This was not a staid, academic project, but rather actors who sought (and some eventually gained) the power to transform U.S. foreign policy strategy and guide it in a particular direction. The most important objective of this political circle was the preservation of the U.S. status as the sole global hegemon. This goal was most strongly articulated in PNAC's "Rebuilding America's Defenses: Strategy, Forces and Resources for a New Century," a document severely critical of the Clinton administration's defense policy, issued only two weeks before the 2000 election. It argued, "At present the United States faces no global rival. America's grand strategy should aim to preserve and extend this advantageous position as far into the future as possible" because "today the task is to preserve an international security environment conducive to American interests and ideals."[10] This was an observation meant not only for the enemies of the United States but also its long time allies.

In direct effect, they were bringing their own interpretation to former President George H. W. Bush's famous call for a "new world order." As the United States assumed the power vacuum left by the fall of communism, an internal debate among conservatives unfolded over how this power was to be wielded and for what purposes. The neo-conservative wing of this debate increasingly found their voice and each other, and slowly began to consolidate a coherent response to the traditionalists. While it is true that all neo-conservatives are not cut from the same cloth, there were and are several unifying themes upon which they agree. From their vantage point, despite the nationalist elements inherent in it, Bush senior's new world order framework still embodied elements that the neo-cons found objectionable and unacceptable: strategic multi-lateralism (as opposed to tactical and contingent multi-lateralism), resolving conflicts primarily through international and regional institutions, and adherence (at least publicly) to international laws, norms, and conventions. For the old school Republicans and conservative Democrats, these elements were necessary though not decisive legitimizing components of U.S. global power. For the neo-cons, they represented unwanted constraints.

Along with PNAC, there were a number of other think tanks and institutes that were and are organizationally, ideologically, and politically linked and committed to reshaping U.S. foreign policy. These include the Center for Security Policy (CSP), Jewish Institute for National Security Affairs (JINSA), Institute for Advanced Strategic and Political Studies, and the older American Enterprise Institute. These research institutions and lobby organizations have interlocking relationships, which facilitates their political mobilization, but more important they have distributed their officials and leaders at the highest levels of security and foreign policy making in the Bush administration. JINSA's board included Cheney, John Bolton (undersecretary of state for arms control) and Douglas Feith (the third highest official at the Pentagon), and Richard Perle (former chair of the Pentagon's Defense Policy Board) among others.[11] Perle, along with former Reagan appointee UN Ambassador Jeane Kirkpatrick, sits on the board of JINSA and CSP. According to *The Nation*, at least twenty-two CSP advisors were given key positions in the Bush administration's security regime.[12]

Another institution engaged in the creation of neo-conservative projects is Harvard University's John M. Olin Center for Strategic Studies. It was formerly led by political scientist and consultant Samuel P. Huntington, best known for his book *The Clash of Civilizations and the Remaking of World Order*, which argued that violent confrontation between the Muslim world and the West was inevitable.

There were other grand strategic thinkers both on the Right and in the center who also argued that U.S. global policy had to move beyond twentieth-century conceptions, that is, a post–Cold War vision needed to be constructed. One critical work in the late 1990s was Zbigniew Brzezinski's *The Grand Chessboard: American Primacy and Its Geostrategic Imperatives*. In this 1997 work, the former national security advisor to President Jimmy Carter argued succinctly but strongly that U.S. preponderance must be maintained particularly in the hot spots of the world. In describing the area that runs from Central Europe and across the Middle East, he wrote, "[I]t is imperative that no Eurasian challenger emerges, capable of dominating Eurasia and thus also of challenging America."[13] Indeed, the multi-national, multi-religious, multi-racial, multi-continental, multi-ideological Eurasia has become ground zero for the most strategic political and military battles confronting the global community.

Importantly, he also noted that the multi-culturalizing of the United States through immigration could play a critical role in the construction and tenor of developing a new foreign policy. The influx of people from across the globe, transforming U.S. racial, ethnic, religious, and potentially political demographics, was a factor not to be ignored. Under these circumstances finding public support for specific foreign policy initiatives could become increasingly difficult unless, he stated with frightening acuity, a unifying occurrence emerged. He wrote, "Moreover, as America becomes an increasingly multicultural society, it may find it more difficult to fashion a consensus on foreign policy issues, *except in the circumstances of a truly massive and widely perceived direct external threat*"[14] (emphasis added). He does not elaborate on this theme, but Brzezinski is aware clearly that organized minority voices could well influence U.S. policy toward particular states or regions, that is, African Americans and Africa, Jewish

Americans and Israel, Hispanic Americans and Latin America, Asian Americans and the Pacific rim, and so on. The implication is that with an increased influx of immigrants to the United States from the Middle East, and Muslims from around the world, U.S. objectives in Eurasia could be challenged internally and compromised absent a more compelling set of circumstances. September 11, of course, would become that external threat that triumphed internal resistance to U.S. political machinations in the Middle East, and, indeed, everywhere. It would also unleash an unrelenting aggressive posture within the United States, at the state level and at the popular level, toward citizens, residents, and visitors of Arab or Muslim background and identity. Brzezinski does not, mercifully, link this growth with the inevitability of increased domestic terrorism, but that has certainly been the view of many, conservative or otherwise, in the United States. The high visibility of two racial minority individuals, Powell and Rice, in the exercise of U.S. hegemony would be a useful strategy and even necessary component of the new policy and mute, in many quarters, charges of racism at home and abroad.

It must be noted that while Brzezinski is a staunch defender of pressing U.S. interests abroad, he is not a neo-conservative and has been sharply critical of the Bush administration's policies not only in Iraq and in prosecuting the war against terrorism, but also more broadly in the erosion of traditional alliances. The consequences of these missteps, he argues, "could produce hegemonic isolation, with old friends cavalierly antagonized and new ones neither truly sharing America's basic values nor capable of becoming genuinely comprehensive partners in coping with the sources of global violence."[15] His concerns echoed the growing alarm of many other foreign policy elites from past Democratic and even Republican administrations, including Brent Scowcroft, who had been national security advisor under George H. W. Bush, and Rice's original benefactor in launching her public policy career.[16]

Powell and Rice Get on Board

> I wouldn't accept the comparison to the Roman Empire, of course, because the United States has no imperial ambitions.
>
> Condoleezza Rice, July 31, 2003[17]

Powell certainly and Rice to a much lesser degree had emerged as popular figures in the black community as a result of their tenure in the Reagan (Powell), George H. W. Bush (Powell and Rice), and Clinton administrations (Powell). While there had been deep antagonism toward Reagan and Bush by black America, Powell and Rice's status as "firsts" in a number of areas allowed them a softer political space in the popular arena. Their racial representational standing of the time was accepted by domestic and global publics alike.

Neither Powell nor Rice were part of those earlier debates in a determinist manner although as noted both had been in the George H. W. Bush administration, he as chairman of the Joint Chiefs of Staff, and she as director, and then senior director, of Soviet and East European Affairs in the National Security Council, and then as special assistant to the president for National Security Affairs. Neither could be considered neo-conservative. During the late 1990s, as the PNAC policies were being forged and plans for a Republican return to power being sorted out, Powell's views on foreign policy were being scorched as his name floated as a possible next secretary of state in a new Republican administration, perhaps led by George W. Bush. For some in the party, Powell's star quality was seen as a needed boost to what was generally conceded to be a lightweight candidate with virtually no foreign policy experience (or thoughts) in his quiver.

Yet, rumors of Powell coming into a new Republican administration enlivened the rancor of the neo-conservatives, particularly those associated with PNAC, who viewed his role in the first Gulf war as nearly traitorous. As PNAC co-founder Robert Kagan wrote in July 2000, after blaming him for Saddam Hussein remaining in power, "Powell's error was no isolated case of faulty reasoning. His judgment during the Gulf crisis fit within a broader doctrine of nonintervention derived from his experience in Vietnam.... The problem with Powell is his political and strategic judgment."[18] He stated further that "on the most important strategic questions of the post–Cold war era, Powell has come up with the wrong answers."[19]

Powell did not join the Bush campaign as early as other key foreign policy advisors, such as Rice, and it was clear that he personally was not close to Bush. His previous negative run-ins with Cheney were legend and recounted bitterly in Powell's autobiography. He writes, for example, of being dressed down by then Secretary of Defense Cheney for speaking above his status at a NSC meeting.[20] These individual conflicts and personal distance would only grow over time. Powell's relationship to Bush was also out of proportion. By reputation, experience, stature, and age, Powell overshadowed the incurious would-be president it was going to be his job to serve.

Neo-conservatives renewed their criticism of what had been termed the "Powell doctrine" on intervention. The key elements of Powell's views included the demand for clear goals and objectives in foreign policy initiatives; the use of force as a last resort; and adequate, overwhelming, and decisive force when used with a considerable measure of public support, domestic, and international.[21] It is misleading, however, to think of the Powell perspective as a doctrine in the classical sense of the term. While it embodies strategy, it is not a strategic or

political framework per se. In that sense, Powell's views are ideologically neb-
ulous and do not constitute any particular vision that addresses key issues of
international political order and boundaries, that is, the nature and contours of
power relations among states and other political actors. Thus his conflicts with
the neo-conservatives appear tactical and contingent, and perhaps even personal,
more so than consistently ideological or long-term strategic. He may genuinely
think of them, to use the words attributed to him by one writer, as "fucking
crazies," but he offers no contending paradigm or even comprehensive critique.[22] While Powell's perspective implies multi-lateralism, military restraint,
and sensitivity to public opinion, those principles certainly appeared to not be
steadfast, and with George W. Bush he would represent an administration that
clearly did not adhere to these beliefs. Yet, even as an operational means or broad
guidelines for carrying out foreign policy, Powell's "doctrine" creates shackles
that the neo-cons find abhorrent and unacceptable. And certainly having Powell
in a position to not only implement his beliefs but also to obstruct other points
of view was not to be tolerated. Yet, as Kagan dismally concluded, it was not
going to be possible to prevent Powell's elevation.

Lawrence Kaplan, a senior editor at *The New Republic* and a well-established
neo-conservative, was even harsher in his criticisms of Powell and his canon.
Kaplan contends that in the first Gulf war, Bosnia and Somalia, Powell's posture
was one of hesitancy and strategic judgments that were flawed through and
through. Writing as Powell was coming into office in January 2001, he states,
"In fact, the Powell Doctrine was already irrelevant when Powell was preaching
it a decade ago. Which is what makes the Bush team's talk of reviving it so
puzzling. As a template for how and when to use force in the post–cold war era,
the doctrine has proved next to useless."[23] He also accused Powell of disloyalty
to both George H. W. Bush and Bill Clinton contending that he used journalists
and others to note his displeasure with certain policies, a no-no in Washington
power circles, an accusation that was not completely without merit.[24]

These arguments were lost on Bush. The Bush team determined correctly that
it had more to gain than lose politically in bringing Powell forward. In selecting
Powell, it also appears that a racial-ideological calculation came into play. At the
time, his popularity among black Americans was higher than most other black
leaders except for perhaps Rev. Jesse Jackson, a fact not lost on a party that had
little black support. While Bush and the Bush team would have undoubtedly
preferred someone more ideological compatible for such an important area, it
was recognized that Powell brought gravitas, popular support from European
and other allies, critical experience, provided a racial safety net, and, most important, could be contained politically. One cleverly selected counter-weight,
though far from the only one, would be Rice.

As George W. Bush and his conservative handlers guiding him began to cobble together his foreign policy team, Rice became a key player. Bush's father had brought Rice in initially to educate his son on the contours and details of international politics. Academically trained in the politics of the Cold War, her orientation toward foreign policy was very much steeped in the "power politics," "balance of power," and "national interests" notions of realists such as political scientist Hans Morgenthau. In his most noted work, *Politics Among Nations*, the bible of realists, he argued that national interest should guide relations among states. Thus, the exercise of power is framed, not by an abstract morality or illusory international community, but by naked national self-interest. He wrote, "World public opinion as a restraint on the struggle for power is a fiction because agencies of national policy that reflect a nation's desire to impose their morality on others mold such opinion."[25] He held similar opinions regarding international law stating that, "International law as a restraint on the struggle for power is a fiction as well, for it only gains its validity in the very sovereignty of nation-states that create the law and mechanisms for enforcing it. Treaties that have sought to outlaw war have always failed."[26]

Morgenthau's impact on Rice was glaring. Prior to Bush II coming to power, she also offered her own views on what should constitute a Bush foreign policy framework and its distinction from what she saw as Clinton's disastrous policies. In a well-known and oft quoted *Foreign Affairs* article, she argues a strong nationalism familiar in realist Republican circles,

> Power matters, both the exercise of power by the United States and the ability of others to exercise it. Yet many in the United States are (and have always been) uncomfortable with the notions of power politics, great powers, and power balances. In an extreme form, this discomfort leads to a reflexive appeal instead to notions of international law and norms, and the belief that the support of many states—or even better, of institutions like the United Nations—is essential to the legitimate exercise of power. The "national interest" is replaced with "humanitarian interests" or the interests of "the international community." The belief that the United States is exercising power legitimately only when it is doing so on behalf of someone or something else was deeply rooted in Wilsonian thought, and there are strong echoes of it in the Clinton administration. To be sure, there is nothing wrong with doing something that benefits all humanity, but that is, in a sense, a second-order effect.[27]

Again, Morgenthau's framework on power would come into play. He contended that politics could essentially be boiled down to the triad of "keeping power, increasing power, and demonstrating power," a thesis that would echo throughout Rice's tenure and perfectly capture the hegemonic practices of the administration.[28]

While few objective observers would agree with Rice's dubious assertion that Clinton put international interests ahead of national ones, her forceful articulation of the accusation served the ideological purpose of preparing for a dramatic shift in the tone and tenor of U.S. international priorities. Back then, her realist inclinations differed from the neo-cons by presenting a softer line than they did on international engagement in a number of areas. She called for regime change in Iraq, which had become a stable hawk demand since the Persian Gulf war, but through more conventional means. She stated,

> As history marches toward markets and democracy, some states have been left by the side of the road. Iraq is the prototype. Saddam Hussein's regime is isolated, his conventional military power has been severely weakened, his people live in poverty and terror, and he has no useful place in international politics. He is therefore determined to develop WMD. Nothing will change until Saddam is gone, so the United States must mobilize whatever resources it can, including support from his opposition, to remove him.[29]

Notably, she does not state categorically that Hussein has WMD nor directly calls for his removal by military means, although she would do so on both counts later citing the transitory impact of September 11.

Rice came into office promoting a security policy agenda that revised a paradigm first proposed under Reagan. As she stated at the Republican National Convention, "It is time to move beyond the Cold War. It is time to have a president devoted to a new nuclear strategy and to the deployment of effective missile defenses at the earliest possible date."[30] In fact, in April 2004, her focus on missile defense, as well as the administration, became the subject of another controversy. As it turns out, on September 11, 2001, Rice was to deliver a speech on national security at the School of Advanced International Studies at Johns Hopkins University. It was cancelled due to that day's events. The focus of her talk was to advocate primarily for building the administration's missile defense program. This news coming out in the middle of the election season and as the administration was defending itself against charges of ignoring the terrorist threat by former national counter-terrorism official Richard Clarke undermined Bush's and Rice's versions of the story that they were focused on addressing: terrorism. The administration refused to release the complete text of the speech that Rice was to deliver.[31]

Yet, despite the differences that existed, she also echoed the view of the neo-cons on the necessity of the United States to act solely from the point of view of national interest and the preservation of U.S. hegemony at all costs. As she told one reporter, "But if it comes to allowing another adversary to reach military parity with the United States in the way that the Soviet Union did, no, the United States does not intend to allow that to happen."[32] Additionally, she refers to the international community and international norms as "illusionary." While stating rhetorically that a Republican administration would be internationalist, her caveat was that it would be from the "firm ground of national interest," which came to mean that while other nations are expected to accommodate themselves to U.S. interests, the reverse is not true. She accused the Clinton administration of failure due to its epidemic references and bows to the "illusionary 'norms' of international behavior." She contends that it is not "isolationist to suggest that the United States has a special role in the world and should not adhere to every international convention and agreement that someone thinks to propose."[33] Rice argued further that the most important approach in conducting U.S. foreign policy was the strategic alliances among great powers—Russian and China—thus relegating other states and interests to observer status. Not only did the U.S.-European allies bristle at these statements but so did much of the world including African states and their supporters in the U.S. black community.

While some black Americans and many in Africa and the Diaspora celebrated the Powell and Rice appointments through the prism of collective racial achievements, others worried that a Clarence Thomas–like Trojan Horse scenario of racial "betrayal" was unfolding. For those progressives who believed that there should be a political rather than or as well as a racial determination in assessing the efforts of Powell and Rice, their strong ties to the previous Reagan and Bush administrations alone raised suspicions. Beyond the domestic issues, there was a jittery distrust about what the new administration would do regarding black American concerns related to Africa and the Caribbean. Yet, even after the appalling events involving black disenfranchisement in the 2000 election in Florida that contributed decisively to Bush gaining the White House generating an anger toward him and his administration that has not subsided, there was, in effect, no substantial organized resistance to the Powell and Rice nominations from the black community.[34]

Upon entering office, Bush faced conflicting inclinations from his foreign policy team leaders of Cheney, the highest ranking neo-conservative in the administration; Powell, represented traditional conservative moderation and Rice was an unreconstructed realist. Lacking strong and well-developed foreign policy views of his own, except for an immature anti-Clintonism, Bush appeared to be trying to accommodate all three perspectives in the first months of his presidency. The administration made it clear that it would be reviewing all of the international commitments made by its predecessor including those to the United Nations and allies. Among its first initiatives, the administration rejected the Kyoto Protocol, unsigned Clinton's agreement on the International Criminal Court, and sent other signals that uni-lateralism was the new game in town. It was less the merits of these agreements, which were being genuinely debated in policy and academic circles, than the posture of hegemonic assertion that drove these decisions. These moves polarized Powell from Rice much of the time and from Cheney, Rumsfeld, Wolfowitz, and other neo-cons nearly all the time although many of the disagreements were turf battles masquerading as political ones. Rice, however, at that point had not fully gone into the neo-con camp and seemed to be more concerned with protecting Bush's ability to be flexible on foreign policy matters and problems than taking sides. Her differences with the neo-conservatives arose around a number of issues including China's stance on Taiwan, Russia's war with Chenchnya, and North Korea's nuclear proliferation and its relations with its neighbors.

Warriors on Terror

> Your government is alert. The governors and mayors are alert that evil folks still lurk out there. As I said yesterday, people have declared war on America and they have made a terrible mistake. . . . My administration has a job to do and we're going to do it. We will rid the world of the evil-doers.
>
> George W. Bush, September 16, 2001

September 11, 2001, settled all disputes in the administration about its foreign policy mandate. Powell's views and Powell himself became even more marginalized than before, if that was possible, and Rice acceded completely to the neo-con perspective. Indeed, she helped to give it some of its more eloquent expression. Clearly befuddled, desperately seeking to project a macho response, and falling back on religious clichés, Bush let the monster of total war loose. He promised revenge on the "evil doers" and the neo-cons provided the rationale and tone. What had seemed nearly politically impossible—an unfettered ability to enact the hegemonic policy of Full Spectrum Dominance—had become the norm virtually overnight.[35] The war on terrorism and its offshoots would not only define the Bush presidency but a new and more perilous stage of U.S. hegemonship. In part fortuitous and in part calculation, it would also be beneficial that two principle actors in this process were black Americans. What better situation to be in than to be able to blunt charges of racist imperialism or religious persecution of Muslims in launching a devastating war against the underdeveloped world than by having Rice and Powell as highly visible and accommodating spokespersons.

From the beginning, Rice set a tone of war without recourse or apology. There is no evidence, both before and since, that she wavered one iota in believing that the questionable elements underlying the war on terror or invading Iraq were the right things to do, unlike Powell who expressed some doubts in the Iraq calamity that has unfolded since the occupation began. Her signature piece was the September 2000 publication of *The National Security Strategy of the United States of America* (NSS). The NSS codifies as official policy the arguments that had been made by the neo-cons for a decade. Though vetted through many hands, the major fingerprints on the document, its lyricist, are those of Rice. It crystallized more sharply a trajectory that was already occurring. The core and distinguishing political assumptions of the strategy are the notion of military preemption and the maintenance of a U.S. hegemonic positioning that makes preemption a permanent option.

Mandated by the Goldwater-Nichols Act of 1986, the NSS was generally ignored by policy-makers and the media alike. Often the reports were late, including the one submitted by Bush that had been due initially on June 15, 2001 and was little more than a brash celebration of the administration's accomplishments. As presented by the various administrations, the NSS reports did not meet the goal of ensuring "greater civilian control over the military and its planning."[36] In fact, given the changing nature of the occupants of the White House and fluid events on the ground, the NSS could never be more than a transitory statement of the political yearnings of the moment masquerading as common national security interests.

It is this context that leads to understanding the qualitative differences between the last Clinton NSS and that of the George W. Bush administration. The Clinton administration's report stated that America's security strategy sought to address three objectives: "To enhance America's security," "To bolster America's economic prosperity," and "To promote democracy and human rights abroad."[37] Distinct from Bush's post–September 11 doctrine, security was, more or less, given equal weight with economic prosperity and human rights. The administration argued that threats would come from a number of different sources including other stable but dangerous states, failed states, terrorists, criminal organizations, weapons of mass destruction, and environmental disasters.[38] Despite Rice's criticism that Clinton failed to give priority to defending the "national interest," much of the NSS is indeed focused on what is termed "advancing the national interest."[39] In reality, the contention is less over whether Clinton addressed national interest and more over how that interest is defined (an international system that the United States unfairly and unilaterally dominates or an international system focused on cooperation and shared interests).

The most notable difference in tone between the two documents is regarding the relationship between the United States and the rest of the international community. The Clinton administration, like Bush, makes it clear that "America must be willing to act alone when our interests demand it," but goes on to state that the United States "should also support the institutions and arrangements through which other countries help us bear the burdens of leadership."[40] This view is emphasized more strongly when the NSS states:

> International cooperation will be vital for building security in the next century because many of the challenges we face cannot be addressed by a single nation. Many of our security objectives are best achieved—or can only be achieved—by leveraging our influence and capabilities through international organizations, our alliances, or as a leader of an ad hoc coalition formed around a specific objective. Leadership in the United Nations and other international organizations, and durable relationships with allies and friendly nations, are critical to our security.[41]

In other words, while the Clinton administration does note its willingness to act unilaterally, it does not highlight the option of "preemption" that anchors the Bush doctrine. The notion of deterrence is ratcheted down as the Bush administration argues that the new threatening forces—rogue states and terrorists—cannot be deterred effectively nor is the possession and use of a weapon of mass destruction to be allowed under any circumstances. Inclusion of the "preemption" option—what Rice has also referred to as "anticipatory self-defense—was strategically deceptive.[42] As Mahajan, Brzezinski, O'Hanlon, and others have pointed out, what the Bush administration was actually adopting was an intervention strategy generally referred to as "prevention" and which has been deemed illegal in international law.[43] While preempting an imminent attack is justified in international law and norms, deciding (especially unilaterally) that a military assault can be launched to prevent an unspecified threat at some unspecified future point is rejected expressively by the international community. And the notion of preventive attack likely would also be rejected by a logically thinking U.S. public, thus the need to hide behind a term that seems both more rational and acceptable to a nation that had just been attacked. The adoption of such a position by other large and even small states—with Russia clearly seizing the doctrine to justify its aggressions in Chenchnya—is a catastrophe for international order. As a political scientist schooled in international relations, it is difficult to believe that Rice was not aware of this distinction giving credence to the suspicion that an ideological point was being fostered rather than a sober assessment of the security issues facing the United States. Ralph Bunche, in his Nobel Prize acceptance lecture, spoke to this issue more than fifty years ago when he stated:

> There are some in the world who are prematurely resigned to the inevitability of war. Among them are the advocates of the so-called "preventive war," who, in their resignation to war, wish merely to select their time for initiating it. To suggest that war can prevent war is a base play on words and a despicable form of warmongering. The objective of any who sincerely believe in peace clearly must be to exhaust every honororable recourse in the effort to save the peace. The world has ample evidence that war begets only conditions which beget further war.[44]

Virtually overnight, Rice morphed from her realist stance of opposing defense of human rights—a "second order effect" as she termed it—as a motivation for intervention and foreign policy determinations to centralizing Hussein's human rights violations as a justification for the war in Iraq as other rationales lost credibility. Her embrace of a central theme of neo-conservatism repositioned her further to the right within the debates inside the administration.

While Powell has been accused consistently by some in the media as well as Bush officials of being off message and not in sync with the administration, he has refuted these accusations and the evidence tends to back him up. Certainly he has played the role of diplomat while other administration officials were welding political sledgehammers. His language has been measured and his deftness at finding ways to get his political and tactical differences into the public domain has been nothing short of remarkable. However, at all the key junctures and on the key political themes of the Bush doctrine, Powell has assented. This has often taken incredible stretches of rhetoric and logic. Perhaps the best example of his effort to argue his loyalty to the administration is in an article that he published in *Foreign Affairs* in January/February 2004. Its purpose was not only to argue that the United States under the Bush administration is not unilaterialist in its approach to foreign policy but also that George W. Bush is a visionary, a posture rarely taken publicly by Powell and much more common for Rice. The article echoes nearly every theme that has come to define Bush's and neo-conservatives' views on foreign policy—the priority of engaging major powers over other states; criticism that Yasser Arafat was an obstructionist; highlighting preemption as an option; viewing free trade initiatives linked to nation building; prioritizing anti-terrorism as the defining element of foreign policy in this period—with the stated aim of proving that the U.S. strategy under Bush has been one of partnerships. Powell's assertions that the United States "strongly affirms" the United Nations, and that its policies regarding the Israeli-Palestine conflict "have brought peace closer" are strains indeed.[45] The tone of the article is defensive throughout as when he writes, "U.S. strategy is widely accused of being unilateralist by design. It isn't. It is often accused of being imbalanced in favor of military methods. It isn't. It is frequently described as being obsessed with terrorism and hence biased toward preemptive war on a global scale. It most certainly is not."[46] Of course, by extrapolation, Powell was defending his tenure at the State Department as well.

Condi Testifies

Perhaps the most controversial moments of Rice's tenure during Bush's first term occurred over whether she would testify before the September 11 Commission (formally known as the National Commission on Terrorist Attacks Upon the United States). Although it sought to rewrite the history of its relation with the commission, the Bush administration opposed the creation of the commission, attempted to block access to critical documents, and when it sought to get public testimony under oath from Rice, clearly a critical player in the events leading up to the terrorist attacks, initially claimed that she was exempt and was not going to let her testify. On February 7, 2004, she had testified in private but it was not under oath and only a few of the commissioners attended because Rice insisted that it be held at her office and on a Saturday. Only after a public outcry, and the bizarre behavior of Rice's giving numerous press conferences about why she could not testify in public, did the administration relent, but only partly. Always seeking a political advantage, White House counsel Alberto Gonzales sent a letter to the commission and fashioned an agreement with it that stated that not only would Rice only testify this one time, but also that no other White House officials would be called not just before this commission but for any in the future! The administration had claimed that in the past no other national security advisor or other White House officials had ever testified before Congress, but this was a fabrication. During the Watergate hearings, several Nixon aides testified. Former Carter national security advisor Zbigniew Brzezinski and former Clinton national security advisor Samuel "Sandy" Berger had both testified before Senate committees during their tenures.[47]

The administration also argued disingenuously that Bush had determined that "he retains the legal authority to decline to make Dr. Rice available to testify in public."[48] In fact, there was no legal basis for his refusal to allow Rice to testify.

The Supreme Court has never ruled on that particular issue and the fact that other White House officials had testified in the past undermines the administration's arguments.

The letter from Gonzales set two conditions for her testimony. It stated, "First, the Commission must agree in writing that Dr. Rice's testimony before the Commission does not set any precedent for future Commission requests, or requests in any other context, for testimony by a National Security Advisor or any other White House official. . . . Second, the Commission must agree in writing that it will not request additional public testimony from any White House official, including Dr. Rice."[49] Rather than admit its embarrassment, the administration attempted to portray its grudging cooperation as an act of generosity. The Gonzales letter called its concession an "extraordinary accommodation."[50] It was anything but, of course.

The decision to let Rice testify was also to counter the accusations made by former White House counter-terrorism expert Richard Clarke, who had worked in the Clinton and George W. Bush administrations. In public testimony before the commission and later in his book, *Against All Enemies: Inside America's War on Terror*, Clarke charged that the White House did not pay attention to the terrorist threat, al Qaeda in particular, although he repeatedly warned of the dangers of an attack as soon as the Bush administration came into office.[51] He grew to believe that the administration became obsessed with Iraq to the detriment of addressing the al Qaeda threat. Clarke's allegations were difficult to dismiss. He had been the nation's top counter-terrorism expert, a Republican, and a critic of both Clinton and Bush.

Clarke had been behind the "Delenda Plan." This was the strategy developed to destroy al Qaeda during the Clinton administration in 1998. This was in response to the al Qaeda bombings of the U.S. embassies in Kenya and Tanzania and other attacks. Military strikes were launched against its camps in Afghanistan and the Sudan. The goals of the plan were to prevent further attacks and prevent al Qaeda from obtaining weapons of mass destruction through covert actions to destroy terrorist cells; identifying and freezing funds; military action where necessary and possible; and diplomacy to force Afghanistan and other states that harbor terrorists to end those sanctuaries. Although the plan was never adopted formally, and key Clinton officials opposed the military component, nevertheless, Clarke sought to implement the other dimensions of the strategy. When Bush was elected in 2000, he stayed on with the new administration until his frustration with what he felt was its refusal to prioritize the al Qaeda threat drove him to leave.

When he went public with his criticisms, the White House launched a full-scale assault on Clarke's credibility with Rice leading the way. A media blitz was unleashed against Clarke in late March 2004, as the controversies over Clarke's book and Rice's testimony grew. Cheney, Rice, and others were dispatched to the media frontlines. On March 22, 2004, the day after Clarke appeared on *60 Minutes*, an interview that was seen by 16 million, Rice made it to all five Monday network morning shows and was booked to appear on fifteen cable news channels and numerous radio shows.[52] Within two weeks, Rice herself would be making the trip to Capitol Hill.

Rice's actual testimony in front of the commission was artful in its ability to obfuscate, mislead, fabricate, and evade. It was also in conflict with statements made by other administration officials and, indeed, by Rice herself. She testified that the White House had a military strategy aimed at al Qaeda, but Deputy Secretary of State Richard Armitage had testified that it did not. Rice stated that Clarke was an important figure in the administration's anti-terrorist efforts, but Vice President Cheney stated that he was "out of the loop." Rice's own statements seem to contradict themselves. At a private press briefing, she said, "We hired him to continue Clinton policies." However, on CNN, she stated that Clinton's anti-terrorist policies had failed and that Clarke had been at the heart of that failure.

In her remarks before the commission, she stated, "I took the unusual step of retaining Dick Clarke and the entire Clinton Administration's counterterrorism team on the NSC staff. I knew Dick to be an expert in his field, as well as an experienced crisis manager. Our goal was to ensure continuity of operations while we developed new and more aggressive policies." This mellowed out perspective was quite a departure from the lambasting that she and Cheney had been giving Clarke in the preceding days and weeks. She also noted that the briefing she and other received from Clinton officials on terrorism and al Qaeda. As early as March 2001, according to Clarke, the new administration and Rice directly had been warned by him that he thought al Qaeda cells were in the United States and seeking a means of attack.[53] There were increased reports on possible al Qaeda attacks including in the United States throughout the spring and summer. Although much of the reporting could not be corroborated the upsurge in warnings, anonymous tips, and CIA-discovered chatter sent signals that were not connected. On May 17, the inter-agency Counterterrorism Security Group that Clarke chaired had as its first agenda item, "UBL: Operation Planned in U.S." UBL stood for Usama bin Laden.[54] In June, reports of a "very, very, very, very" big and imminent attack were non-stop. Clarke sent messages to Rice and her assistant Steve Hadley about these intelligence reports.[55]

The most heated exchange during her testimony occurred regarding the August 6, 2001, Presidential Daily Briefing. The PDB was titled, "Bin Laden Determined to Strike in US." The administration, including Rice, attempted to hide the name of the PDB, and most observers only heard the title for the first time during Rice's testimony. After being pushed by Commissioner Richard Ben-Veniste, she begrudgingly stated the title. It was clearly embarrassing to the administration to admit that it had received a memo only a month before September 11 indicating that al Qaeda had set its sights on targets inside America. The first line of the PDB read, "Clandestine, foreign government, and media reports indicate Bin Laden since 1997 has wanted to conduct terrorist attacks in the US."[56] The PDB went on to state, after noting that U.S. intelligence agencies could not verify anything beyond the general nature of the threats, that "Nevertheless, FBI information since that time indicates patterns of suspicious activity in this country consistent with preparations for hijackings or other types of attacks, including recent surveillance of federal buildings in New York."[57] Bush and Rice both claimed that the document was "historic" in nature and did not reflect any specific knowledge or actionable intelligence. The memo had first surfaced in May 2002 in a discussion with reporters where Rice clearly did not mention the disturbing title of the document, a title that the administration would classify.[58] While it was true that the memo was broad and general, and in and of itself not a specific indicator of the upcoming September 11 events, the administration's efforts to hide or mislead regarding the memo indicates its fear that it would be perceived as not doing enough to prevent the attacks. Taken with other information about its failure to connect the dots, the PDB underscores critics' claims that the administration is more concerned with its image than with admitting its errors.

There were other glaring contradictions in Rice's portrayal of events. Although Clarke had told the new administration many months earlier that al Qaeda had a presence inside the United States, incredibly and dubiously, Bush told the commission that his advisors had never told him that there was a cell in the United States.[59] While Rice and other officials stated that the PDB gave no information specific to September 11, she also noted in her testimony that "The FAA issued at least five Civil Aviation Security Information Circulars to all U.S. airlines and airport security personnel, including specific warnings about the possibility of hijackings."[60]

While it was relatively clear that the administration had not given urgent attention to the possibility of a terrorist attack inside the United States, it would continue to claim that it was doing everything possible before September 11 to go after al Qaeda. Rice told the commission, "We decided immediately to continue pursuing the Clinton Administration's covert action authorities and other efforts to fight the network."[61] However, media reports demonstrated that the Bush administration cut several anti-terrorist programs specifically aimed at al Qaeda. *Newsweek* reported, "In the months before 9/11, the U.S. Justice Department curtailed a highly classified program called 'Catcher's Mitt' to monitor al-Qaeda suspects in the United States," and "though Predator drones spotted Osama bin Laden as many as three times in late 2000, the Bush administration did not fly the unmanned planes over Afghanistan during its first eight months," thus eliminating another program started under Clinton.[62]

There were other statements made during her testimony that did not ring true. For instance, she stated, "We increased funding for counterterrorism activities across several agencies." However, according to the *New York Times*, when Bush came into office, his 2002 budget proposed to cut more than half a billion dollars from counter-terrorism at the Department of Justice. The paper reported that the new administration "did not endorse F.B.I. requests for $58 million for 149 new counterterrorism field agents, 200 intelligence analysts and 54 additional translators" and "proposed a $65 million cut for the program that gives state and local counterterrorism grants."[63]

In the end, Rice simply refused to acknowledge any mistakes made on the part of the Bush administration, instead blaming bureaucratic roadblocks and inadequate laws—resolved in her view by the civil liberties–challenging Patriot Act—for the government's failure to intercept or prevent the strikes. Her refusal to apologize to the families of victims of September 11 during her testimony, following the lead of Bush, Cheney, and other officials, was a sore point for many of those family members who fought to establish the commission in the first place and attended its hearings.

Aftermath

Rice and Powell were at the center of the administration's planning and implementation of its war on terrorism. Within a few months of the attacks, the United States had invaded and occupied Afghanistan overthrowing the hated Taliban regime and chasing al Qaeda forces out of their camps. Osama bin Laden managed to escape as did many of his top aides. At this juncture, much of the world still held sympathy with the United States although differences abounded with little sign that Bush would seek a more accommodationist relationship with the United Nations and European allies. Rice and Powell both were central in advancing the arguments built to support the war on terrorism including incorporating the unilateralist approach that had come to define the foreign policy strategy of the administration. With Afghanistan under its belt, the war drums grew even louder as new targets entered the public discourse.

While the September 11 attacks would be the first large disaster shaped by the ideological ambitions of the new administration, it would not be the last. While Powell and Rice expressed little public disagreement over how to press the war against terrorism, the ever growing shift to focus on Iraq would position the former in the most difficult time in his career and the latter more solidly linked to the neo-conservative agenda. And while there had been a remarkable surge of black support for Bush in the immediate period after September 11, within a very short time, the black community would be the most opposed to the war in Iraq and the administration's foreign policy overall.

Five

The Clash: Iraq in the Crosshairs of Hegemony

When tomorrow comes will you be the perpetuators of war or of peace?

John Rice (Condoleezza Rice's father)[1]

Despite his befuddled initial reaction to a question on "Meet the Press" about why the United States went to war against Iraq, when Bush eventually responded, he stated that Iraq was a war of necessity. In truth, his decision to invade Iraq, built on a mountain of fabrications, distortions, and manipulation, was a war of choice. And that choice had little substantially to do with fighting terrorism, finding illusionary weapons of mass destruction, ending Hussein's human rights abuses or his purported ties to al Qaeda, or even primarily opening Iraq's oil reserves to the West. The seizure of Iraq was the opportunistic execution of a long-planned, determined global geopolitical strategy, that is, the furtherance of U.S. hegemonic power manifest in the imposition of free markets dictates, U.S.-styled and defined political systems, and establishment of permanent U.S. military bases. The ever changing justifications for the war by Bush and British prime minister Tony Blair were fluid because they were mostly irrelevant. The theatre of going to the United Nations and, in the case of Britain, plagiarized reports and dubious legality, never had a chance at stopping a war whose decision to conduct had already been made long before the first troops crossed Iraq's borders. For the Bush administration, the issue of international legality or legitimacy was never a determinant factor. UN Resolution or not, it was going to take advantage of the post–September 11 political atmosphere and remove Hussein from power. In the post–Cold War period, containment has been abandoned as a strategy and opportunity targets will be taken out—pre-emptively, if possible. September 11 made what had been politically tenuous a foregone conclusion.

Iraq is the defining event of the George W. Bush presidency, a defining occurrence of Powell's career, and a defining moment of Rice's political and ideological transformation. When Bush used the phrase "mission accomplished" on May 1, 2003, in one sense he was speaking of a broader objective than the military effort, which had not been accomplished. More important, the invasion and occupation of Iraq is the end of a phase of hegemonization in which securing a permanent military and political presence in Eurasia has been achieved, and it is the beginning of an era of power projection and regional political remapping that will extend past the Bush tenure for as long as it can. The corrupt and repressive dictatorship in Saudi Arabia, despite its longstanding alliance with the United States and even longer unholy financial partnership with the Bush family dynasty, was an unreliable partner in the long run. Though dependent upon the United States in many ways and its strongest collaborator in the region, Israel's tendency to give priority to its own interests also makes it a difficult alliance at times. Given its strategic location, oil resources, access to waterways in the North, and history of resistance, Iraq was the prize to be seized more so than Iran, Syria, and any other state in the region. The 1998 "Iraqi Liberation Act," which had been a key lobbying effort by neo-conservatives associated with the Project for the New American Century, had made "regime change" in Iraq official U.S. policy and inevitable. Expressions of a peaceful solution to the Iraq situation were hollow on the part of Bush administration officials.

A critique of the process by which Bush went to war should never assume that an alternative was considered by the administration or most of his key aides. While Blair and other Western governments who backed Bush may or may not have believe one of the various arguments being suggested, though not likely, the White House certainly had no such illusions. The UN Security Council process for seeking a first and then second resolution coincided with the military buildup, which was fortuitous for those like Blair who need a degree of political cover, but it was not decisive in determining whether war was going to happen or not because, as Rice stated, "The United States needs to speak so that the U.N. knows that America is capable of acting with or without U.N. authorization."[2] The Bush administration was generally concerned to some degree that the Blair government could tumble for backing his aggression. However, that concern had less to do with Bush's personal friendship with Blair than with the necessity to maintain in power the chief ally and facilitator of U.S. hegemony among large states. And, ultimately, as Secretary of Defense Donald Rumsfeld let slip, Britain was not needed to win the military battle against Hussein. It was needed, however, to foster the fiction that a broad international coalition was behind the war. Poll data in the fall 2002 revealed that Bush only won majority support for the war by the American people if they believed that other nations also were behind it. When that belief was taken out of the equation, support fell dramatically. Blair was in on the game nearly from the beginning if one is to believe former British ambassador Christopher Meyer who states that on September 20, 2001, Bush told Blair that "I agree with you, Tony. We must deal with this first. But when we have dealt with Afghanistan, we must come back to Iraq."[3]

Even more devastating to the official narrative was a dagger in the form of a memo from a meeting on July 23, 2002 by Blair and his top foreign policy and security officials. This included Defense Secretary Geoffrey Hoon; Foreign Secretary Jack Straw; Attorney General Lord Goldsmith; the head of MI6 [Britain's "CIA"] Richard Dearlove; head of the Joint Intelligence Committee John Scarlett; Chief of the Defense Staff Admiral Sir Michael Boyce; Blair's Chief of Staff Jonathan Powell; Blair's Director of Strategy and key political advisor Alastair Campbell; and Director of Government Relations Sally Morgan. The meeting was organized to discuss the growing Iraq crisis and just where the Bush administration stood. The key passage from the memo derives from Dearlove's—referred to as "C" in the memo—report on his meetings in Washington. The memo reads:

> There was a perceptible shift in attitude. Military action was now seen as inevitable. Bush wanted to remove Saddam, through military action, justified by the conjunction of terrorism and WMD. But the intelligence and facts were being fixed around the policy. The NSC has no patience with the UN route, and no enthusiasm publishing material on the Iraqi regime's record. There was little discussion in Washington of the aftermath after military action.[4]

This memo documents that at least eight months before the invasion, and clearly even longer than that given that this was a report being discussed in Britain, Bush had decided to go to war. Everything that followed, from the public relations campaign to win popular support to going to the United Nations were constructed around a decision that was already on the table. The British discussion was not how to stop Washington—Straw stated at the meeting that "the case was thin"—but how to create a political climate and argument that would allow it to participate in the war. Straw would ultimately suggest that "We should work up a plan for an ultimatum to Saddam to allow back in the UN weapons inspectors. This would help with the legal justification for the use of force." In other words, while Washington initially saw no use for the United Nations in its war drive, the British conceived a plan by which the United Nations would facilitate, rather than prevent, Washington's machinations. Straw suggested discussing this proposal with Powell, the one administration official who would likely not be so blinded by antipathy toward the United Nations that he could see the double benefit of obtaining UN cover and keeping Britain on board.

Neo-Conned into War

The administration built its case on going to war against Iraq on three arguments: Iraq possesses weapons of mass destruction (WMD) and that cannot be tolerated in the post–September 11 period; Hussein has ties to terrorist groups including al Qaeda; and Hussein has committed massive human rights violations including the deliberate spreading of poison gas in a massacre of the Kurds. And Bush insisted that he had world opinion and the United Nations behind him on each of these charges. These arguments and claims, later proved false and misleading, would be pushed relentlessly by Bush and the others. In the buildup to the war, they would be successful enough in spinning these yarns to convince a large majority of the population to support the invasion in March 2003 as the war began.

In a study by the Program on International Policy Attitudes (PIPA) and Knowledge Networks, it was demonstrated that support for the war was directly correlated with the degree to which individuals believed those arguments.[5] And belief or rejection of those arguments was linked to specific news sources including Fox, CNN, NBC, ABC, CBS, PBS/NPR as well as the print media. Powell and Rice were two of the most visible proponents in the media making the administration's case. The PIPA study conducted polls before and after the invasion and found that significant proportions of Americans, sometimes majorities, believed one or more of the three misconceptions that they were asked about: Iraq or Hussein's involvement in September 11, Iraq's possession of WMD, and the degree of international support for the U.S.-led invasion. As the study notes, "In the run-up to the war with Iraq and in the postwar period, a significant portion of the American public has held a number of misperceptions that have played a key role in generating and maintaining approval for the decision to go to war."[6] In January 2003, the survey found that 68 percent believed that Iraq was involved in September 11. By summer 2003, the number had dropped but was still a substantial 57 percent who thought that Iraq was directly involved (22%) or gave substantial support to al Qaeda (35%).

Initially, the central argument proffered by Bush and company was that Iraq had nuclear, biological, and chemical weapons of mass destruction and could use them against not only its own citizens and neighbors, but also against the United States. Bush and other administration officials spoke with absolute certainly that WMD existed, and Hussein's refusal to let UN inspectors see them was a violation of Security Council resolutions that was no longer tolerable. They spoke with such certainty that in lieu of any real evidence still managed to convince large numbers of people that they did exist. PIPA found that even months after the invasion, when it was clear that WMD had not been found, roughly a quarter of those polled continued to believe that WMD had been found as did a poll by NBC/*Wall Street Journal*.[7] Indeed, a substantial number of individuals, 20 percent in September 2003, believed that chemical and biological weapons had not only been discovered but actually used by Iraq in the war.

A second important misconception was that there was worldwide support for Bush's and Blair's call for war. However, one of the most notable features of the Bush era was the dramatic change in global support for the United States that unfolded immediately following the September 11 attacks and then a precipitous fall globally as Bush drove toward war. The falloff between late 2001 and 2002 of favorable views of the United States was stunning: in France from 63 percent to 31 percent, in Italy from 70 percent to 34 percent, in Russia from 61 percent to 28 percent, in Turkey from 30 percent to 12 percent, and in England from 75 percent to 48 percent.[8] World opinion on every continent was against the increasing military buildup and rhetoric of the United States. By 2003, with war drums beating non-stop at the White House, Bush's global popularity sank to new lows for a U.S. president. From political and business elites to people in the streets, across the world the Iraq war was alienating tens of millions against the United States. According to one study by the University of Miami, nearly 90 percent of more than 500 elites in half a dozen Latin American countries rated Bush negatively with many giving him the lowest rating of "poor."[9] In some countries, the souring on Bush was almost total with scores of 98 percent in Brazil, 93 percent in Argentina, and, in one of Bush's favorite states, about 92 percent in Mexico.[10]

European polls conducted by the research group Eurobarometer found similar disapproval of Bush and the Iraq conflict. According to one report, more than two-thirds of those interviewed felt that the war in Iraq was "not justified."[11] In Asia, similar numbers existed. Only 15 percent of those polled in Indonesia and Turkey had a favorable opinion of the United States, 13 percent in Pakistan, and a whopping 1 percent in the Palestinian territories.[12]

Polls by Gallup International, Pew, Zogby, and others all demonstrated that there was very little global backing for Bush before the war and after it had began. On February 15, 2003, tens of millions around the world, in what was the largest coordinated demonstration in world history, protested the Bush and Blair war. In London, Bush's closest ally, more than 1 million took to the streets in one of the largest, if not the largest, demonstration in British history. In Spain, Portugal, Australia, and other nations where the governments supported

Bush, large demonstrations were also held. In Africa, the Middle East, and the Americas, protests were also held.

One of the most important conclusions of the PIPA study is that the more misconceptions held by individuals the more likely they were to support the war. The study found that of those who held none of the misconceptions only 23 percent supported the war, while those who held one misconception supported the war by 53 percent, those with two misconceptions by 78 percent, and those who held all three misconceptions by 86 percent. Where did these misconceptions derive?

Media Correlations

The Air Force defines "perception management" as "actions to convey and (or) deny selected information and indicators to foreign audiences to influence their emotions, motives, and objective reasoning. . . . In various ways, perception management combines truth projections, operations security, cover, and deception, and [psychological operation.]"[13] "Perception management" by the Bush administration was not just applied to foreign audiences. The misconceptions noted above were a direct consequence of the deliberate bombardment of the U.S. media, particularly conservative media outlets, with lies perpetuated by administration officials.

The PIPA study discovered that there was a strong correlation between the principle news source that individuals watched or listened to and their holding one or more of the misconceptions. The media outlets that were identified as the principle source of news for individuals were ABC, CBS, CNN, Fox, NBC, PBS/National Public Radio, and the print media generally. As it turned out, those who held the most misconceptions and were most likely to support the administration received their major news information from the Fox network, while those who were least likely to have any of the misconceptions got their news from PBS/NPR. The latter were least likely to support the administration. The research demonstrated that one or more misconception was held by 80 percent of Fox watchers in the survey, 71 percent of CBS, 61 percent of ABC, 55 percent of NBC, 55 percent of CNN, 47 percent of those who read the print media, and 23 percent of PBS/NRP consumers.[14]

While one has to be careful in overreading this poll data because other variables come into play, however, it is reasonable to assume that the more conservative Fox network would disproportionately air the administration's relentless spin while PBS/NPR would strive to be more politically objective (as they are legally required to be). Fox is owned by conservative media mogul Rupert Murdock who also owns a worldwide chain of over 140 tabloid newspapers that feed off sensationalism, sleaze, and hysteria. All of Murdoch's newspapers and "FOX News" took editorial stands supporting the Bush administration and the invasion.[15]

UN-Believable: Powell Presents to the World

> My colleagues, every statement I make today is backed up by sources, solid sources. These are not assertions. What we are giving you are facts and conclusions based on solid intelligence.
>
> Colin Powell, February 2, 2003[16]

During his tenure in office, it was reported consistently that Powell had serious reservations about going to war against Iraq as the neo-conservatives, especially Cheney and Wolfowitz, pushed for the invasion. Powell stated in a December 2001 interview that Saddam "is no longer the threat to the region that he was ten years ago."[17] He seemed to indicate that, while not totally satisfactory, the sanctions should stay in place and the administration would prefer but not precipitate a regime change. He certainly did not advocate, parsed or otherwise, a military invasion. Although there were clearly those in the top echelons of the administration who were contending that Iraq had to be next, Powell continued to state publicly that no decisions regarding Iraq had been made. On December 11, 2001, in press remarks with Foreign Minister Hubert Vedrine of France, Powell stated, "The President has made no decision as to what actions we should take in the next phase of our campaign against terror, nor has he received any recommendations as to what the next step should be and that specifically includes Iraq."[18]

His notion of an Iraq as a virtual non-threat was not held by others in Bush's top circle of foreign policy officials and Bush himself all of which left Powell marginalized in many respects. In Bob Woodward's account of the effort to bring regime change in Iraq, Powell is so far out of the loop that he was informed about the final decision to go to war after the Saudi ambassador, Prince Bandar bin Sultan, was told.[19] Denials all around notwithstanding, the story has a high believability factor because Powell was seen widely as the administration's dove. This was all the better, for Powell would play a decisive role in the evolution and furtherance of the new policy.

In a shrewd and devilishly brilliant move by the administration, in February 2003, Powell was tasked to make the U.S. case for war against Iraq at the United Nations in the struggle to get a second Security Council resolution that would legitimize the Bush and Blair invasion. Although Blair had told Parliament that he was on legal grounds with the elastic Resolution 1441, there were enough skeptics in his own party who wanted an ironclad act of the United Nations before committing to war. A statement of "serious consequences" if there was a breach by Iraq had been put in the resolution, but that was still open to interpretation as to whether it meant war or if it triggered a second, more definitive resolution. The British ambassador to the United Nations, Sir Jeremy Greenstock, had stated explicitly, "There is no 'automaticity' in this Resolution. If there is a further Iraqi breach of its disarmament obligations, the matter will return to the [Security] Council for discussion as required."[20] While Bush claimed that 1441 (and other past resolutions) were all that he needed, one last effort at coercion of the United Nations was warranted primarily at the insistence of Blair who was facing open revolt even among his own cabinet members. Conscious that more than any other U.S. official, Powell was perceived as the least hawkish, the administration sent him to do their dirty work. According to an extensive investigation by *Vanity Fair*, Vice President Cheney, aware of the shoddy nature of their evidence and of the disparagement of the administration's motives by the international community, told Powell a few days before the speech, "Your poll numbers are in the 70s. You can afford to lose a few points."[21] Powell's standing among European and other world leaders was also high.

Although reportedly, he rejected presenting some of the more outlandish accusations and questionable evidence the Bush administration wanted to put forward, Powell nevertheless orated for seventy-six minutes with audio tapes, charts, and pictures an argument for belligerence against Saddam Hussein, arguments that turned out to be untrue in nearly all aspects.[22] Whatever differences existed between Powell and the rest of the administration, that speech locked him into a position defending the Iraq war that he could not abandon with any credibility. As time passed, even in the face of opposing world opinions and perpetual isolation from with the administration, he mostly held steady.

However, as the evidence mounted that his UN presentation was a tower of fabrications and misrepresentations, Powell began to recant. In April 2004, he stated, "Now it appears not to be the case that it was that solid. But at the time I was preparing that presentation it was presented to me as being solid" acknowledging that his address was based on "faulty sources."[23]

Powell's presentation did little to give any credibility to the war cry and despite an unprecedented assault of pressure on a number of the small states on the Security Council, the Bush-Blair alliance could not secure the nine out of fifteen votes needed for a second resolution. Bush and Blair had also not counted on Hussein allowing the UN weapons inspectors back in, a strategy they advocated with the hope that the criteria would be too high for Hussein to meet. Their extensive searches were not turning up any WMD, and instead of the United States interpreting that as Iraq telling the truth, it was seen as a failure of the inspection process. Powell also made it clear that it did not matter what the inspectors found or did not find. He stated, "U.S. policy is that, regardless of what the inspectors do, the people of Iraq and the people of the region would be better off with a different regime in Baghdad. The United States reserves its option to do whatever it believes might be appropriate to see if there can be a regime change."[24] Blaming the French, incompetent weapons inspectors, and the always tricky Hussein, the United States and Britain withdrew their effort, declared that the first Security Council resolution gave enough legal cover, and set about launching their war.

In part, Powell's failure was due to the fact that he, Rice, and the other administration officials had been unconvincingly making the same arguments for months with very dubious evidence. Indeed, Powell was making assertions that were not facts and were drawn on questionable and sometimes manufactured intelligence, half-truths, and lies.

Powell and Rice on the Record

Powell was not alone. There are a number of works that rigorously examined the lies and misleading campaign of the administration to win public and congressional support for the Iraq war. The sheer number of books with "lies" in the title underscores the popular view among many that the administration was dishonest in its explanation of why it went to war against Hussein. This includes David Corn's *The Lies of George W. Bush*, Christopher Scheer's *The Five Biggest Lies Bush Told Us About Iraq*, Jerry Barrett's *Big Bush Lies*, Paul Waldman's *Fraud: The Strategy Behind the Bush Lies and Why the Media Didn't Tell You*, and Malachy McCourt's *Bush Lies in State* among others. These works are not only a critique of Bush, but also of the media, which failed to investigate the claims of the administration, and congressional leaders, who gave it a blank check to conduct the war. A more insightful behind-the-scenes examination is the *Vanity Fair* article by Evgenia Peretz, David Rose, and David Wise.[25] They clearly show how the administration did not hesitate to exaggerate faulty intelligence to press for war.

A study by Rep. Henry Waxman examined the public statements by Bush and his top four foreign policy officials of Cheney, Powell, Rice, and Rumsfeld and the accuracy and veracity of their remarks in the media. It found that each of these, including Bush, had lied and mislead on numerous occasions related to the main arguments discussed above. According to the time period under investigation, the study found that between March 2002 and January 2004, in 40 speeches, 26 press conferences and briefings, 53 media interviews, 4 written statements, and 2 testimonies before Congress, the five gave 237 misleading statements where they distorted the truth but also included 10 statements that were wholly false. Bush made 55 misleading statements, Cheney 51, Rumsfeld 52, Powell 50, and Rice only 29, although, according to the study, she made the most blatantly false statements—8.[26]

Weapons of Mass Destruction

> Going into the war against Iraq, we had very strong intelligence. I've been in this business for 20 years. And some of the strongest intelligence cases that I've seen, key judgments by our intelligence community that Saddam Hussein . . . had biological and chemical weapons. . . .
>
> Condoleezza Rice, July 31, 2003[27]

On numerous occasions, including his UN harangue, Powell claimed that the United States had found mobile labs in vans that were for the purpose of producing biological weapons. This assertion was one of his central and most dramatic claims during his UN speech. Using cartoons and blurred satellite photos, he stated, "One of the most worrisome things that emerges from the thick intelligence file we have on Iraq's biological weapons is the existence of mobile production facilities used to make biological agents. . . . The trucks are easily moved and are designed to evade detection by inspectors. In a matter of months, they can produce a quantity of biological poison equal to the entire amount that Iraq claimed to have produced in the years prior to the Gulf War."[28] This alarmist assertion, as it turns out, had little basis in fact. Although Defense Intelligence Agency engineers would later examine the trailers and concluded that they were most likely used for non-military purposes and probably to produce hydrogen for artillery weather balloons, Powell continued to spread this story.[29] In virtually every media outlet available, Powell repeated the story of the mobile vans.[30]

Sometimes he equivocated, but more often, he declared with surefooted authority that the mobile vans and evidence of Hussein biological weapon ambitions had been discovered. On "Fox News," the principle media vehicle for the administration, Powell stated, "We have uncovered the mobile vans and we are continuing to search."[31] He repeated this assertion on CNN stating, "One element that I presented at that time, these biological vans, all I could show was a cartoon drawing of these vans, and everybody said, "Are the vans really there?" And, voila, the vans showed up a few months later. We found them."[32]

Powell cited two witnesses for his evidence. One was deemed unreliable by U.S. intelligence agencies even before the presentation. The second turned out to be a relative of a senior official in the highly suspect Iraqi National Congress. This person had not even been interviewed by any U.S. intelligence operations.[33]

At the United Nations, Powell consistently and repeatedly misrepresented the facts regarding Iraq's WMD. However, he did correctly identify a chemical plant called Falluja 2 that may have produced mustard and nerve gas that was used against the Iranian army. The facility was located at the Tariq state company. Ostensibly the plant was to produce chlorine, which has legitimate uses, but it is also a necessary agent for the production of chemical weapons. Powell stated, "Iraq has rebuilt key portions of the Tariq state establishment. Tariq includes facilities designed specifically for Iraq's chemical weapons program and employs key figures from past programs. That's the production end of Saddam's chemical weapons business."[34]

In his blustering against Saddam, Powell failed to mention the links of the United States and Britain to Iraq's weapons industry. The Tariq plant was built by the British in 1985, and its existence kept secret not only from the British public but also its U.S. allies. With approval from the former Prime Minister Margaret Thatcher's government, the plant was installed by the Hounslow, Unde Ltd, a British company. In March 1988, thousands of Kurdish villagers and Iranian soldiers were gassed in the infamous incident at Halabja, gas that may have come from the facilities built by the British (see discussion of this incident below).[35]

Iraq's anthrax capabilities were born in the United States during the Reagan era. As *Foreign Policy in Focus* noted, Powell "did not bother mentioning that the seed stock for Iraq's anthrax was sold to Saddam Hussein back in the 1980s by the United States."[36]

In other instances, Powell referred to ghost towns as sites of WMD. He cited a compound in northeastern Iraq as a venue for "terrorist chemicals and poisons factory," yet when UK journalist Luke Harding went to visit the site only three days after Powell's presentation, he found "a shabby military compound [of a] dilapidated collection of concrete buildings at the foot of a grassy sloping hill. . . . There is a bakery. There is no sign of chemical weapons anywhere—only the smell of paraffin and vegetable ghee used for cooking."[37]

Powell's assertions about the mobile labs were often repeated by Rice. On June 8, 2003, in an interview on *This Week with George Stephanopoulos*, she declared, "Already, we've discovered, uh, uh, trailers, uh, that look remarkably similar to what Colin Powell described in his February 5th speech, biological weapons production facilities."[38] On that same day on *Meet the Press*, with the administration's spin machine on full blast, she said, "We are confident that we—I believe that we will find them. I think that we have already found important clues like the biological weapons laboratories that look surprisingly like what Colin Powell described in his speech."[39] Waxman's study found that she made this claim on a number of other occasions.[40]

While Powell was most identified with the mobile labs argument, Rice would be the strongest advocate of the storylines related to Iraq attempting to obtain "yellow cake" uranium ore from Niger and its unlawful use of aluminum tubes. In a January 23, 2003, *New York Times* article, Rice also rants against Iraq's "efforts to get uranium from abroad."[41] Five days later, in his 2003 State of the Union address, in the buildup to the invasion, Bush stated, "The British government has learned that Saddam Hussein recently sought significant quantities of uranium from Africa."[42] It turns out not only that Rice and Bush were lying, but also that the knowledge that the story was not true was known long before their January 2003 assertions. Rice, who was one of the top officials responsible for clearing information that would be used by Bush in speeches, stated after the story was exposed, that "The intelligence community did not know at that time or at levels that got to us that this, that there was serious questions about this report."[43] On *Face the Nation*, she stated, "My only point is that, in retrospect, knowing that some of the documents underneath may have been—were, indeed, forgeries, and knowing that apparently there were concerns swirling around about this, had we known that at the time, we would not have put it in. . . . And had there been even a peep that the agency did not want that sentence in or that George Tenet did not want that sentence in, that the director of Central Intelligence did not want it in, it would have been gone."[44]

In fact, there was a great deal of evidence that the story was not true. In February 2002, former U.S. ambassador Joseph Wilson was sent to Niger by the administration to investigate the charges made in documents possessed by the CIA that Iraq had attempted to purchase yellow cake uranium from Niger. Wilson concluded that the story had no basis and reported his conclusions back to the administration. It was later determined that the documents were forged.[45] Nevertheless, Cheney and other Bush officials continued to make the allegation. When Wilson went public in the *New York Times* with his story, the White House outed his wife as a covert CIA operative to some friendly media reporters ruining her career, but also initiating an investigation that by the end of 2005 resulted in an indictment of Cheney's chief of staff I. Lewis "Scooter" Libby. In September 2002, Blair's government issued a "white paper" that included the false allegation that Iraq tried to get uranium from Africa, the report cited by Bush in his State of the Union address. Nervous about Bush's public statements regarding the charge, CIA director Tenet had the statement removed from a speech Bush gave in Cleveland, and he sent two memos to Rice's office and had a phone conversation with her assistant Steven Hadley stating that the yellow cake claim could not be sustained.[46]

The existence of the memos was revealed in a story that broke in July 2003. As *Slate*'s Timothy Noah points out, after being confronted with the memos and no longer able to claim that no one knew the statement was false, she retreated to the defenses of "I didn't read the memo," "I don't remember reading the memo," "I read the memo and then forgot about the yellowcake part," and "There was no reason for me to read the memo."[47] Wilson would also go public when denials about being aware of the forged documents continued. For his troubles, someone in the White House leaked information exposing his wife Valerie Plame as a CIA operative, an illegal action under the Intelligence Identities Protection Act that is still under investigation.

When all else failed, Rice and the White House tried to blame the yellow cake scandal on the British government. Rice told the press, "The president quoted a British paper. We did not know at the time—no one knew at the time, in our circles—maybe someone knew down in the bowels of the agency, but no one in our circles knew that there were doubts and suspicions that this might be a forgery."[48]

This is not to get the British off the hook. The dossier that Powell referred to in his UN speech—"the fine paper that the British distributed"—and Bush in his State of the Union address was discovered to not only be full of inaccuracies and misinformation, but also significant parts were plagiarized. Four of the nineteen pages of the February 3, 2003, document, *Iraq: Its Infrastructure of Concealment, Deception and Intimidation*, had been lifted from a September 2002 article by Ibrahim al-Marashi in the *Middle East Report of International Affairs*.[49] There were other parts as well as they were unaccredited. Marashi's article was not just copied, but modified to make Iraq appear more sinister. Marashi states, for example, that he wrote "they support organizations in what Iraq considers hostile regimes," but the doctored government document read, "they support terrorist organizations in hostile regimes." This document and others released by the government in its supportive role to Bush's campaign drew derision and references to Blair as "Bush's poodle."[50]

There were other charges related to WMD made by Rice and Powell that proved to be false. With absolute conviction Rice declared, "We do know that he is actively pursuing a nuclear weapon" and "We know that he has the infrastructure, nuclear scientists to make a nuclear weapon."[51] The International Atomic Energy Agency (IAEA) and other experts refuted these claims as did the *Comprehensive Report of the Special Advisor to the DCI [Director of Central Intelligence] on Iraq's WMD* or popularly called the "Duelfer Report" after its principle investigator, Charles Duelfer.[52] As Duelfer stated in testimony before Congress on the report, in terms of Iraq and WMD, the administration was "almost all wrong" including Rice's assertion that he was pursuing actively a nuclear weapon, and that Hussein not only had no weapons of mass destruction and had not made any since 1991, but that he had no capability for making any either.[53]

On a number of occasions before and during the war, Rice charged that Hussein illegally obtained aluminum tubes. On the *NewsHour with Jim Lehrer*, she stated, "[H]e had...an active procurement network to procure items, many of which, by the way, were on the prohibited list of the nuclear suppliers group. There's a reason that they were on the prohibited list of the nuclear suppliers group: Magnets, balancing machines, yes, aluminum tubes, about which the consensus view was that they were suitable for use in centrifuges to spin material for nuclear weapons."[54] As the Waxman study noted, "This statement was misleading because it suggested that Iraq sought aluminum tubes for use in its nuclear weapons program, failing to mention that the government's most experienced technical experts at the U.S. Department of Energy concluded that the tubes were 'poorly suited' for this purpose."[55]

Iraq's al Qaeda Links

It is easy to see why so many erroneously believed that there was a connection between al Qaeda and Saddam Hussein because administration officials stated it so often. A typical statement by Rice, before the invasion, characterized the unconditional allegations propagated by Bush officials. On *Fox News Sunday*, she stated, "Well, we are, of course, continually learning more about these links between Iraq and al Qaeda, and there is evidence that Secretary Powell did not have the time to talk about. But the core of the story is there in what Secretary Powell talked about. This poisons network with at least two dozen of its operatives operating in Baghdad, a man who is spreading poisons now throughout Europe and into Russia, a man who got medical care in Baghdad despite the fact that the Iraqis were asked to turn him over, training in biological and chemical weapons."[56]

In another instance, on "Larry King Live," she stated, "There is no question in my mind about the al Qaeda connection. It is a connection that has unfolded, that we're learning more about as we are able to take the testimony of detainees, people who were high up in the al Qaeda organization. And what emerges is a picture of a Saddam Hussein who became impressed with what al Qaeda did after it bombed our embassies in 1998 in Kenya and Tanzania, began to give them assistance in chemical and biological weapons, something that they were having trouble achieving on their own, that harbored a terrorist network under this man Zarqawi, despite the fact that Saddam Hussein was told that Zarqawi was there." Abu Musab al-Zarqawi is a Jordanian militant who is leading one of the many factions fighting the U.S. occupation in Iraq. He is the leader of Ansar al-Islam, which during Hussein's era was located in northern Iraq in areas under the control of Hussein's Kurdish adversaries. The administration has yet to provide any evidence that Hussein or anyone in his government gave Zarqawi assistance in chemical and biological weapons procurement.

One of the "high ups" that Iraq was supposedly in touch with in the al Qaeda organization was September 11 hijack ringleader Mohammad Atta. Naturally, the mere mention of Atta in association with practically anyone, especially Saddam Hussein, was an automatic guilt-by-association. In October 2001, a few weeks after the attack, a report from some Czech officials speculated that Atta had met with a senior Iraqi official at the Iraqi embassy in Prague in April 2001. By April 2002, however, the FBI both had debunked the story and, later in October, Czech president Vaclav Havel would do the same. In fact, according to records examined by the FBI, Atta was in Virginia Beach, Virginia, at the time he was rumored to be in Prague.[57] These definitive investigations notwithstanding, both before the invasion and after the occupation, Rice, Cheney, Wolfowitz, and other officials peddled the story through rumors, hints, vague references to classified documents, or were simply mendacious about it.[58]

Months after the invasion and there was still no clear evidence of either an operational link or sustained relations between Hussein and al Qaeda, but Rice and others continued their argument. In a September 2003 interview, she stated in response to a question about the connection, "Absolutely.... But we know that there was training of al Qaeda in chemical and perhaps biological warfare. We know that the Zarqawi network was out of there, this poisons network that was trying to spread poisons throughout.... And there was an Ansar al-Islam, which appears also to try to be operating in Iraq. So yes, the al Qaeda link was there."[59] In fact, not only was the U.S. intelligence community and that of other states wary of this alleged connection, and with certainly did not see any operational connection, Rice and others often cited Zarqawi and Ansar al-Islam but failed to mention that Zarqawi despised Hussein as does Osama bin Ladin, and that Ansar al-Islam was located in the northern region of Iraq in Kurdish territory that was not under Hussein's control.

Rice, of course, was reflecting the politics of Bush who also made these charges. In his 2003 State of the Union speech, Bush conjured up an image of Hussein giving vials of biological or chemical weapons to terrorist hijackers, and accused that he "aids and protects terrorists including members of Al Qaida."[60] Other times, he stated that there had been a "whole series of high-level contacts" between the two, and that "an Al Qaeda operative had been sent to Iraq several times in the late 1990s for help in acquiring poisons and gases, and that Zarqawi was a "senior Al Qaeda terrorist planner."[61] These statements as well as those of Rice, Powell, and others were contradicted by the report from the 9/11 Commission that included testimony from former CIA director George Tenet.[62]

Iraq's Human Rights Violations

Even before the March 2003 invasion, the argument that Hussein had WMD was already falling apart as inspectors were unable to locate any of the nuclear, biological, or chemical weapons that the administration claimed existed. Increasingly, the administration fell back on the argument that it did not matter because Hussein was a tyrant who had used WMD on his own people, case number one meaning the Kurds in northern Iraq and specifically in the town of Halabja in March 1988 near the Iraq-Iran border. In that incident, 5,000 had been killed by poison gas during a battle between Iraq and Iran. This charge has been repeated so often that it has essentially become background noise, always there and quietly accepted without challenge or critical thought.

This example was cited time and time again by Bush, Rice, Powell, and the other top officials. Powell stated, "It isn't a figment of anyone's imagination that just 15 years ago they gassed and killed 5,000 people with sarin and VX at a place called Halabja I visited just a few weeks ago. They never lost that capability."[63]

Like pretty much everything claimed by the administration, this accusation also requires a critical eye and upon examination also collapses under the weight of investigation and research. First, it is never mentioned that at the time, the United States was backing Hussein and providing him with military and economic support, which was not cutoff as a result the Halabja incident.

Second, it is also never raised that there are contending versions of what happened there in March 1988 even within U.S. intelligence, military, and political circles. While the administration argues that Hussein deliberately targeted the Kurds who lived in this village near the border of Iran for supporting their enemy, a former CIA senior political analyst on Iraq, Stephen Pelletiere writes in the *New York Times* that the actual target of the gassing was the Iran army and that it is misleading to state, in this particular instance, that the Kurds had been the main target.[64] This is not to say that Hussein sought to protect the Kurdish people or even cared, but that to say he ordered their killings is a distortion of the known facts.

Perhaps most devastating to the administration's use of this incident is the issue of even whether it was the Iraqi gas that killed the Kurds as opposed to that of the Iranians. According to a Defense Intelligence Agency report that Pelletiere cites, it was conceivable and maybe probable that Iranian gas, which contained a cyanide-based gas known to be in the type used by Iran had been responsible for the deaths. The Iraqis used mustard gas in the fight that was not known to have blood agents in it at the time.

None of this, of course, exonerates Hussein's murderous tenure, and there are plenty of human rights violations of which he is guilty, but it does indict the dishonesty of the administration and its sully manipulation of the tragedy. As it did on countless occasions, it presented as certainty information that had been debated and left uncertain even within the administration. By cooking the numbers, the administration attempted to make its case on going to war against Iraq stronger than it actually was, and, in fact, had no case to make at all that was sellable to either the U.S. public or the global community.

Conclusion

> I agree with Paul Robeson absolutely, that Negroes should never willingly fight in an unjust war. I do not share his honest hope that all will not. A certain sheep-like disposition, inevitably born of slavery will, I am afraid, lead many of them to join America in any enterprise, provided the whites will grant them equal right to do wrong.
>
> W.E.B. Du Bois, 1950

Powell and Rice willingly and actively participated in the farcical drama of rationalizing a war that did not need to happen, deaths that should not have occurred, and a political argument that had no merit. The overwhelming majority of the world, both before and after the aggressions of the U.S.-coalition, rejected the arguments and politics of Bush and Blair. Their "coalition of the willing" (to be bribed and bullied) laughingly consisted of states who disgraced themselves and ignored the popular wishes of their citizens. It included states such as Albania, Azerbaijan, the Dominican Republican, El Salvador, Eritrea, Ethiopia, Kazakhstan, the Marshall Islands, Nicaragua, Palau, Poland, Rwanda, Uganda, and Uzbekistan, who wisely, if not morally, saw an opportunity for political or economic benefit. As secretary of state, Powell coordinated and defended this fictive coalition.

Rice, already under the gun for arguably the most massive security failure in the country's history that occurred on her watch as national security advisor, would also come under fire for her role in intelligence clearing and interpretation regarding the Iraq debacle. Her main rejoinder to critics has been that the United States was not alone in believing that Hussein had WMD and was willing to use them. That argument does not hold, however, not only because of the incidents cited above that disproved assertions by Bush officials, but also because it was the United States alone that determined that the clearly inconclusive evidence warranted a war that would cost tens of thousands of lives. Rice was put in charge of a project known as the "Iraq Stabilization Group" whose existence seems to have come and gone with the speed of the case regarding Iraq's WMD.[65]

Powell and Rice would also excuse, defend, and obfuscate the scandals that erupted over prisoner treatment at Abu Ghraib and Guantanamo Bay, Cuba. While condemning the brutality and depravity of the abuse, neither expressed the logical conclusion that they were the inevitable results of the tone and tenor of the campaign used to build the war, not isolated aberrations as Bush and other Republicans stated. At the most fundamental level, they united with the objectives and ideological framework of the hegemonists, indeed, they became charter members. Rice was much less wavering in her conversion than Powell, embracing her newfound stance with nary a nod to her past political positions. Powell, reluctant to a fault, came along nevertheless sans a tantrum or two.

For Powell, however, his reward for being insufficiently loyal and committed to Bush's strategy of hegemony was a quick pro-forma and staged exit at the end of Bush's first term that belied the White House spin about Powell's heroic and stellar tenure. Her recompense for these calamities was promotion to secretary of state.

Unfortunately, Iraq was not the only spot in the world where Powell and Rice left their marks. With the 2002 National Security Strategy, the Bush doctrine concepts of "preemption" and "uni-lateralism" were declared the guiding strategy options of U.S. hegemony. With the war in Iraq that declaration became a matter of fact. From Africa to Latin America and beyond, the Bush doctrine was being promoted and implemented, and always at the center of these campaigns were Powell and Rice.

Six

Counter-Hegemony in the Global South: Africa Challenges the Powell, Rice, and Bush Doctrine

We should cease to talk about such vague and—for the Far East—unreal objectives as human rights, the raising of living standards and democratization. The day is not far off when we are going to have to deal in straight power concepts. The less we are then hampered by idealistic slogans, the better.

George Kennan, 1948[1]

So it is the policy of the United States to seek and support the growth of democratic movements and institutions in every nation and culture, with the ultimate goal of ending tyranny in our world.

George Bush, Inaugural Address, January 21, 2005

It would appear on first blush that there is a great gap between George Kennan's realpolitik of the late 1940s and Bush's idealistic notion of a cascading global democracy driven by the United States as the defining feature of the new millennium. The gap narrows and disappears, however, when the veil is removed, and it is revealed that the hegemonic thrust of contemporary U.S. foreign policy—encapsulated in the National Security Strategy's objectives of "opening societies and building the infrastructure of democracy"—is deeply rooted in the straight power concepts that Kennan advocated.[2] In the end, Bush's anti-tyranny rhetoric and "idealist slogans," as Kennan would frame it, cannot conceal the real agenda of hegemonic self-interest.

Hegemony, however, gives rise and is linked directly to counter-hegemonic movements and politics. Though unevenly enacted, ideologically miscellaneous, geographically dispersed, organizationally varied, strategically wide-ranging, and historically unpredictable, counter-hegemonic resistance emerges from the ongoing practices of those at the bottom for freedom from exploitation, oppression, and domination from above. Rather than the passive actors who accept their fate of powerlessness inaudibly, a global imaging broken by the occasional "terrorist" act or protests against faux elections, the global South constructs innumerable sites of resistance to the hegemonic desires and aims of international power centers. Neo-conservative fantasies of the end of history notwithstanding, there are no moments of pure, unchallenged hegemony, and in the current era, arguably, the pendulum has swung toward an escalating defiance on the part of southern civil society, government, and even private-sector players against the axis of Western and domineering states (led by the United States and the G8), international finance institutions (led by the IMF, World Bank, and World Trade Organization), and global capital. That the United States has become the focus of this resistance is a response to not only a long historic trend but also to the policies and politics of the specific contemporary configuration of U.S. hegemony: the George W. Bush administration.

In the Bush era, U.S. policies toward the global South boil down to two words and inter-related processes: security and resources. The securing—nee military commandeering—of resources of other states that have been designated as in the national security interests of the United States forms the argument that fundamentally underpins U.S. foreign policy. Issues identified as priorities by those who live in the regions of Africa, the Americas, and Asia have been marginalized or corrupted as the United States has increasingly used the "war on terrorism" as the means by which to further neo-liberal economic policies and pressure states in the South to compromise their political, economic, and military independence. Cooperation in the U.S.-led war on terrorism has become a litmus test for receiving aid and the political blessings of Washington. At the same time, states have been forced to open their economies to market reforms dictated by global capital and to make their resources available to Western corporations on terms favorable to those entities. Perhaps even more so than during the Cold War, the United States has linked open markets with security and anti-terrorism concerns seeing the former as constitutive of the latter. Consistent with the administration's unilateralist orientation it has approached dealings with the global South primarily through bi-lateral (and grossly uneven) relations rather than through international or regional institutions. And overall, the U.S. personality in these relations has been arrogant, belligerent, and insensitive.

Campaigns solely in the name of the war on terrorism, however, have limited utility in areas where no identifiable terrorist activities or groups exist such as in many areas of Africa, the Americas, and elsewhere. Thus, in Bush's second iteration, anti-terrorism has been parsed into a broad call for the expansion of "democracy" and "freedom," phrases that both President Bush and Secretary of State Condoleezza Rice emphasized at the beginning of the new term. A demand for democratization appears more palatable and popular and is framed by a contention that bringing democracy to oppressed peoples is not only the responsibility of the world's only superpower, but also it is the morally right thing to do. Former Secretary of State Powell's scolding of deposed Haitian president Jean-Bertrand Aristide, Rice's ongoing berating of Venezuelan president Hugo Chavez, and condemnations of other political figures are projected by the administration as criticisms of anti-democrats who, though democratically elected, abused their power. In fact, these are attacks on leaders who disagreed with the Washington consensus and who sought self-determination and to maintain national sovereignty, an unacceptable stance in the Bush era. Hypocritically, at the same time, Bush built close ties with some of the most undemocratic and repressive states in the world including Pakistan, Egypt, Uzbekistan, Russia, and others.

In the George W. Bush era, no such concessions are necessary nor are they being given. While Afghanistan and Iraq have been thus far the only countries actually invaded and forcibly and militarily occupied by the administration, many other states and political leaders have also been in the crosshairs of U.S. hegemony. Whether under the banner of anti-terrorism or behind a placard shouting "democracy," the United States has made it clear that it will pre-empt any border it deems necessary. Defense of the Iraq occupation, as other justifications have evanesced, is now framed in terms of defending its democratic trajectory, one drawn, determined, and dependent on the United States. In its second term, the Bush administration has been even more explicit that through the prism of U.S.-imposed and defined democracy, it will seek to reshape the world. As Rice stated ominously during her confirmation hearings, "we will spread freedom and democracy throughout the globe."[3] This is not idle chatter; it is the ideological foundation of U.S. hegemony in this period that rationalizes and exercises intervention and occupation.

Powell and Rice unite with this fundamental thesis and bring to it a unique quality. From the administration's first days in office, Powell and Rice were its most visible spokespersons on foreign policy, and both were extremely conscious of the racial imagery embedded in their positions. This conjunction of race and policy would have important political, ideological, and cultural significance in interactions with the global South (as well as the rest of the international community). It was reported that the very first section of the State Department that Secretary of State–designate Colin Powell visited after being nominated for the position was the Africa section.[4] This symbolic act was to demonstrate that Africa and its issues would not be ignored by the new administration or, at least, by its highest diplomat. Although Powell had spent little time in Africa during his career, he later confessed to feeling some sense of kinship. As he told allafrica.com,

> There is a little bit of additional pressure and there are the expectations that are placed upon me because I'm black. But I'm Secretary of State of the United States of America first. . . . So, I try to do what is right as Secretary of State of the United States. But it will always be shaped, to some extent, by the fact that, even though my parents came from Jamaica, their parents came from somewhere off the west coast of Africa. So, there is a connection here and I'm sure that connection will always give me that little bit of added pressure to do what I can for Africa.[5]

Powell hoped that his gesture would signal strongly that he could find the appropriate balance between being secretary of state and implementing U.S. policies toward Africa, and, on the other hand, express a racial connection, that is, "that little bit of added pressure," which would also be beneficial to the peoples of Africa. And during his tenure, it is fair to say, Africa received more attention than in previous administrations, Republican or Democratic. More attention, however, did not necessarily translate into fairer and more just policies on the part of the United States, and, in fact, Powell and Rice's blackness (and that of other top black U.S. foreign policy officials) often masked and diverted attention from policies that aggravated the dire conditions faced by Africa and much of the global South.

As did Powell, then National Security Advisor Rice also acknowledged a personal linkage with Africa. In meeting with the press before Bush's 2003 trip to Africa, she stated in response to a question about the legacy of black slavery and Africa that "Slavery was, of course, America's birth defect. We've been trying to deal with the consequences of it every [*sic*] since and to bring about reconciliation. . . . The President is going to talk about and acknowledge what has—what slavery has meant to Africa and has meant to America. But there is plenty of blame to go around about slavery."[6] While she does not elaborate on the distribution of blame that she alludes to or what exactly "reconciliation" meant, for many Americans and many around the world, Rice's racial heritage provides a legitimizing dimension to her remarks unavailable to other Bush foreign policy officials except for Powell.

These statements and others gave hope initially to many in Africa as well as in the Caribbean, Latin America, and other regions of the global South, particularly to communities of peoples of African descent in these areas. While recognizing, as Powell stated, that their first obligation was their responsibility as secretary of state and national security advisor, some desired desperately that his and Rice's experiences as black Americans provided an edge of sensitivity that was lacking historically in U.S. foreign policy and that could translate into a more beneficial and honest relationship with the United States. However, as the Bush doctrine unfolded, key elements of which were drafted by Rice and implemented by her and Powell, among others, those hopes were gutted and binned. Under Bush, U.S. policy toward the global South was characterized by a number of features that had little to do with the interests of the peoples in the region and more concern with opening markets for foreign investments and exploration, particularly involving oil-rich states, a serious beatdown of recalcitrant political leaders, moral commandments on issues such as birth control and homosexuality, and U.S. military expansion in the name of anti-terrorism and national security.

Out for Africa: The Bush Doctrine and the Struggle to Advance Africa

> And I am here today to say on behalf of President Bush that Africa matters to America, by history and by choice.
>> Colin Powell, May 25, 2001[7]

> I sincerely hope that people will focus on this tremendous positive agenda that this President has, over the last two-and-a-half years, developed for Africa. It's broad. It is a positive agenda.
>> Condoleezza Rice, July 3, 2003[8]

Strong rhetoric, public pledges and promises, vacuous meetings with African heads of state, and even a visit to Africa by the president could not veil the brutal truth: the policies of the Bush administration have failed to address substantially and, in a number of instances, exacerbated the calamitous conditions faced by the peoples of sub-Saharan Africa. Bush's "positive agenda" for Africa, as Rice puts it, had little to do with what the people of African considered their urgent needs and more to do with U.S. access to Africa's resources. As a number of observers note, Africa's priorities and interests "have been fairly consistent in recent years," and so has been the tendency of the policies of the United States to ignore them.[9]

In 2000, the United Nations passed the Millennium Declaration that was adopted by 189 countries, which generated the Millennium Development Goals (MDGs), a set of eight goals, eighteen targets, and forty-eight indicators agreed upon by UN members to reduce and eliminate hunger and poverty eventually, and to promote health care, education, and development. These 2015 targets seek, among other objectives, to cut infant mortality by two-thirds; reduce by half the number of people living on less than $1 a day; achieve primary education for every child; eliminate gender disparities at all levels of education; reduce by three-quarters maternal mortality; and cut in half the proportion of people without access to safe drinking water.[10] The MDGs by themselves will not eliminate poverty in the developing South let alone spur sustained development. Ultimately, it will not be the generosity of the North, but the restructuring of global economic and political relations that must occur. However, the MDGs are important benchmarks of what is needed if progress is to be made. For a number of states, the goals have helped to shape and focus government, private sector, and civil society actions to address the needs of society's more marginalized sectors.

Sub-Saharan Africa is struggling to meet these goals, a struggle that it is losing on many fronts. In mid-2005, the United Nations reported that 3 million more children will die in sub-Saharan Africa as a result of failing to meet the targets set by the MDGs. Current projections are that due to lack of funding and resources, the reality will fall far short of the goals. Instead of reducing the number of deaths of children under the age of 5 to 2 million, the number will rise from the current 4.8 million to more than 5 million without emergency intervention. Sub-Saharan Africa is the only region in the world where the number of child deaths under age 5 is growing. At the current rate, the goal will not be achieved in the region until 2115. It also projected that 115 million children will remain out of school, 43 million in sub-Saharan Africa, and an addition 219 million will fall into the ranks of the poorest.[11] According to the United Nations Development Program, while the life expectancy at birth in the United States is 77 years, it is 46.3 for sub-Saharan Africa and in many cases dropping due to AIDS and poverty-related deaths.[12] The infant mortality rate in the United States, overall, has been reduced to 7 per 1,000 while in sub-Saharan Africa the rate is 108 per 1,000.[13]

There are a number of African states that have seen important progress since the 1990s including Cape Verde, Mauritius, Mozambique, and Uganda. These states have all had economic growth rates of more than 3 percent per year despite being burdened with mammoth debts and other concerns. Ghana and Mozambique both achieved substantial reductions in hunger rates.[14] Despite these important advancements, too many other states are losing ground rapidly.

A real effort to demonstrate that "Africa matters to America" as Powell claims would be to implement policies that:

- provide adequate resources for a serious war against AIDS, including affordable life-saving drugs;

- cancel Africa's unsustainable and largely illegitimate debts;

- back attempts by African diplomats and civil society to resolve conflicts, manage peace negotiations, and achieve lasting peace;

- support efforts to move beyond formal elections toward increased participation and accountability for national and multi-national institutions;

- invest development resources not only in health, education, and other sectors that build African human resources, but also in communications and transportation infrastructure necessary to make human resources economically productive.[15]

These minimum requirements have a consensus not only across Africa but also in much of the rest of the world, but have been given more talk than action by past and current U.S. administrations. Powell's and Rice's praise of the Bush policies are unwarranted, and his administration continues a dual pattern of abandonment and exploitation that has long been the record of the United States and the West in general. Most recently, during Clinton's two terms (1993–2001), his "new African leaders" strategy selected a few states and a few leaders—specifically Ethiopia's Meles Zenawi, Eritrea's Isaias Afwerki, Rwanda's Paul Kagame, and Uganda's Yoweri Museveni—to promote as role models of self-help and bootstrap responsibility.[16] This strategy not only collapsed in the face of deadly conflicts and political ineptitude in several of these states, but also exposed the lack of any other comprehensive achievements by the Clinton administration and its failure to address critical issues confronting other states in sub-Saharan Africa. On the issues of AIDS, debt relief and cancellation, development resources, and humanitarian intervention, Clinton consistently provided empty symbolism, compromised with congressional conservatives, provided paltry amounts of aid, or did nothing at all as in the horrible massacres that took place in Rwanda in 1994. Though a grand step above Reagan and George H. W. Bush's farcical policy of "constructive engagement," generous support of tyrants and murderers, and starve-the-children legacy, Clinton's Africa policies left many frustrated and unsatisfied. His "Africa Growth and Opportunity Act" (AGOA), which sought to increase U.S. trade with Africa, fluttered but ultimately received tepid support from the Africa policy community mostly because it was felt that this was the best that was going to come out of a reluctant conservative Congress and an embattled president. And just when it was believed that U.S. policies could hardly get any worse, along came Bush and company.

In 2002, in the unilaterialist manner that has come to characterize the administration, and rather than promote or fully donate its fair share to the MDGs, Bush created the Millennium Challenge Account (MCA). Theoretically, the MCA was created to increase foreign aid funding so that it would double eventually the 2002 level by 2006. By mid-2005, the MCA had not distributed a single penny in aid although it had approved one state, Cape Verde, for receiving funding through a $110 million five-year compact between the United States and the island nation. MCA's economic and political eligibility criteria are cumbersome and created delays even for states that were favored by the administration. As Salin Booker and Ann-Louise Colgan point out, "The eligibility criteria are based on sixteen indicators: six for 'governing justly,' four for 'investing in people,' and six for 'promoting economic freedom.' These eligibility criteria, unilaterally dictated by the United States, are not dissimilar to the conditionalities of previous aid programs and, like prior restrictions, are likely to be overridden by political priorities, such as the 'war on terrorism.'"[17]

It was within this policy and political context that Powell and Rice functioned and defended the administration. Their rhetoric of advancing African interests and that of Bush has grown stronger under pressure from the global South and European and Japanese leaders, but finds little reflection in actual U.S. policy. As noted below, Bush has resisted the overtures of even his close ally—Blair—embarrassing his most loyal supporter and has misled the public concerning what the administration has actually done to address Africa's needs.

Powell in Africa: Selling the Bush Doctrine

In May 2001, five months after being in power, Powell traveled to four African countries, Kenya, Mali, South Africa, and Uganda. He also met with Presidents Paul Kagame of Rwanda and Joseph Kabila of the Democratic Republic of the Congo. These early gestures were meant to be a message to the peoples of Africa that the United States would give serious attention to the issues faced by millions who have been historically ignored, abandoned, and subjugated by the United States and other Western governments.

On May 25, 2001, Colin Powell spoke before an audience at the University of Witwatersrand in Johannesburg. With a great deal of enthusiasm on his first official trip to Africa as secretary of state, he stated,

> We have almost 35 million and one citizens of African descent. Last year, the total US-African trade approached $30 billion, and America is Africa's largest single market. The United States is the leading foreign investor in

Africa. Over 30,000 Africans are studying in the United States today. Our pasts, our presents and our futures are closely intertwined, and as America's 65th Secretary of State and her only African-American Secretary of State so far, I will enthusiastically engage with Africa on behalf of the American people.[18]

Would Powell's empathy translate into a new era of enthusiastic engagement? Would his and Rice's declared connection be visibly and substantially advantageous? Would the "compassionate conservative's" compassion actually make an appearance? The answer to these questions would be in the negative.

By August 2001, the Bush administration would anger much of Africa and the world by pulling out of the UN World Conference against Racism, Racial Discrimination, Xenophobia, and Related Intolerance being held in Durban, South Africa (see details in chapter 3). In September 2002, at the UN-sponsored World Summit on Sustainable Development, also held in South Africa, Powell was booed robustly.[19] By fall 2002, as would much of the world, many in Africa opposed the increasing signals by the Bush administration that it was preparing to invade Iraq on dubious assertions that it possessed weapons of mass destruction and was linked to al Qaeda. African states that were on the Security Council at the time—Angola, Cameroon, and Guinea—also resisted the enormous pressures and threats by the Bush and Blair administrations to support a second Security Council resolution to go to war, a campaign highlighted by Powell's infamous February 5, 2003, UN presentation. The hopes that many Africans had regarding Powell had waned, and his stature and that of the administration deteriorated rapidly. As one journalist in Zambia wrote, "When Powell was appointed first black U.S. Secretary of State, the whole non-white world had high expectations. Why? Because we thought that Powell will be our spokesperson to moderate white domination in world affairs. But Powell's language on African affairs have [sic] not so far given us a feeling of relief that we have a black brother in top U.S. administration."[20]

However, the fact that Powell and Rice were officials in the conservative Bush administration gave rise to skepticism to many regarding how much their race would impact on policies toward Africa. While acknowledging Powell's and Rice's heritage, most critics in Africa soberly understood that relations between the United States and African states, those two notwithstanding, were devoid of racial sentimentality or allegiance. *The Star* (South Africa) commented on Powell's tour of Africa stating, "That Powell is an African American, and felt an 'emotional twinge' on landing in Mali before heading for Pretoria, adds a poetic note only. Any business discussed will be guided only by national interest."[21]

Another *Star* writer noted of Powell's visit, "Watching this African American, we may well ask: more African or more American? The answer to that one is obvious. Colin Powell is first and foremost a representative of the most powerful country in the world. His visit to Africa may be emotive and sentimental, but he is here to further the policies of the Republican government in Washington."[22]

On every issue, Powell and Rice facilitated the administration's misleading and detrimental policies toward Africa. This includes reluctance to address the causes and resolutions to African development, access to Africa's oil resources, the AIDS crisis, and the conflicts in Darfur and Zimbabwe. An examination of how the administration approached these issues gives rise to concern and apprehension about its Africa policy more so than the so-called "positive agenda" that Rice raved about and that thus far has failed to make an appearance.

Justice, Not Charity: Ending Africa's Debt and Pursuing Development

As the writer George Monbiot points out, "the rich owe the poor far more than the poor owe the rich."[23] Global poverty, including that in Africa, has its legacy and continuing existence in the economic, political, and military histories of the relations between the global North and the global South, histories in which the exploitation of southern resources and the accompanying human costs were the priority. Contemporary efforts at ending African poverty remain low on the list of Western agendas despite recent declarations to the contrary. In 2004, the world's richest countries spent $1 trillion on arms while providing, in the same period, $78.6 billion in aid to the developing world. The United States, which bought $455 billion worth of weapons, increased its arms budget by 12 percent over 2003. A report from the Congressional Research Service documented that five Group of Eight (G8) members—United States, Britain, France, Germany, and Russia—provided 89 percent of the arms sales to developing countries.[24] Meanwhile, U.S. foreign aid funding constitutes a paltry 4.1 percent of its arms budget. And in terms of the African continent, "Only one-hundredth of one percent of the entire U.S. budget (that is, $1 billion) is spent on aid to sub-Saharan Africa."[25] Furthermore, MCA or not, the United States ranked at the bottom of all donor nations with only 0.1 percent of its GNP—just over $10 billion in 2004—being spent worldwide, and half of that goes to Israel and Egypt.[26] With Bush, as writer Ann-Louise Colgan dryly points out, it was more "compassionate showmanship" than real effort on the part of the administration.[27]

These despairing figures help to put in perspective an agreement reached by the G8 in June 2005 to cancel about $40 billion worth of debt owed by eighteen developing countries. The G8, representing the top industrial nations in the

West plus Japan and Russia, agreed to cancel the debt of eighteen eligible countries almost immediately and another twenty others eventually who owe massive and unpayable debts to the World Bank, IMF, and the African Development Bank. Of the first eighteen countries, fourteen are in Africa.[28] For these countries, they will save a total of about $15 billion in debt payments over the next ten years if the deal holds.[29] The need for debt cancellation is painfully obvious and urgent. African states are spending millions on interest payments alone while unable to fund education, housing, and health care needs. It is estimated that African countries spend about $14 per person on debt payment compared to less than $5 per person on health care. Overall, sub-Saharan Africa owes a staggering $333 billion in foreign debt.[30]

Debt cancellation has long been a demand of African activists and governments. U.S.-based organizations, such as TransAfrica and Africa Action, and international NGOs, such as Jubilee 2000 and Oxfam, helped to lead global education campaigns to end debt for states that realistically had little hopes of ever paying off what they owed. However, the debt cancellation deal constructed by the G8, while resolving some issues, has severe limits as well. First, the agreement only covers a small number of countries that need debt cancellation. The agreement also did not include many poor countries, such as Kenya and Nigeria in Africa and Haiti and Indonesia elsewhere, which are all on the brink of economic collapse. Aid advocates argued that at least sixty-two countries need debt cancellation and increased aid to have a ghost of a chance of rising out of poverty and meeting the MDGs.[31] The eighteen countries constitute only 5 percent of the population of the developing world, and, even if the other potential twenty or so countries are included, the figure only rises to about 11 percent.[32]

Second, as in the past, the G8 agreement came with a number of conditionalities. In the Structural Adjustment Program loans forced on the developing world during the 1970s and 1980s by the international finance institutions, there were a number of conditions that nations had to meet in order to qualify for funding. While all contracts entail some degree of conditions and requirements, more often than not the conditions imposed by the IMF, in particular, on developing countries had more harmful effects than helpful ones. These often included downsizing the public sector, opening local markets to foreign goods, ending or reducing local subsidies (while foreign subsidies are maintained that provide an unfair competitive advantage to U.S. and European-based corporations and agribusinesses), cutting tariffs, and other provisions that furthered debt rather than eliminated it. Specifically, the G8 agreement, *inter alia*, calls for "the elimination of impediments to private investment, both domestic and foreign."[33] The conditions imposed by the G8 grow out of the 1996 World Bank "Heavily

Indebted Poor Countries" (HIPC) initiative. These eighteen countries have reached the so-called HIPC "completion point," meaning that they have met the harsh reforms set down by the bank. Norm Dixon points out how these nations have suffered already in their efforts to accommodate their World Bank overlords. He notes:

> In Tanzania, 45,000 public sector jobs have been lost due to privatization. In Zambia, the figure is 60,000. To reach the H.I.P.C. "completion point" Tanzania and Ghana were both required to privatize their urban water supplies. Mali was forced to agree to privatize its railways and cotton industry. The World Bank insists that Mali's state cotton company pay producers the "world market price," which is a big drop in income. Mali's railways are now owned by a Canadian-French consortium, which has shed 600 jobs, closed two-thirds of the stations and decimated passenger numbers, sharply curtailing the livelihoods of thousands who relied on the lines as a source of customers and a way to get their products to markets.[34]

These circumstances are compounded by Western protectionism. Washington and other Western states still refuse to open fully their markets to African products without severe restrictions, high tariffs, and other obstacles. At the same time, according to recent data, the EU and the United States provide over $300 million a year in subsidies to domestic farmers and corporations.[35] While keeping Western markets closed or tightly controlled, developing countries have been forced to open their markets to foreign commodities that additionally have an unfair advantage due to subsidies. As noted above, the principle legislation for advancing trade with Africa is the AGOA and its extension, the "AGOA Acceleration Act" (2004). These two pieces of legislation essentially force African countries to pursue not only free market economic policies, but those that are specifically beneficial to U.S. corporations. Although the administration extols the growth in trade with Africa, the reality is that only a very small number of African states actually trade with the United States, and about 80 percent of that trade is related to oil, core minerals, and metals.[36] U.S. subsidies and protectionism prevent African agricultural products from being competitive; a devastating arrangement given that "agriculture supports 70–80 percent of the people, employs some 60 percent of the labour, accounts for 20 percent of merchandise exports and 17 percent of GDP."[37]

Most important, the debt cancellation agreement did not include increases in aid. Not one poor country will suddenly turn into a Canada or a Sweden because their debt has been erased. Separately, the British had proposed to double the aid that goes to Africa and other poor regions to $50 billion, and to have rich nations commit to increasing their official development assistance (ODA) for poor countries to 0.7 percent of their gross domestic product (GDP) by 2015, proposals that Bush seemed to find personally repugnant. The United States currently commits only a miserly 0.16 percent of its GDP to ODA, the smallest of all major industrialized nations.[38] Bush stated that such an increase "doesn't fit our budgetary process."[39] In a special trip to Washington in early June 2005, Blair personally lobbied Bush to raise the percentage of U.S. foreign aid given to Africa but was rebuffed. Aware of the public relations disaster of dissing his most loyal and long-suffering ally, Bush attempted to mollify critics by declaring "Over the past four years, we have tripled our assistance to sub-Saharan Africa."[40]

As is so often his habit, Bush was again untruthful. A Brookings Institution report, written by former Clinton Africa policy specialist Susan Rice, documents that in real dollar terms, the increase has been far less than Bush claimed. She writes, "U.S. aid to Africa from FY2000 (the last full budget year of the Clinton administration) to FY2004 (the last completed fiscal year of the Bush administration) has not 'tripled' or even doubled. Rather, in real dollars, it has increased 56 percent (or 67% in nominal dollar terms)."[41] Additionally, about 53 percent of that increase was in emergency food aid rather than in overseas development assistance needed for long-term sustainable development.[42]

Bush's canard was aimed at distinguishing his record from that of his predecessor as well as throwing a bone to Blair. The claim of "tripling" would make its way into the final agreement of the G8, which included a listing of the increased development aid that members and the European Union were making to Africa.[43] With his legacy in mind, Blair has scrapped to become identified as the world leader most concerned and committed to bringing Africa out of poverty. His political credibility has been tarnished by his puppet relationship with Bush, and his Africa efforts perhaps represents his last opportunity before leaving office to be known for more than his Iraq downfall.

Above All Else Oil Rules

> African oil should be treated as a priority for U.S. national security post 9-11, and I think that post 9-11 it's occurred to all of us that our traditional sources of oil are not as secure as we once thought they were.
> Rep. Ed Royce (R-CA), Chair, House Sub-committee on Africa[44]

Prior to her appointment as national security advisor, Rice had virtually no foreign policy experience or academic interest in sub-Saharan Africa; in fact, her first trip ever to Africa occurred in July 2005. However, she was connected to Africa in another manner. She had been a member of the board of Chevron that had massive investments in Nigeria and other parts of the continent. During her tenure on the board—1991 to 2001—the Ogoni people in western Nigeria and elsewhere in the country fought against the deadly collusion between the corrupt regime of Nigerian dictators and Western oil companies including Chevron, Shell, and others that suppressed the rights of workers, harmed the environment, and committed massive human rights violations. The government response, when protests against Chevron intensified, was to crack down on the protesters with arrests, imprisonment, beatings, and even murder (working in close collaboration with the oil company). In 1998–1999, when local Nigerians rose up against the destructive and exploitative policies of Chevron, they were suppressed brutally by the Nigerian military with the company's assistance. Reportedly, on January 4, 1999, Chevron transported about 100 soldiers on its corporate aircraft to areas where the protests were most active. In one instance, in May 1998, two workers died at Chevron's Parabe Offshore Platform in the context of demonstrations against the company. In 2000, the New York–based Center on Constitutional Rights filed a lawsuit on behalf of a group of Nigerians who had been victims of Chevron's corporate policies.

During this period, from 1999–2001, Rice chaired Chevron's Committee on Public Policy whose mission was to protect the corporate image. Rice not only failed to speak out against these atrocities or apologize for the company's role in them, but she actively defended the position of Chevron. As far as the public record goes, she did not address the issues raised by the Nigerian people or demonstrate a visible concern to what was happening under her company's name. She opposed resolutions that sought to force the corporation to address environmental and human rights concerns in Nigeria and elsewhere. As occurred with other loyal and valuable board members, such as former Secretary of State George Schultz and Bush trade secretary Carla Hills, in 1995 Rice had an oil tanker named in her honor that had much to do with the pivotal role she played in helping to advance Chevron's interest in Eastern Europe and elsewhere. It was rechristened the *Altair Voyager* after she became national security advisor, in part, because it embarrassingly but truthfully reinforced the intimate ties of the administration to the oil industry. Popular discussion over this curiosity in the media diverted discussion from her substantial role as a corporate apologist and champion of a major corporation that was willing to link arms with dictators, destroy the environment, and facilitate human rights violations.

Beyond an oil interest, it is difficult to find any discourse on Africa from Rice in either her academic or policy work prior to her joining the George W. Bush administration. In her pivotal January/February 2000 *Foreign Affairs* article, a 6,500-word plus piece that outlined Bush's projected foreign policy agenda and priorities should he win the 2000 presidential contest, Africa, nor any of the issues it faces, was not mentioned at all.[45]

Rice's oil ties were an appropriate prelude to what would be a major component of the Bush administration's Africa policy objective: securing access to Africa's substantial, but mostly untapped oil reserves. As Africa policy expert Ann-Louise Colgan notes, "In reality, the twin perceived priorities of oil and strategic military relations have been the driving forces of Africa policy under the Bush team, and the pursuit of this agenda is likely to continue to define U.S. Africa policy in the second Bush term. The appointment of Condoleezza Rice as the new Secretary of State only confirms the centrality of these priorities in the definition of U.S. interests in Africa."[46]

The administration has defined African oil as a strategic national interest making countries such as Nigeria, Angola, Gabon, and even Sudan as high security priorities. As Assistant Secretary of State Walter Kansteiner stated, "African oil is of national strategic interest to us, and it will increase and become more important as we go forward."[47] He went on to say, "that's really the primary focus of what our policy is."[48] U.S. dependence on African oil is growing. It now constitutes about 15 percent of U.S. oil imports and that it will likely grow, according to government studies, to perhaps as much as 25–30 percent by 2015, a higher percentage than what currently comes from the Middle East.[49] According to the *Washington Times*, "Nigeria is the seventh largest world oil exporter and the fifth biggest supplier of oil to the United States."[50] West Africa contains about 10 percent of the world's oil resources. While the administration has heralded the increase in imports from Africa to the United States, about 70 percent of those are oil imports.[51]

Powell would also play a key role in the American scramble for African oil. After his brief appearance at the UN World Summit on Sustainable Development he rushed off to visits in Angola and Gabon. These two oil rich countries have become favorites for the administration. The purported purpose was to "encourage continued peace in Angola and to take a 10-minute photo-op walk in a rain forest in Gabon," but the real agenda was to solidify U.S. interests in the development of the oil reserves in these nations.

Prevarication and Politics: Bush and the African AIDS Pandemic

Many believe that the most urgent issue facing sub-Saharan Africa is the HIV/AIDS pandemic. As Booker and Colgan noted,

Africa is ground zero of the global AIDS crisis—home to just over 10 percent of the world's population but more than 70 percent of the world's HIV/AIDS cases. In many southern African countries, HIV prevalence rates now stand at over one-third of the population. While almost 30 million Africans are living with HIV/AIDS, less than 2 percent of these people have access to life-saving treatments that have cut death rates so dramatically in the United States and other wealthy countries.[52]

All of the issues surrounding the medical dimensions of the crisis are exacerbated by the continent's unrelenting poverty. Lack of access to life-extending drugs, prevention education programs, and the general lack of public health ensure that the crisis grows more deadly by the minute.

Although late and still substantially underfunded, the global community and international institutions have mobilized to address the crisis primarily through multi-lateral strategies. In 2002, the United Nations established the "Global Fund," an international organization established in 2001 to fight AIDS, tuberculosis, and malaria. This mechanism was setup to coordinate multi-lateral efforts around these diseases. In 2001, the World Trade Organization passed the Doha Declaration, which stated that public health should be given primacy over intellectual property rights when it comes to providing low-cost medicines for the poor who are afflicted with the virus. This position was fought by Western pharmaceutical companies who make millions in the West on these drugs.

In 2002, Bush created the "President's Emergency Plan for AIDS Relief" (PEPFAR) as an alternative to the Global Fund. In his State of the Union address that year, he stated, "I ask the Congress to commit $15 billion over the next five years, including nearly $10 billion in new money, to turn the tide against AIDS in the most afflicted nations of Africa and the Caribbean." Although this clearly was intended to convey the message that the United States was about to commit $15 billion to fight AIDS in Africa and the Caribbean, the administration later "clarified" that it meant that it was proposing $15 billion as its total global AIDS budget.[53] To add insult to injury, Bush's budget request only a few weeks later was only for $450 million for the new initiative, far short of the $3 billion he had brashly declared in his speech. Congress would ultimately approve more than what Bush requested.

The corporatist nature of the Bush regime also manifested itself around this initiative. In late 2003, the U.S. Global AIDS Initiative (USGAI) was formally housed in Powell's State Department and Randall Tobias, a former pharmaceutical executive for Eli Lily and Company, was put in charge. He was criticized by some activists as a less than objective player, and that he "consistently avoided making a commitment to using the lowest-cost generic medicines available, and instead will likely give preferential consideration to the procurement of brand-name medicines."[54] In addition, the administration's favored strategy in dealing with HIV/AIDS was abstinence rather than treatment, education, and condom distribution, choices that are the preferred options of most activists and experts.

The *New York Times* pointed out that the proposed increase in HIV/AIDS funding was to come, in part, by cutting about $500 million from international child health programs. It wrote, "The White House should not be forcing the babies of Africa to pay for their parents' AIDS drugs."[55] Other parts of the funding would come from the MCA. This game of shifting funds from one program to another and calling it "new" and "additional" funding is the kind of dishonesty that has led Africans and others to not put a great deal of faith in the promises of the United States.

Double Standards: Powell, Rice, and Human Rights in Darfur

Conflicts in parts of Africa were mostly skirted by the Bush administration. It was rare that Bush, for all of his meetings with African leaders, would speak out on these issues. The war in Darfur, Sudan, is a typical example of the strategy of rhetoric and avoidance carried out by the administration.

In 2003, two new rebels groups emerged, the Justice and Equality Movement (JEM), and the Sudan Liberation Movement (SLM), both fighting to gain more resources for those in the South, and perhaps independence from the Khartoum regime. After JEM and SLM attacked government offices in February 2003, the government responded with bombing attacks. It also support the murderous assaults by the Janjaweed, an Arab-based militia linked to the Khartoum government, on villages allegedly supporting the rebels. The Janjaweed's campaign of murder, pillage, and rape ignited a massive refugee crisis. It is estimated by the United Nations that by 2005 as many as 200,000 had died, though many suggest a much higher figure, and more than 2.25 million were driven from their homes and into refugee camps throughout western Sudan and in Chad.[56] In particular, the Fur, Massalit, and Zaghawa ethnicities were targeted for attacks.

On September 9, 2004, in testimony before the U.S. Senate Foreign Relations Committee, Powell stated that the violence then occurring in the Darfur region constituted genocide. He stated, "We concluded that genocide has been committed in Darfur and that the government of Sudan and the Janjaweed bear responsibility and genocide may still be occurring."[57] This statement was echoed in a press release by Bush also declaring "we have concluded that genocide has taken place in Darfur."[58]

Reports issued by the U.S. State Department, Human Rights Watch, International Crisis Group, and the United Nations strongly argued and documented that the government and the Janjaweed militia were perpetuating acts that met the criteria for genocide as elaborated in the 1948 Convention on the Prevention and Punishment of the Crime of Genocide (the Genocide Convention), and in rulings from the International Criminal Tribunal for Rwanda (ICTR), and the International Criminal Tribunal for Yugoslavia (ICTY). As human rights scholar Jamal Jafari writes, "The atrocities in Darfur clearly constitute genocide" according to these legal standards.[59]

Powell in his Senate testimony described the three criteria used to identify genocide under the Genocide Convention: "Specific acts are committed—killing, causing serious bodily or mental harm, deliberately inflicting conditions of life calculated to bring about physical destruction of a group in whole or in part, imposing measures to prevent births or forcibly transferring children to another group; such acts are committed against members of a national, ethnic, racial or religious group, and; such acts are carried out with intent to destroy, in whole or in part, [the group] as such."[60] Unfortunately, Powell also stated that the administration's position was that the Darfur genocide did not mean that either the United Nations or the United States should intervene militarily.

Powell's statement was significant because usage of the term "genocide" has very specific meaning under international norms and international law. In the post–World War II period, revulsion against the atrocities committed by the Nazis led to universal agreement among nations of the world that they had an obligation to intervene in any situation where genocide or crimes against humanity were occurring. This commitment was compromised subsequently when the larger states, those with the capacity to intervene in a meaningful way, hesitated to label certain situations genocide in order to avoid sending troops. This hesitation was infamously on display during the Rwandan crisis in spring 1994. As it became clear that genocide was being carried out by the Hutus against the Tutsis and moderate Hutus, the State Department resorted to creating new terms and phrases to avoid the trigger word of "genocide." Officials at the State Department referred to the situation in Rwanda as "acts of genocide."[61] When reporters asked State Department official spokesperson Christine Shelley exactly how many "acts of genocide" add up to genocide itself, she dismissed the question by stating,

That's just not a question that I'm in a position to answer. . . . I have guidance which I try to use as best as I can. There are formulations that we are using that we are trying to be consistent in our use of. I don't have an absolute categorical prescription against something, but I have the definitions. I have phraseology which has been carefully examined and arrived at as best as we can apply to exactly the situation and the actions which have taken place.[62]

Shelley's garbled answer was the kind of official State Department gibberish that allowed the United States (and other governments) to sidestep their responsibility to intervene. Powell's use of the term "genocide" was controversial because it did not trigger an increase of U.S. involvement in the Darfur situation, and it put the onus on the United Nations to handle the crisis.

The West had fiddled while the crimes in Darfur in the Sudan are rising. Although his own former secretary of state Colin Powell declared in fall 2004 that genocide was occurring in Darfur, by summer 2005, Bush had managed to speak of it only once publicly and that was in passing at a White House photo opportunity. In addition to the killing of villagers, a policy of systematic rape was also occurring. Medecins sans Frontieres (Doctors Without Borders) issued a report in March 2005 that documented about 500 rapes that the group had treated in only a four-and-a-half month period that represented only a tiny fraction of the rape incidents.[63]

The Congressional Black Caucus would also demonstrate concern about the lack of urgency on the part of the administration to address the Darfur crisis. In a press release in July 2004, it wrote, "Today, several Members of the Congressional Black Caucus held a very serious and substantive meeting with U.S. Secretary of State Colin Powell regarding the man-made human catastrophe unfolding in the western region of Darfur, Sudan."[64] The CBC pushed for Powell to be more forceful in getting the administration to declare honestly what was truly occurring in Darfur. It stated, "Additionally, in the meeting, we strongly urged the Secretary to recommend to President Bush that he join the Congress in recognizing the crisis in Sudan for what it is—GENOCIDE."[65]

Once in office as the new secretary of state, Rice would backslide on Powell's charge of genocide. In March 2005, UN Resolution 1593 referred the situation to the International Criminal Court (ICC) on a Security Council vote of 11 to 0 with the United States and three other countries abstaining. Under Rice, rather than support any effort with the ICC, the United States called for an ad hoc tribunal to be setup in Tanzania that would investigate if genocide, war crimes, or crimes against humanity had occurred and who was responsible. There was a deliberate shift from the charge of genocide made only months earlier. It is believed by many that the changed U.S. posture toward the Darfur situation has to do with growing U.S. ties with the Sudanese government related to its cooperation in the war against terrorism and to the vast untapped oil reserves in the country. The *Los Angeles Times* reported that the "Bush administration has formed a close intelligence partnership" with the Khartoum regime, which is still on the U.S. official list of states that sponsor terrorism.[66] This growing relationship has included not only U.S. intelligence officials going to the Sudan to interview suspected terrorists captured by the Lt. Gen. Omar Hassan Ahmed Bashir's government, but also has flown Sudan's intelligence chief, Maj. Gen. Salah Abdallah Gosh, to the United States for secret meetings.[67]

While Powell may have fudged on compromising African lives with Bush administration security interests during his tenure, there have been few qualms with Rice in office. In a March 2005 letter to the Khartoum regime, while criticizing its role in Darfur, she wrote of a future "fruitful relationship" and her satisfaction of the "close cooperation" that existed regarding the war on terrorism.[68] Most important, the Bush administration has did little to stem the atrocities that continued to mount throughout 2005 with the president virtually unable to mention the word "Darfur" although it was a central issue of African politics.

Conclusion

Under the presentation policy configurations, Africa will be seen more and more as a continent serving as a frontline for U.S. hegemony. African states are already forced to trade off aid and political goodwill in exchange for compromised sovereignty, foreign capital dominance, and reduced capabilities to address their pressing social and economic needs. Beyond the rhetoric, there is little sensitivity to the genuine concerns that have been raised consistently by the people of Africa themselves.

Bush stated that ending African poverty "is a central goal of my administration."[69] As are many of the assertions of the Bush administration, these words echo hollow down the long tunnel of lies, evasions, and misrepresentations that characterize it.

The appointments of Powell, Rice, and other black diplomats have had one great benefit: the clarification that racial affinity is irrelevant to U.S. policy interests. Few in Africa now believe that simply having high-ranking black American officials opens the door to a more just relationship with the United States. In fact, harboring such illusions blinds one to the real political agenda that is being articulated and carried out. The Bush administration has been a disaster for sub-Saharan Africa. It failed to lead or support, and in many instances sabotaged, a wide range of issues from the genocide in Darfur to genuine, widespread debt cancellation, needed trade reforms, environmental degradation, land reform, and increased development aid. It misled about its funding for Africa's HIV/AIDS crisis, much of which is fiduciary sleight-of-hand, and remains inadequate, cumbersome, and symbolic. Bush's "positive agenda" for Africa, as Rice put it, exists in press releases and speeches and virtually nowhere else.

Seven

Counter-Hegemony in the Global South: The Americas Say "No Pasaran" to the Bush Doctrine

Powell, in whom so much was originally expected by this region of that American son of Jamaican roots, has not proven particularly helpful either in advancing the agenda in U.S.-Caribbean relations.

Caribbean Journalist Rickey Singh, September 3, 2004[1]

Condoleezza Rice brings a marked lack of experience in Western Hemisphere affairs to her post. Her training in Cold War mentality feeds into the president's messianic vision of foreign policy to create a dangerous tendency to prejudge events.

Counterpunch Journalist Laura Carlsen, February 5/6, 2005[2]

Powell is a son of the Caribbean islands. Almost. Both of his parents, Luther and Maud Ariel Arie (McKoy), were born in Jamaica and both migrated to New York in the early 1920s where they met and married. With deep affection and a sense of identity, Powell has written about his visit to his father's birthplace at a small village called Top Hill and meeting many, many relatives. His mother's side of the family is from Westmoreland, another small village. The Jamaica of small, but incremental prosperity that Powell's parents knew and that he heard of as he grew up is no more. Like virtually all of the Americas, years of forced structural adjustment programs and political intervention from the United States have retarded development, distorted economies, and ruptured social progress. In addition, in Latin America, those of African descent and indigenous peoples occupy the bottom rungs of society across the board as they face racial discrimination as well as class oppression. The Bush years have done little to erase social inequalities, and, indeed, have exacerbated political tensions and instability.

For many in the Americas, Colin Powell and Condoleezza Rice were to become large disappointments. The region found little to celebrate during the years of their appointments as they carried out the Bush doctrine that included attacks on those leaders perceived to be insufficiently subservient to U.S. interests, imposition of detrimental trade policies, and political pressure to adopt U.S.-defined anti-terrorism policies. Powell's involvement during the Reagan era in what he called "working hard to support the Contras" [who were terrorizing the Nicaraguan people in their effort to overthrow the Sandanistas] and invading Panama already had left some bitter residue.[3] Rice, on the other hand, had never demonstrated any interest in her entire career in the region. In addition, neither Powell nor Rice acknowledged, let alone supported, the progressive democratic movements of black and indigenous peoples against racism and discrimination.

While the Bush administration was concentrating its energies on the Middle East, leftist and progressive movements in the Americas blossomed and declared their independence from a long history of Washington domination. In Argentina, Brazil, Chile, Peru, Uruguay, and Venezuela progressive and left-leaning governments came to power who expressively challenged what has become known popularly as the Washington Consensus—dictates really—of harsh neo-liberalist economic policies and political hegemony. The phrase, "Washington Consensus," has been the subject of numerous debates about its meaning within policy and scholarly circles including from economist John Williamson who coined the phrase in 1990. He states that he originally used the term "to refer to the lowest common denominator of policy advice being addressed by the Washington-based institutions to Latin American countries as of 1989." He advocated privatization, trade liberalization, interest rate liberalization, and other reforms that have become associated with neo-liberal economic policy. While there is no consensus on the term "Washington Consensus," a distinct set of policies from Western governments and international financial institutions have functioned as a consensus in practice.[4]

In the face of belligerent diplomacy by former Secretary of State Colin Powell and his successor Condoleezza Rice, many have opened up relations with Cuba, spurned the IMF, rejected unfair trade agreements, advocated or implemented moderate social welfare programs, strengthened ties with the hated Chavez government in Venezuela, and been reluctant to join Bush's war on terrorism and war in Iraq. There has been a high price to pay for these stands due to the constrained resources confronting even the most economically stable states let alone the poorer ones. The Bush administration is vengeful pathologically and seeks aggressively to punish states that oppose its overtures. While the sobering reality is that few have the capacity to carry on long-term resistance to the financial incentives or punishments being offered, the movements for democracy, inclusion, transparency, and justice have demonstrated remarkable resiliency and have grown during the Bush era.

This period has also coincided with the rise of Afro-Latino movements in many states in the region. In Brazil, Colombia, Peru, Venezuela, Mexico, and even in a state considered lily-white, such as Argentina, progressive black voices have emerged. While Bush, Powell, and Rice gave an inordinate amount of attention to African issues with Powell and Rice strategically floating their racial lineage when useful, there has been little acknowledgment by either of the latter two of the black populations in Latin America and their issues of social exclusion, human rights abuses, land seizures, and racial discrimination. A vibrant Afro-Latino civil society is challenging not only the racial norms of states in Latin America but also their fundamental commitment to democracy and willingness to include civil society in the critical decisions that govern their lives. Afro-Latino communities, often in unison with indigenous communities, have fought for affirmative action, land rights, and other reforms that move society forward as a whole. The logic of these changes, in many ways, go against the policies being advocated by the Bush administration such as privatization, less government intervention, end of social welfare, limited labor rights, environmental minimalism, and security interests over human rights.

This chapter looks at U.S. efforts related to the politics, economics, and security agendas toward the Americas that have arisen during the George W. Bush years, the role of Powell and Rice in implementing that agenda, and the response by states and civil society. The discourse regarding their race, except in the Caribbean, was more muted than in Africa but the surge of black consciousness throughout the region served as an important context for assessing their impact and legacy.

From the Monroe Doctrine to the Bush Doctrine

> [T]he American continents, by the free and independent condition which they have assumed and maintain, are henceforth not to be considered as subjects for future colonization by any European power.
>
> From the Monroe Doctrine[5]

On December 2, 1823, President James Monroe delivered his seventh annual message to the U.S. Congress. He sought to address, among other items, a proposal by the British for a joint U.S.-British alliance that would block France and Spain from intervening in the affairs of the newly independent states of Argentina, Bolivia, and Venezuela including any attempt at re-colonialization. His secretary of state, John Quincy Adams, had argued that an alliance was unnecessary and that it was time that the United States asserted its authority over the region. In his address, Monroe made it clear that the Americas were off limits for the European powers. The paradox, of course, was that while Monroe was defending the "free and independent conditions" of nations to the South, millions of blacks were enslaved and the indigenous people of the United States (and the rest of the Americas) had been slaughtered and robbed of their land with more seizures, in the most violent ways possible, to come.

A message was also being sent to the new nations in the region that the United States would respect their sovereignty. Madison stated, "It is still the true policy of the United States to leave the parties to themselves in the hope that other powers will pursue the same course."

The words were barely out of Monroe's mouth before the United States launched nearly two centuries of direct intervention into the affairs of the states and territories of Central America, South America, and the Caribbean. In the post–World War II period alone, this included occupations and military interventions (Haiti, Grenada, Panama, Nicaragua, Colombia, Guatemala, Peru), assassinations or attempted assassinations (Cuba, Chile, Costa Rica, Nicaragua), election rigging (Haiti, Guyana, Ecuador, El Salvador, Jamaica), and coups and attempted coups (Guatemala, Brazil, Dominican Republic, Uruguay, Bolivia) on a regular basis as well as economic hegemony. Virtually every nation and territory in the region has been victimized by its neighbor to the north. In particular, the latter years of the Cold War were bloody and murderous. There was hardly a day that went by when one or more of these strategies were not in full operation. In the final decade of the Cold War, the 1980s, during the Reagan and George H. W. Bush eras, countless individuals died, were displaced, and had their lives and communities destroyed by the direct and indirect intervention of these administrations in Central America through supporting dictatorships and sponsoring terrorist groups. The Clinton years were marked by benign neglect except for the billions spent in Colombia on a drug war that seemed more focused on counter-guerilla objectives more than anything else.

Thus, it is difficult for those in the region to believe the assurances of Bush and his key officials about promises of equal partnerships and support for democracy. Both Powell and Rice elide any responsibility for the role that the United States played in the damage to democracy that existed during previous Republican (and Democratic) administrations. Rice notes how "we must not lose sight of how far our hemisphere has come in 25 years. Back then, 14 military dictatorships oppressed citizens throughout the region. Violent insurgencies raged in nine countries. Corrupt statist economies impoverished millions of people."[6] She fails to mention that the overwhelming majority of those dictatorships were not only supported by the United States but in many instances it was their creator and their lifeline, and the political progress occurred in spite of the United States not because of it.

The Bush administration had little doubt that it had the capacity and indeed the right to intervene in the political affairs of the region. In Venezuela, Haiti, and Cuba in particular, it blatantly sought to overthrow those governments or provide aid and encouragement to those who would. In policies and actions, Bush and his officials betrayed its own rhetoric about promoting democracy, ignored regional and international laws and norms regarding sovereignty, and attempted to thwart the democratic wishes of millions.

Venezuela: The Bolivarian Revolution Meets the Bush Doctrine

Since the early days of the administration, one of its top priorities has been the downfall of the Hugo Chavez Frias government in Venezuela. Chavez is a former army lt. colonel who tried to overthrow the government in 1992 and install a progressive government—what he has termed a "Bolivarian Revolution," named after the heroic Latin American liberator Simon Bolivar—that would address the needs of the poor and marginalized. He served two years in prison when it failed, but reformed his strategy and later won the presidency in 1998. He brought with him a radical agenda and was able to rewrite the Venezuelan constitution to include an expansion of rights for ordinary citizens, more control over the country's oil, and even renamed the country to the Bolivarian Republic of Venezuela. His massive popularity gave him the support to initiate a significant number of executive decrees that included land reform, new taxes on the rich, and other changes. He also initiated an effort to improve the housing, education, and health care provided by the state for working-class and poor people.[7] When Chavez came to power, about 80 percent of the population was officially designated as poor. The oil wealth of the country, estimated at over $30 billion annually, was in the hands of one of Latin America's most selfish and arrogant elites. The positive impact of the Chavez government was real despite the barrage of negative accusations coming from its internal and external opponents. As journalist Conn Hallinan wrote, "He increased economic growth by 4 percent. Infant mortality and unemployment dropped, and literacy and minimum wages increased."[8] Within a few years of being in office, Chavez had brought about 1 million children into the school system, mostly rural children who had been abandoned by previous administrations.

While his domestic policies angered the local elite, his foreign relations drew Washington's attention. His friendship with Fidel Castro and rejection of U.S. military adventures in Iraq and elsewhere were fumed at by Bush and his officials.

Venezuela has become Cuba's largest trading partner to the anger of the administration, and Chavez is virtually never mentioned by administration officials without a reference to his links to Cuba.

From Washington, Chavez was criticized regularly by Bush, Powell, and Rice for his association with Castro. Rice stated, "It is beyond me to understand why anybody who believes in democracy or wants people to believe that they believe in democracy would want to have anything in that regard to do with Fidel Castro."[9] In testimony before the Senate Foreign Affairs Committee in February 2002, Powell charged, "Chavez turns up in some of the strangest countries; Iraq, Iran, Libya, Cuba."[10] His insinuation was that Chavez was cavorting with America's worse enemies for what must have been unsavory reasons. In fact, Iraq, Iran, and Libya, just like Venezuela, are all members of OPEC and were logical, indeed, necessary venues for meetings between members.

As relations with Venezuela continue to sour, U.S. officials have implied that Chavez is cultivating relationships with terrorist groups. In a *U.S. News & World Report* article, unnamed senior U.S. military and intelligence officials stated that "Venezuela is emerging as a potential hub of terrorism in the Western Hemisphere, providing assistance to Islamic radicals from the Middle East and other terrorists."[11] There was not one shred of evidence to support this brazen assertion, but it is clearly part of the strategic thinking that if a tale is told often enough it will take on an air of truth. The Bush administration, led by Secretary of State Condoleezza Rice, has characterized Chavez as a danger and has placed Venezuela near the top of its list of security threats in the Americas. During her testimony for confirmation as secretary of state, Rice stated that Chavez "has been unconstructive" and called him "a negative force" in the region.[12]

The country's elite, and their allies in Washington, soon began to mobilize to oust Chavez after he came to power. The bankers, oil executives, corrupt politicians, and the media owners in particular launched a campaign to demonize Chavez. The counter-revolution went into full motion.

Political support and funding for opposition groups came from the Bush administration and U.S. government. From 2000 to 2003, the National Endowment for Democracy (NED) provided $2.2 million to anti-Chavez groups in Venezuela.[13] The NED was created on November 6, 1982, by the U.S. Congress with the expressed mission to "strengthen democracy throughout the world," and though primarily funded by the U.S. Congress under the State Department budget, it operates as a private, non-profit entity. In addition to congressional funding, it has also received funds from the Smith Richardson Foundation, John M. Olin Foundation, and Lynde and Harry Bradley Foundation, three major backers of conservative organizations and institutions in the United States. Ominously, the three key Bush administration Latin American officials that have been running policy, Otto Reich, John Negroponte, and Elliott Abrams, have all been associated with the NED either as board members or other officials. In addition, NED Board of Directors chairman, Vin Weber, is a long-time fundraiser for George W. Bush and the Republican Party as is NED president Carl Gershman.

Among the anti-Chavez groups that received NED funding were the notoriously corrupt Confederation of Venezuelan Workers ($154,377); Assembly of Educators ($55,000), whose leader Leonardo Carvajal was made minister of Education during the April 2002 two-day coup; and the radical conservative party, Prodel ($50,000).[14] In a more direct manner, the International Republican Institute (IRI), a NED institution, opened an office in Caracas with a budget of $339,998 in 2001, up from $50,000 in 2000.[15] The IRI was involved in bringing together anti-Chavez groups with Bush administration officials and flew several of the groups to Washington for meetings.

On April 11, 2002, after months of agitation and support from Washington, Chavez's opposition seized power in a coup that lasted about forty-eight hours. In the days before the coup, protests against the Chavez government, organized by striking oil executives and the conservative private media provoked counter-protests by those who supported Chavez. Violence occurred, likely provoked, and more than a dozen were killed thus providing a pretext for the pre-planned seizure of power. Late that evening and into the next day, Chavez was arrested by several military leaders, held hostage, and pro-U.S. businessman Pedro Carmona, was installed as the faux new president. The Venezuelan people were informed falsely that Chavez had resigned and was on his way out of the country though no resignation letter was presented nor was Chavez allowed to talk to the media.

Carmona and the coup leaders moved quickly to destroy the Chavez government. The National Assembly and the Supreme Court were dissolved, presidential edicts were overturned, and even the name of the country was changed back to the Republic of Venezuela. This all occurred within the first twenty-four hours of arresting Chavez.

As these events were unfolding, Powell's State Department issued a statement that essentially endorsed the coup and the "new" government. It stated, "Yesterday's events in Venezuela resulted in a transitional government until new elections can be held. Though details are still unclear, undemocratic actions committed or encouraged by the Chavez administration provoked yesterday's crisis in Venezuela."[16] The Bush administration's statement also made unsubstantiated charges that Chavez and his allies precipitated a massacre stating that "Chavez supporters, on orders, fired on unarmed, peaceful protestors, resulting in more than 100 wounded or killed."[17] There was no evidence to support the accusation that there were "orders" to fire on demonstrators, and, as it turned out, more Chavez supporters were killed in the incident than those who opposed him. The State Department accepted and spread the lie that "Chavez resigned the presidency."[18]

There was also a celebratory statement from the IRI. George Folsom, IRI president issued a statement full of untrue and, for this U.S.-sponsored non-profit organization, partisan assertions. Folsom claimed that, "Last night, led by every sector of civil society, the Venezuelan people rose up to defend democracy in their country," however, subsequent events would demonstrate that when the majority of people did rise up it was to support the restoration of Chavez.[19] Before the coup was even twenty-four hours old, Folsom was gushing about future elections that would not include Chavez. Writing as though he had intimate knowledge of the objectives and plans of the coup plotters, Folsom wrote, "Today the National Assembly is expected to meet to lay the groundwork for the transitional government to hold elections later this year."[20]

Not only did the Bush administration and IRI support this blatantly un-democratic action, so did many of the U.S. major newspapers. On April 13, 2002, the *New York Times*, calling Chavez a "ruinous demagogue," wrote with some satisfaction that he "had stepped down after the military intervened and handed power to a respected business leader."[21]

The only countries to recognize the coup leaders as a new government were El Salvador, Colombia, Spain, and the United States. Their anointment of the illegal regime was received with great hostility in the rest of the Americas. The coup overtly violated provisions of both the Inter-American Democratic Charter of the Organization of American States (IADC) and the Organization of American States (OAS) Charter. Article 19 of the IADC states, "Based on the principles of the Charter of the OAS and subject to its norms, and in accordance with the democracy clause contained in the Declaration of Quebec City, an unconstitutional interruption of the democratic order or an unconstitutional alteration of the constitutional regime that seriously impairs the democratic order in a member state, constitutes, while it persists, an insurmountable obstacle to its government's participation in sessions of the General Assembly, the Meeting of Consultation, the Councils of the Organization, the specialized conferences, the commissions, working groups, and other bodies of the Organization." Ironically, the IADC was established on September 11, 2001, the day of the terrorist attacks on the United States, and included the full participation and approval of then Secretary of State Colin Powell, who was in attendance at the signing in Lima, Peru.

Rather than endorse the coup, the United States and others should have adhered to Article 9 of the OAS Charter that states, "A Member of the Organization whose democratically constituted government has been overthrown by force may be suspended from the exercise of the right to participate in the sessions of the General Assembly, the Meeting of Consultation, the Councils of the Organization and the Specialized Conferences as well as in the commissions, working groups and any other bodies established."[22]

Indeed, not only were the coup leaders in violation of the OAS agreements, so was the United States. Congressional and administration direct aid to anti-Chavez groups desecrated Article 19 of the OAS charter that states, "No State or group of States has the right to intervene, directly or indirectly, for any reason whatever, in the internal or external affairs of any other State. The foregoing principle prohibits not only armed force but also any other form of interference or attempted threat against the personality of the State or against its political, economic, and cultural elements."[23]

On April 12, as word spread about the capture of Chavez, his massive base of supporters from the poor and working-class sectors of the society began to flood the streets and voice opposition to the coup. By April 14, the coup had lost its helium, its leaders discredited, Chavez was restored, order was reestablished, and the revolt was over. After Chavez was reinstated to power, rather than apologize for its inappropriate interference, condemn the plotters, or acknowledge its strategic miscalculation, the administration argued that the coup should serve as a warning. Rice stated, "We do hope Chavez recognizes that the whole world is watching and that he takes advantage of this opportunity to right his own ship, which has been moving, frankly, in the wrong direction for quite a long time."[24]

Initially, the Bush administration attempted unsuccessfully to deny any involvement in the coup. Bush officials, including Powell and Rice met with opposition leaders on a number of occasions including those directly involved in the short-lived coup. The *London Observer* wrote, that according to its sources in the OAS, that in these meetings, "The coup was discussed in some detail, right down to its timing and chances of success, which were deemed to be excellent."[25] Elliott Abrams, Otto Reich, and John Negroponte, all former Reagan officials who were involved in the Central American wars of that period, and now high-ranking Bush administration operatives, were key in these discussions. These three essentially ran the U.S.–Latin American policy despite Powell being overall in charge of the State Department.

More than two years after the coup attempt, a "Senior Executive Intelligence Brief" (SEIB) and other documents obtained under the Freedom of Information Act (FOIA) by freelance journalist Jeremy Bigwood and posted on the www .venezuelafoia.info website revealed that the CIA had advance knowledge of the coup and had passed it along to a large number of administration officials. According to the *New York Times*, SEIB documents are read by about 200 officials in the Bush administration.[26] In a document labeled, "Senior Executive Intelligence Brief," and dated April 6, five days before the coup, it was noted that the plotters of "disgruntled senior officers and a group of radical junior officers are stepping up efforts to organize a coup against President Chavez, possibly as early as this month." The CIA analysis also stated that they would try to "exploit unrest stemming from opposition demonstrations slated for later this month."

In August 2004, a recall election cheered on by the Bush administration backfired and Chavez won 59 percent of the vote giving him even more authority and legitimacy. In the lead-up to the election, while Powell expressed "hopes that the Government of Venezuela will allow this process to move forward," he also stated that the United States was "not interfering in it."[27] In contrast, his supposedly subordinate, then assistant secretary of state for Western Hemisphere Affairs Roger Noriega, threatened reprisals if the recall did not happen or go in the direction that the United States wanted. Although a number of Chavez's enemies declared that the election had been rigged, it was certified by official observers from the OAS as well as the U.S.-based Carter Center, the pro-democracy institution founded by former President Jimmy Carter.

The Overthrow of Haiti and Aristide

> Representatives of Caribbean governments do not know her well, and just how much she knows about the region is an open question.[28]

The administration had more success in the elimination of another of its perceived adversaries, Haitian president Jean-Bertrand Aristide. He first came to power in 1990 with a great deal of hope and optimism that for the first time in modern Haitian history, there would be a popular leader who would advance the economic and social interests of the nation's poor and impoverished. In 1991, Aristide was overthrown by a coalition of former military officers and corrupt political officials and forced into exile in Washington, D.C. Efforts at negotiation, such as the July 3, 1993, Governor's Island Agreement, faltered as the junta consistently reneged on its promises to give up power. After years of pressure by black American and human rights activists and political leaders, a hunger strike by former TransAfrica executive director Randall Robinson, a rise in the flow of Haitian refugees to Florida, demands by the OAS, and unrelenting brutality by the coup leader Gen. Raoul Cedras and his military dictatorship, in September 1994, Clinton sent 20,000 U.S. troops to Haiti—"Operation Restore Democracy"—to return Aristide to power.

In his September 15, 1994, speech to the nation detailing the regime's horrors and why it was necessary to bring back the elected president, Clinton stated,

"Haiti's dictators, led by General Raoul Cedras, control the most violent regime in our hemisphere. For three years, they have rejected every peaceful solution that the international community has proposed.... Cedras and his thugs have conducted a reign of terror. Executing children. Raping women. Killing priests."[29] Speaking in superpower tones, he stated, "Now the United States must protect our interests—to stop the brutal atrocities that threaten tens of thousands of Haitians, to secure our borders and to uphold the reliability of the commitments we make, and the commitments others make to us."[30] Recognizing the unpopular nature of his decision to send troops with a wide section of the U.S. public and likely attacks from the Right, he linked his action to that of former Republican presidents stating, "Restoring Haiti's democratic government will help lead to more stability and prosperity in our region, just as our actions in Panama and Grenada did.... Our mission in Haiti, as it was in Panama and Grenada, will be limited and specific."[31] The Clinton administration was also working under the auspices of UN Security Council Resolution 940, passed on July 31, 1994, which authorized the creation of a multi-national force empowered to use "all necessary means" to restore Aristide to his office.

On September 16, Powell, then retired, was part of an advance team that included Jimmy Carter and Sam Nunn, former chair of the Senate Armed Services Committee. Their mission was to tell the coup government in no uncertain terms that it was time to go. They convinced Cedras to leave shortly before U.S. troops began arriving on September 19.

While many applauded the United States returning Aristide to Haiti, little note was taken of the conditions that Aristide was forced to agree to in order to be restored to power. Operating under a framework similar to the Governor's Island Agreement, Aristide agreed to a number of conditions that would imprison his government economically and facilitate the growth of his opposition. In a devastating analysis by Lisa McGowan, she systematically lays out the role of the international financial institutions (IFIs)—specifically the IMF, World Bank, Inter-American Development Bank, and U.S. Agency for International Development (USAID)—in controlling Haiti's economy and, in effect, Aristide's destiny.

Referring to the privatization demands of the donor community, McGowan writes: "Before President Aristide even returned to Haiti, donor aid was explicitly conditioned on his agreement to privatize nine entities out of a list of over 40 state assets. The priority list included the telephone and electricity companies, a cement plant and flour mill, the nation's airport and sea ports, a cooking oil plant and two state banks."[32] The Emergency Economic Recovery Program (EERP), the plan under which Aristide was forced to commit, was a structural adjustment program that also required that the government "lay off public-sector workers, cut fringe benefits of those remaining, remove petroleum subsidies, suspend licensing requirements for sugar and rice imports, reduce import taxes, and move toward eliminating customs tariffs."[33]

When he first came into office, Aristide attempted to implement several progressive reforms that would benefit Haiti's poor, who comprised over 75 percent of the population. In a nation where 1 percent of the population controlled 50 percent of the wealth, it was prudent on Aristide's part to try to push through the imposition of price controls on basic foodstuffs; raising the hourly minimum wage to a combined cash and benefit total of US$.75 cents per hour as well as the enforced payment of legally required Social Security taxes, but these provisions were undermined and eventually compromised or abandoned under the weight of the IFI controls.[34]

Disappointment with Aristide by his base was not simply because he became repressive and undemocratic as the Bush administration and its allies claimed, but specifically it had to do with his acquiescence to the harsh and harmful demands of global capital and international finance. As McGowan tragically notes, "The high level of compliance by the Aristide [and Preval] Administration with IMF and donor demands has brought almost no benefit to the Haitian people, while yielding little in the way of private investment."[35] Backed into an economic corner, Aristide had little choice but to give into the demands of the international donor community and seal his fate.

Under the EERP, the priority was establishing "a stable macroeconomic environment and an incentive framework for private sector development" that locked Aristide into a future that could only turn out badly.[36] While the United States and Western Europe, through subsidies and other programs protected and aided their farmers, Haiti was forced into allowing economic rape, that is, "market liberalization," on its peasants.

It was also a condition of the agreement that Aristide would not run in the next presidential election in 1996, a provision that was in the constitution that he honored. Rene Preval, an ally of Aristide, won the election. It would be Preval that would continue to attempt to implement the demands of the IFIs and the U.S. government and repair the damage left by years of military rule. The privatization of public enterprises by Rene Preval would be only one catalyst for demonstrations. Protesters included Aristide who founded the Lavalas Family Party in January 1997 on his way back to power.

In 2000, he won the presidency again in a contest boycotted by the opposition and with low turnout. However, his radical rhetoric, refusal, and inability to build a coalition government with his opposition, and the natural hostility of a Republican-controlled U.S. Congress and soon-to-be Republican president to any leader not subservient to U.S. interests as they perceived them set him on a collision course with the United States. In the 2000 elections, questionable results regarding seven senators in Aristide's Lavalas Family Party gave the U.S. Congress the pretext it needed to pass legislation putting a hold on badly needed aid to Haiti. The United States also blocked a $145.9 million development loan from the Inter-American Development Bank (IADB).[37] Even though the politicians in question resigned or were removed eventually from office, the U.S. Congress refused to lift the sanctions and continued to squeeze Aristide's government.

The Convergence and Group of 184 were the two main opposition groups to form against the Aristide regime. The Convergence was led by Guy Phillipe, Louis Chamblain, and Jean Pierre Baptiste, all of whom had been involved in the 1991 coup. They were also the former leaders of the para-military group FRAPH. Reportedly, the Convergence had also received funding from the IRI. The Group of 184, named after the number of organizations and groups that had come together to depose Aristide were led by Andy Apaid, a factory owner who had been active in the Duvalier government and a fierce opponent of Aristide's efforts to increase the minimum wage and expand worker's rights.

Further exacerbating the situation was an unsuccessful assassination and coup attempt in December 2001 at the National Palace. The incident further strained relations between Aristide and the OAS, which released a report stating that the assault was not an attempted coup as he claimed.[38] Many believe that following that incident Aristide grew more resistance to cooperation and inclusion. Regardless, the situation began to deteriorate rapidly in 2003, and by the end of the year, a student revolt, growing political opposition, and an armed assault by former military individuals was launched from the Dominican Republic. Many involved had been convicted or were wanted on crimes of murder, embezzlement, and other serious offenses. By November 2003, Powell was saying that he was "very disturbed" by the deteriorating situation in Haiti, but he also stated to the Senate Foreign Relations Committee that, "It is the policy of the government that it is not for regime change."[39]

The intransigence of the opposition, the seizure of towns by the rampaging invading army, and an economic crisis isolated Aristide more and more with few options. Powell supported a power-sharing proposal, fully agreed to by Aristide, which would establish a "Council of Advisors" who would help him govern until new parliamentary elections could be held. The proposal had the backing of the OAS, the Caribbean Community (CARICOM), Canada, and France. But sniffing blood, the proposal was rejected by the opposition who were aware that the United States would only go so far in preserving Aristide's government. Meanwhile, the murderous insurgency in the North continued.

On February 26, 2004, eighteen CBC members went to the White House to meet with Bush, Powell, and Rice to advocate for an intervention involving a

U.S.-led international force that would save Aristide and stop the bloodshed that was happening. The administration was non-committal, Bush claiming that he was waiting for a "political solution," and the CBC members left the meeting frustrated with a sense of foreboding.

Two days later, the day that the final phase of the coup began, according to the U.S. State Department, the situation became increasingly untenable, and it was made clear to Aristide that the United States would accept no solution other than his resignation and departure. Former Rep. Ron Dellums reported that he received a call from Powell on that day warning that Aristide would be killed if he stayed in Haiti and that he had to leave with the American troops when they came to get him later that evening.[40] Around 11:00 P.M., U.S. ambassador James Foley in Haiti called Aristide and told him it was time to go. After writing and signing a resignation letter, Aristide and his wife Mildred were flown out of Haiti around 6:45 A.M. (EST) the following morning to the Central African Republic.[41] The White House directly blamed Aristide for the situation, with spokesman Scott McClellan stating, "This long-simmering crisis is largely of Mr. Aristide's making."[42]

Powell's version of the events of February 28–29, which is substantially different from Aristide's, is couched in more "humanitarian" terms. While rejecting any kind of official inquiry into what occurred, he claims,

> [T]hat on that evening, the situation was deteriorating rapidly in the country and especially Port-au-Prince. We were on the verge of a bloodbath and President Aristide found himself in great danger. He got in touch with our Ambassador and arrangements were made at his request for him to depart the country. He drafted, wrote, signed his letter of resignation all by himself and then voluntarily departed with his wife and his own personal security force. And we were able to provide transportation for him to depart.[43]

Although Powell had stated earlier that the United States would defend Haiti's democracy, the day after Aristide left, Powell called him "a president who really was running a flawed government, a flawed presidency."[44] Assistant Secretary for Western Hemispheric Affairs Roger Noriega stated that Aristide's departure "may eventually be considered his finest hour."[45]

Rice was also active the evening of the coup. According to the *Washington Post*, she telephoned Bush around 1:30 A.M. and woke him up to tell him that Aristide was ready to go and to have him call Secretary of Defense Donald Rumsfeld to authorized a deployment of Marines.[46] Following Aristide's ouster, on *Meet the Press*, Rice stated bluntly, "We believe that President Aristide forfeited his ability to lead his people because he did not govern democratically."[47]

Aristide states in no uncertain terms that he was essentially kidnapped by the U.S. government and forced to leave the country. He stated that Luis Moreno, deputy chief of mission at the U.S. embassy in Haiti, arrived at his home with Marines and presented him with an ultimatum: leave or be killed by his enemies.

The response by African American leaders and activists was unremitting anger. Rep. Elijah Cummings (D-MD), then chair of the Congressional Black Caucus, stated, "By the inaction of the United States government and our allies over the last several years, the democratically elected president of Haiti has been undermined and forced to leave his country."[48] Rep. Maxine Waters (D-CA), who talked with Aristide and his wife in the hours after he had left Haiti, stated in a press release, "The thugs and military criminals have accomplished their mission of deposing Aristide with the overt approval and support of the Bush administration. . . . This should have been prevented and could have been prevented if the Bush Administration had acted to help stabilize the situation in Haiti."[49] In the aftermath of the coup, Randall Robinson called Powell "the most powerful and damaging black to rise to influence in the world in my lifetime."[50] Robinson and others also expressed anger toward Rice. According to Robinson, Rice threatened Jamaica and other governments in the Caribbean for harboring Aristide after he flew back to Jamaica, for a period, after being first taken to the Central African Republic.[51]

On April 5, 2004, after Aristide's departure, Powell went to Haiti to give support to the new government. He praised the new government of interim Prime Minister Gerard Latortue, who Africana.com referred to as "out with the bad and in with the worse," and pledged U.S. political and economic support for the new regime.[52] Caribbean nations refused to recognize the new government and were demanding an investigation into Aristide's ouster to which Powell stated dismissively, "I don't think any purpose would be served by such an inquiry." He returned to Haiti in December 2004, one of his last trips as secretary of state. During his one-day visit shots were fired outside of the palace in Port-au-Prince while he was meeting inside. As CNN reported, "Without offering evidence, a senior State Department official said the gunfire was believed to have come from supporters of ousted President Jean-Bertrand Aristide's Lavalas Family Party."[53] Even in his absence, the State Department blames Aristide for Haiti's continuing woes.

Contumacious Cuba

Of all the states in the Americas, Cuba remains the sharpest political thorn in the side of the United States. Since 1959, every U.S. president, Republican or Democratic, has desired to be the one who brought down Fidel Castro, and everyone has failed. In 1962, the United States succeeded in having Cuba removed from participation in the OAS. Contrary to popular belief, it still remains a member of the OAS according to its website. Congress has joined in the drive to isolate and castigate Cuba and over the years passed harsh legislation related to economic and trade sanctions, travel restrictions, preferential immigration, punishment, and threats toward states that had relations with Cuba, as well as other policies that it has never imposed on even some of the most dedicated U.S. foes. Its documented efforts to assassinate Castro have generated rebukes from around the world.

Driven as much by domestic politics as well as ideological rigidity, the blind spot toward Cuba is fed by a rabid base among the Cuban American population in a number of states, but especially in Florida. In 1998, this political state of affairs was made even more taut with the election of the anti-Castro Jeb Bush, brother of George W. Bush, as governor. In the United States, a tipping point occurred in 1999–2000 surrounding the case of Elian Gonzales, the little Cuban boy who was rescued from the sea after his mother and others died while attempting to leave Cuba illegally. His relatives in Miami, uncompromising anti-communists, along with other anti-Castro activists, refused the request by the boy's father that he be returned to Cuba. After months of fruitless negotiation with the Miami relatives and their refusal to abide by a legal order to surrender Elian, the Clinton administration sent federal agents to forcefully take Elian and eventually reunite him with his father. This incident was thought to symbolize an end of an era where Cuban-American politics dictated completely U.S. policy toward the country. U.S. popular opinion was overwhelmingly in favor of Elian being returned to his father. It was believed that a thaw in Cuban-American relations was on the horizon.

However, the arrival of the Bush administration halted any progress toward advancing relations between the two countries. In May 2004, the administration passed new policies that had more of a harsh impact on the Cuban people (and Cuban Americans) than on the Cuban government. These changes were the result of a commission established by Bush, which was setup in October 2003—Presidential Commission for Assistance to a Free Cuba—headed by Colin Powell and tasked to make its report in spring 2004. Its May 2004 report stated unambiguously that U.S. policy toward Cuba aims to "bring an end to the ruthless and brutal dictatorship," assist the Cuban people in a transition to representative democracy," and "assist the Cuban people in establishing a free market economy."[54] Bush authorized $59 million over a two-year period to implement the commission's recommendations that included more trade sanctions, travel restrictions, and radio broadcasts into Cuba. The administration has made the embargo and other policies more permanent and immune to presidential waivers.

Rice, who has consistently called Cuba an "outpost of tyranny," announced in early August 2005 that she had created a position within the State Department known as the Cuba Transition Coordinator and that a Republican operative Caleb McCarry would be appointed to the job. His job, in part, will be to distribute funding to anti-Castro groups, which according to the Council on Hemispheric Affairs is approaching the $100 million mark.[55]

The Bush administration initiatives complemented the "Cuban Liberty and Democratic Solidarity Act of 1996" (PL 104–114) also known as the Helms-Burton Act. Under the law, even after Castro is out of office, Cuba must meet specific U.S.-defined obligations, such as establishment of a free market system, hold "free and fair" elections, release political prisoners, and legalize noncommunist political parties and activities.

Cuban Americans are now allowed only one visit every three years, only to visit immediate relatives, have more restrictive spending limits while in Cuba, have a reduction in the number of gifts allowed, and still must apply for a U.S. Treasury Department license. U.S. military aircraft are transmitting signals of Radio Marti and TV Marti to get around Cuba's jamming of those broadcasts.

The result of all of these activities, in terms of the political objectives of the United States, has been one colossal failure. Castro remains in power, maintains domestic popularity, has improved ties to other states in the Americas, and has seen calls for normalizing relations, even among some Republicans, increase inside the United States. The Bush administration remains stubbornly undaunted, however, and, like past administrations, refuses to move toward normal and practical relations, and is waiting for Castro to be overthrown or to die, either option being acceptable. The official policy line toward Cuba, as it was in Iraq and is in Venezuela, is for "regime change."

The Bush administration considers Cuba as a full member of its other "Axis of Evil" group. Cuba is one of six countries—Iran, Libya, North Korea, Sudan, and Syria being the others—on the State Department's official list of "terrorist-sponsoring states" (see Table 1), although there is scant evidence to back such an assertion. The political nature of the list is marked by the exclusion of states such as Saudi Arabia, Colombia, and, well, Iraq, all allies of the United States, where evidence of government officials' links to those who have targeted civilians for murder and mayhem is overwhelming. At the same time, the Bush administration has had strong and increasing relations with Libya, Sudan, and even North Korea.

No other contemporary incident reflects the double standards and hypocrisy of the administration's ersatz war on terrorism than the case of Bay of Pigs veteran Luis Posada Carriles. In 1976, Posada was behind the bombing of a Cuban airliner—"the first act of airline terrorism in the hemisphere"—that

Table 1
State Department Listing of "Terrorist-Sponsoring States"

Country	Designation Date
Cuba	March 1, 1982
Iran	January 19, 1984
Libya	December 29, 1979
North Korea	January 20, 1988
Sudan	August 12, 1993
Syria	December 29, 1979

Source: U.S. State Department

murdered seventy-three people including the Cuban national fencing team.[56] He was involved in other terrorist attacks on Cuban civilians as well as in the Iran-Contra debacle. At the time, Posada and other right-wing anti-Castro terrorists were working closely with the CIA. The Cuban-born Posada, who has a Venezuelan passport, was arrested and jailed there on the airline bombing charge but escaped from prison in 1985. For the next twenty years, Posada was on the run. He surfaced at one point as part of Oliver North's contra operations in Nicaragua. In November 2000, Posada was arrested in Panama for plotting to assassinate Castro who was to attend the Ibero-American Summit being held there. In April 2004, Posada and his henchmen were pardoned by President Mireya Moscoso of Panama who is close to the Bush administration and the Miami Cuban exile community.

In March 2005, it was revealed that despite all the supposedly state-of-the-art security at U.S. borders, Posada had entered the United States illegally and was in Miami. As an internationally known fugitive, Posada should have been arrested immediately. Instead he was welcomed and treated as a hero by Miami's hardcore anti-Castro Cubans. He was brazen enough to give an interview to the *Miami Herald*. The public embarrassment of having a very public terrorist providing soundbites in the middle of the "war on terrorism" finally led authorities to arrest him on May 17, 2005, nearly three months after it was known that he was in the country. He was sent to Texas where he was held on immigration charges. His arrest initiated another fierce round of exchanges between the Chavez government, who demanded his extradition back to Venezuela, and the Bush administration that appeared hesitant to grant the request. The administration found itself caught between protecting a well-known international terrorist or turning a former CIA asset over to someone it considered the ideological equal of Castro.

According to an article by Oscar Corral and Jay Weaver in the *Miami Herald*, in September 2005, a U.S. Texas Homeland Security judge ruled that Posada could not be deported to Venezuela because he faced a threat of torture ("U.S. Arrests Alley of Posada," November 21, 2005).

Little Carrots and Big Sticks: The U.S. Battles the Left and "Radical Populism"

These three instances of Bush-era aggression reflect a new desperation on the part of Washington as it has witnessed its influence and capacity to shape political events in the region wilt. The new configuration of power was on display in the drama that emerged in spring 2005 over the leadership of the OAS. Historically, although the United States has never had someone from the United States as secretary-general of the OAS, it has ensured that all previous SGs have been favorable to its interests. The battle over the SG position would also be Rice's first major effort as secretary of state to advance the Bush doctrine.

Tensions between the OAS and the Bush administration had been growing for some time. Regional rejection of the attempted coup in Venezuela, coup in Haiti, war in Iraq, and, in 2003, the refusal by the OAS General Assembly to give the United States a seat on the Inter-American Commission on Human Rights all demonstrated that this was not the OAS historically that had given into U.S. demands with barely a whimper. CARICOM, as an organization, and key members of the OAS have demanded an investigation on the ouster of Aristide, which Rice continues to refuse to support, and CARICOM has not recognized Haiti's interim government, seeing it as a puppet regime installed with dubious legality by the United States.[57]

In 2004, after former Costa Rican president Miguel Angel Rodriguez, a U.S. ally, was forced to resign from the office of Secretary-General after he was indicted on corruption charges back in Costa Rica, three candidates emerged to take his place: former president of El Salvador Francisco Flores, Mexico's foreign minister Luis Ernesto Derbez, and Chile's interior minister Jose Miguel Insulza. The United States initially supported Flores, the most conservative of the three. He had been the only Latin American leader to join the United States in supporting the coup leaders in Venezuela and had actively supported the Iraq war and sent troops from El Salvador to join the occupation.[58] Derbez's backing came from Mexico, and states, such as Bolivia and Peru, which sought to mitigate the rising power of Venezuela and Chile.

The United States strongly opposed the leftist-oriented Insulza from Chile who was favored by Argentina, Brazil, Uruguay, and Venezuela. Insulza is a socialist who advocates full participation of Cuba in the OAS and had opposed the war in Iraq. He would also receive the support of the majority of Caribbean states who, although traditionally predisposed to U.S. interests, had growing economic ties with oil-rich Venezuela and a new sense of independence. At least ten of the fourteen CARICOM states supported Insulza. With about fifteen votes in hand of the eighteen that were needed—to the consternation of the Bush administration and the new secretary of state—Insulza was emerging as the favorite.

The election was scheduled for April 11, 2005, in Washington. As it became clear that Flores could not win, Rice desperately sought to unite the opposition and build a winning coalition of eighteen votes. On April 8, Flores dropped out of the contest, undoubtedly under pressure from the United States, and efforts went into securing the seat for Derbez. However, the vote deadlocked on five consecutive ballots at 17–17. Skillful political maneuvering by Brazil, Chile, and Venezuela had resulted in the United States being unable—for the first time in the history of the OAS—to have its preferred candidate as SG. Bribes, threats, and other tactics had failed to achieve the outcome Rice desired. Even reliable allies such as Haiti and Paraguay were believed to have abandoned the United States.[59]

A second election date was scheduled for May 2. In the interim period, Rice had scheduled a trip beginning April 25 to the region to visit Brazil, Chile, Colombia, and El Salvador. Officially, she was attending the Community of Democracies gathering in Chile, and on a "charm offensive" similar to the one she took to Europe after the 2004 U.S. elections. Politically, the trip had several objectives including lobbying around the Derbez candidacy, further ranting against Chavez, and giving a visible show of support to Colombia and El Salvador, the two most important allies in the region of the United States. She was rebuffed on a number of fronts. According to the *Progreso Weekly*, in Brazil and Chile she was informed that support for Insulza would remain, and in Colombia, she was warned that Derbez was likely to be embarrassingly defeated. Colombian's president Ricardo Lagos informed her that previous Derbez supporters, the Bahamas, Haiti, and Paraguay, had switched their votes to Insulza.[60]

Brazil may have been more flexible if the United States had given support to Brazil's desire to become a permanent member of the United Nations Security Council. However, in media interviews, Rice evaded and deflected the issue each time it was raised. When asked directly by TV Globo, "Do you support a bid for Brazil to become a permanent member to the U.N. Security Council?," Rice spoke of the need for "broader U.N. reform" and "There's no doubt that Brazil is an emerging and important player regionally, increasingly globally. And international institutions will have to begin to take that into account."[61] While never directly answering the question, there was little doubt that Brazil was out-of-favor at that moment.

In the middle of these events, a political crisis arose in Ecuador. On April 23, President Lucio Gutierrez dissolved the country's Supreme Court in an effort to protect two of his cronies and ignited a firestorm of protests and demonstrations. Within twenty-four hours, he was forced to resign and was given asylum by the Brazilian government. Gutierrez had been close to the Bush administration and his departure opened the door for the substantial left-leaning popular movement to vie for power. In the immediate situation, it meant that Ecuador's vote had become unstable.

Rice, on her trip, continued to voice strong championship of Derbez in interviews with Latin American media—CNN en Espanol, UCTV (Santiago), and Television Nacional (Chile)—and Derbez arrogantly asserted that he expected Insulza to withdraw, not him, but behind the scenes a different scenario was unfolding.[62] On April 29, after a two-hour meeting with Rice in Chile, it was Derbez who announced that he was withdrawing from the race. The United States won a minor concession from Insulza who wrote, in part, in a statement after Derbez's quit the race, "I believe it is essential that governments that are elected democratically govern in a democratic way," words that are almost verbatim the mantra carried by Rice, specifically as it related to Chavez.[63] In a meeting before the Council of Americas on May 3, 2005, she stated, "The real divide is between those who are elected and govern democratically, and those who do not."[64] Speaking before the OAS a month after the Insulza victory, she attempted to draw a more politically pragmatic line by stating, "The divide in the Americas today is not between governments from the Left or the Right. It is between those governments that are elected and govern democratically—and those that do not."[65] However, Insulza's words of concession were absent when he gave his formal acceptance speech after officially being named SG.[66]

Although the Bush administration attempted to spin the climbdown as a diplomatic victory, what the *New York Times* called a "calculated retreat in response to warnings to Ms. Rice in Brazil and Colombia earlier in the week," it was in fact a defeat of major proportions for the United States and Rice.[67] The elevation of Insulza reflected the consolidation of a new alliance of resistance by southern cone states, a number of Caribbean nations, and progressive social movements in Central America. It would have been inconceivable a decade ago that enough political opposition could have been brought to bear to defeat a U.S. initiative of such gargantuan importance.

The battle over the OAS Secretary-General was emblematic of the rise and increasing alliance among the Americas' neo-leftists and those seeking more independence from the United States. The election of Chavez in Venezuela, Tabare Vazquez in Uruguay, Luiz Inacio Lula da Silva in Brazil, and Néstor Kirchner in Argentina brought progressives into power across the region. Strong workers' movements in alliance with other sectors have also grown as radical power bases in Bolivia, Peru, Nicaragua, and elsewhere. One effort at consolidation, though perhaps more symbolic than real, was the formation of the twelve-nation (Argentina, Bolivia, Brazil, Chile, Colombia, Ecuador, Guyana, Paraguay, Peru, Suriname, Uruguay, and Venezuela) Community of South American Nations alliance on January 9, 2005. A number of states, such as Uruguay, Brazil, and Venezuela among others, have asserted boldly their right and intention to have full diplomatic, political, and economic relations with Cuba.[68]

The neo-leftists are riding to power on the abysmal record of the neo-liberal economic model that has failed to end poverty, stunted growth, and degraded living standards in the regions. At the same time, however, a defining characteristic of the neo-left has been the acceptance and even embracing of a market economy approach. This sets up an inevitable confrontation between the realization of a progressive social agenda, on the one hand, and the constraining, anti-labor precepts of conservative economic policies, on the other. In the immediate period though, the new governments and movements distinguish themselves from the Bush doctrine by calling for labor rights, maintenance of government control over state-run industries, some protectionist policies, and fair trade agreements.

States in the region including some that have otherwise been accommodating have been penalized for not signing bi-lateral agreements shielding the U.S. military from the jurisdiction of the International Criminal Court (ICC). Although the overwhelming consensus among international law experts is that there is little chance that the United States would ever face the court, the Bush administration wants to signal that it is not going to be subject to international law wherever possible. As a consequence, Congress passed a law in 2002, "American Servicemembers' Protection Act," and added an amendment to it in 2004 that cuts aid to countries that have ratified the ICC but not signed an immunity agreement with the United States. Aid cuts are authorized related to military training, social and health care programs, such as AIDS education and peacekeeping, refugee assistance, and judicial reforms.[69] This has resulted in twelve countries in the Americas losing tens of millions of dollars in aid including Ecuador, Uruguay, Coast Rica, Bolivia, Dominica, Peru, Barbados, and several others. The Bush administration has exempted from punishment countries such as Australia, Britain, Germany, and Japan, all of whom have also ratified the ICC.

Both Powell and Rice have been in sync with the administration's anti-left agenda. Powell's history in the region has left a number of bitter moments. In 2003, Powell wrote, "Twenty years ago, Central America was in turmoil. Civil wars wracked El Salvador, Guatemala, and Nicaragua. Foreign-supported guerrilla movements on the left and death squads on the right terrorized the people of the region."[70] The turmoil he writes about, to a significant degree was driven by policies from Washington, specifically the Reagan administration's determination to destroy every political movement or action it considered leftist. Peasant groups and trade unions that sought basic justice were labeled "guerrilla movements on the left" and the death squads, some of whom worked directly with the CIA and were sponsored by Reagan and U.S. allies in Guatemala, El Salvador, Argentina, and Honduras. Powell was a key figure in these developments. He also wrote, proudly, "Serving as national security advisor in the late 1980s, I was part of the effort backing Honduras against its Sandinista neighbors and supported the Nicaraguan Resistance—the Contras—whose pressure paved the way to free elections in 1990."[71]

Secretary Rice would continue, under the auspices of the Bush doctrine, to again apply double standards and unilateralism. In spring 2005, the Bush administration withdrew from the Optional Protocol to the Vienna Convention on Consular Relations. The protocol, which was drafted in 1963 by the United States itself, gives individuals imprisoned in foreign countries the right to consult with their own consular officials during the process of imprisonment and trial. It mandates the UN's International Court of Justice with the authority to intervene in cases in which that right has apparently been violated. Under that authorization, the court had directed a "meaningful review" of fifty-one convictions and sentences of Mexican citizens sentenced to death in the United States. It turns out that none of the condemned had been allowed to consult with a consular official. Following that decision, Washington announced that it would simply remove itself from the court's jurisdiction.[72] In her May 2005 visit to Mexico, Rice told her hosts, "We will continue to believe in the importance of consular notification," but international court jurisdiction has "proven inappropriate for the United States."[73]

Under the Bush administration, respect for national sovereignty only applies to the United States. Through Rice, the administration continues its political push of hegemonic aggression, and to attempt impose a neo-liberal economic framework, the source of much of the perpetual opposition to Washington, on a resistant region.

Free Trade or Fair Trade: The Resistance to Neo-Liberalism

For many years, Jamaican banana workers worked loading bananas on boats to be shipped to markets around the world. This profitable business provided much needed income and jobs and functioned as an important industry on the island. However, as dramatically documented in the film, *Life and Debt*, the

Jamaican banana industry—and that of other parts of the Caribbean—has been decimated by the unfair dynamics of economic globalization as embodied in the policies of the IMF and inequitable trade agreements.[74] Potatoes, milk, and other commodity markets in the developing world have been overwhelmed by the tidal wave of globalization flowing from the North to devastating effect.

The grim situation and the long-term destructive human consequences have fueled the movement for global justice that has sought to challenge and create a more transparent and just international economic balance. In the Americas, the global justice movement has been fighting to intervene in, reform, and stop a number of trade proposals being sought by the United States. These proposals seek to lock states in the region into a neo-liberal, market-oriented future in which they surrender their economies to the corporate juggernauts of the North. There are a number of bi-lateral and sub-regional proposals, but the centerpiece is the Free Trade Agreement of the Americas (FTAA), a grand scheme to incorporate all the states of the Americas—with the notable exception of Cuba—into one seamless market.

In 1994, several years of hard negotiation had finally come to a close and the three-way trade agreement between Canada, Mexico, and the United States, the North American Free Trade Agreement (NAFTA), was now on the books.[75] The negotiations had been acrimonious with non-governmental organizations (NGOs), such as human rights groups, environmental organizations, trade unions and others, charging that the three governments had colluded with transnational corporations to push through an agreement that would result in lower wages, job flight, relaxing of environmental safeguards, and less rights for workers. Proponents of NAFTA argued that the deal would increase jobs, end unprofitable trade barriers, and, in the long run, set the stage for a broader agreement for the rest of the Americas.[76]

NAFTA became law in 1994 and had an immediate impact not only on jobs, trade, and investment in and between Canada, Mexico, and the United States, but also other countries in the Americas. NAFTA cut and burned nearly 800,000 jobs in the United States that were replaced by about 400,000.[77] In Mexico, there was also initial job downsizing, particularly in manufacturing. Wages fell by 21 percent from 1995–1999 and, according to economists, are just now turning around.[78] Despite the agreement, more than 280,000 jobs were lost when more than 350 maquiladoras closed as businesses pulled up and went for even cheaper labor costs in places such as Haiti and Guatemala.[79] NAFTA also gave rise to the Ejercito Zapatista de Liberacion Nacional (Zapatista National Liberation Army)—the Zapatistas—in Chiapas in southern Mexico led by indigenous groups and others who expressively rejected arguments that the agreement would lead to greater economic prosperity. As Manuel Castells notes,

Mexico's economic liberalization policies in the 1990s "ended restrictions of imports of corn, and eliminated protection on the price of coffee. The local economy based on forestry, cattle, coffee, and corn, was dismantled."[80] These policy changes in Mexico and throughout the region induced widespread economic suffering—and resentment.

The Caribbean was hard hit by NAFTA. Even the U.S. government admitted that many of the countries in the Caribbean suffered disinvestment and slower export growth as a consequence of NAFTA. As the *New York Times* noted in 1997, "Three years after the United States, Canada and Mexico agreed to become a single market as part of the North American Free Trade Agreement, their exports to each other are booming. But here in the Caribbean, the economies of the United States' much smaller neighbors are reeling from the impact of that success and finding it nearly impossible to compete. From the apparel plants of Jamaica to the sugar-cane fields of Trinidad, NAFTA has already resulted in the loss of jobs, markets and income for the vulnerable island nations of the region."[81] The Caribbean apparel industry, in particular, was slammed by NAFTA. More than 150 plants and over 100,000 jobs disappeared directly due to the impact of the trade agreement.[82] Jamaica's stunning growth in this arena, from $10 million to over $600 million in garment exports over a fifteen-year period fell dramatically in the years after NAFTA.[83]

The Caribbean Basin Initiative (CBI) could not stop this slide. Begun under Ronald Reagan and updated under Bill Clinton, CBI is a series of trade agreements between most of the Caribbean and the United States to promote economic development through privatization and investments. By the time of NAFTA, however, the rules governing CBI trade could do little to stem the harm of the former.

Despite the evidence that NAFTA was actually causing many jobs to be lost, environments to deteriorate, and workers' rights to be eroded, other nations in the region, particularly Chile, began lobbying for a similar deal. The FTAA proposal is the child of that history. For more than a decade, there has been a concerted effort to create a FTAA involving representatives from thirty-four nations that have been working on developing a new trade regime. At the same time, the trade unionists, environmental groups, and other NGOs that fought to stop or rewrite NAFTA have again engaged in battle raising many of the same issues as in the early 1990s. One critical difference this time, however, is that the movement for global justice—sometimes erroneously referred to as the "anti-globalization" movement—is a lot stronger and more organized than a decade ago.

In April 2001, in Buenos Aires, an initial draft of the FTAA emerged out of the sixth ministerial meeting, and it was published on the official FTAA website. The sensitive issue of non-corporate, non-governmental organizations' inclusion, the concern that had made NAFTA so controversial, was addressed by the FTAA negotiators. They created the Committee of Government Representatives on the Participation of Civil Society whose task was to assist states in developing productive consultative relationships with NGOs such as trade unions, environmental groups, consumer groups, and human rights organizations. NAFTA was opposed, in part, because the process lacked transparency, that is, open and public negotiations. Opponents criticized the "behind-the-closed-doors" process out of which the agreement emerged. In the end, NAFTA became a corporate written policy that ignored the massive outcry for input by workers' organizations, NGOs, policy-makers, and others directly affected by the pact.

Along similar lines, the FTAA negotiations also offer little in terms of civil society participation. A tepid and inadequate process for soliciting citizens' views—what some have called derisively a "suggestion box" approach to inclusion—is a long way from genuine representation and consultation, which the states clearly seek to avoid. Meanwhile, as Global Exchange notes, "hundreds of corporations are advising the U.S. negotiators and other government representatives and have advanced access to the negotiating texts. While citizens are left in the dark, corporations such as Monsanto, Pfizer Pharmaceuticals, Citigroup, WorldCom, Raytheon, and Shell are writing the rules of FTAA."[84]

An agreement developed without input from those who are going to be most affected is simply undemocratic, unfair, and unacceptable to the activists in the global justice movement. The locking out of those with a genuine concern about the content of FTAA is one of the reasons the meetings to negotiate FTAA have seen consistent and strong protests by tens of thousands. Also, just as reformers sought to get environmental and human rights protections in NAFTA, similar concerns have been raised regarding the FTAA. It is no secret that unchecked and unregulated transnational corporations have wrought disaster on the environment across the world, but especially in the global South. Deforestation, polluted waters, chemical spills, and other never ending travesties have impacted negatively the economic, social, and personal health of the developing world. States such as Puerto Rico, Guatemala, and Brazil, which have lost an area of forest the size of France, have gone and are going bald in environmental terms.[85] As noted, activists from the Americas and around the world have demonstrated against FTAA. In November 2002, thousands descended upon Miami where the latest round of negotiations were being held. Brutal and unprovoked attacks by Miami police, which are being investigated by the courts, sought to blunt the passion that protesters brought to the streets and media in opposition to being excluded.[86] The talks themselves were inconclusive.

For the most part, demonstrators are not against trade in principle, but they call for fair trade, that is, trade agreements that are inclusive, transparent, democratic, and in the interests of those most impacted by these compacts. "Free" trade has not and is not working for the majority of people in the developing world. In February 2004, a report issued by the World Commission on the Social Dimension of Globalization of the International Labour Organization drew several important conclusions. The report, "A Fair Globalization: Creating Opportunities For All," argued that the central policies advocated by the IMF and World Bank and embodied in trade agreements such as NAFTA and FTAA—market liberalization and open, minimally regulated investment—may not lead to economic growth in developing nations. And, second, even when there is economic growth, it does not necessarily translate into social growth and stability.[87]

Joseph E. Stiglitz, former World Bank official and 2001 Nobel Prize winner in economics, wrote perceptively in the *Financial Times*, "If globalisation is managed better, the world can come closer together and become more prosperous. If it continues to be poorly managed, discontent with globalisation will grow . . . we need a more inclusive debate about globalisation, in which its social dimensions are given their proper emphasis."[88] He sums up well the deepening passions of billions around the world that concessions to profit at the expense of peoples' livelihoods and, indeed, their very lives is unacceptable and will be resisted.

Resistance to FTAA led to a retreat on the part of the United States and to two new proposals: the Central America–Dominican Republic Free Trade Agreement (CAFTA) and Andean Free Trade Agreement (AFTA). Negotiations on the former began in 2003. CAFTA's objective is to end trade barriers between the United States and Costa Rica, El Salvador, Guatemala, Honduras, Nicaragua, and the Dominican Republic for U.S. goods.

Despite an unprecedented effort by the Bush administration, it took extraordinary measures on the part of the U.S. House Republican leadership to squeak by a victory. Normal procedure allows a fifteen-minute time limit on voting, however, the vote was kept open for an hour to permit Bush and Republican leaders to pressure resistant Republican lawmakers to vote for the bill. After the first fifteen minutes the count was 180 to 175 against the bill. In the end, the legislation passed on a 217 to 215 count with fifteen Democrats crossing the line to vote for the bill and twenty-five Republicans crossing the line to vote against it.[89] Among the Democrats who crossed over were three black members, William Jefferson (D-LA), Greg Meeks (D-NY), and Edolphus Towns (D-NY). The Central American Free Trade Agreement is an effort to get around the criticisms emanating from the southern cone and the Caribbean and sway the more compliant nations of Central America.

Both Powell and Rice have been strong vocal advocates of CAFTA linking it to issues of democratization and security. Powell was involved in the early drafting and promotion of CAFTA. He openly acknowledged its potential harm stating, "CAFTA will require structural change. There are always some losers, as well as many winners in those kinds of agreements, and our experience with NAFTA and other bilateral trade agreements is that the benefits will outweigh the structural—and usually temporary—disadvantages that come in when you're going through the process of entering into a free-trade agreement."[90] Rice declared that "CAFTA will also help our Central American neighbors to strengthen environmental and labor standards, because only democratic governments truly deliver on the popular desire for a clean environment and guaranteed rights for workers and only free markets and free trade protect the common goods that all people share and enjoy together."[91]

Importantly, CAFTA was more about sending a message than a real impact on the economic relationship between Central America/Dominican Republic and the United States, which is predicted to be rather small. According to the Center for Economic and Policy Research, the most significant impact of CAFTA will be to depress wages in the region in the years to come.[92]

It was the administration's hope that the passage of CAFTA would lead to the Andean Free Trade Agreement (AFTA) that involves Colombia, Peru, and Ecuador and perhaps the troublesome Venezuela and Bolivia. Popular uprisings in the Peru and Ecuador, however, have spoiled the drive to push through the agreement and efforts to isolate Venezuela, Argentina, and even Brazil. A further complication is that in July 2005, the Andean Community of Nations, a sub-regional trade group, appointed Chavez as its chairman making it highly unlikely that the United States would have an easy and quick process of negotiation and ratification.

Anti-Terrorism and Security

In the Americas, Bush's war on terrorism has met a wall of resistance. In part, it has been difficult to make a case for anti-terrorism, at least the Bush variety, in a region where the only "terrorists" of any sort seeking to violently overthrow the state are in Colombia and Peru, insurgencies that are decades old. Efforts to link Cuba or Venezuela to terrorists have appeared ridiculous to even supporters of the Bush administration both domestically and throughout the region.

The administration has strained to connect terrorism with anti-drug activities and other crimes of an international nature as a means by which to bring the region on board. In its 2004 report on global terrorism, the State Department's reference to the Americas states,

Terrorists in the region are becoming increasingly active in illicit transnational activities, including the drug trade, arms trafficking, money laundering, contraband smuggling, and document and currency fraud. The

Western Hemisphere's lightly-defended "soft" targets—its tourism indus-try, large American expatriate communities, thriving aviation sector, and busy ports—as well as systemic disparities between countries in border security, legal and financial regulatory regimes, and the difficulty of maintaining an effective government presence in remote areas—represent targets and opportunities for domestic and foreign terrorists to exploit.[93]

The State Department lavishes excessive praise on most states in the region for cooperating with the United States in the war on terrorism although this pri-marily means that many have included the word "terrorism" in their laws, participated in joint counter-terrorism trainings and exercises, and have accepted anti-terrorist funding. States in the region have been encouraged to be on the lookout for groups engaged in "domestic subversion," a broad label that could and has been used to include trade unions, peasant groups, environmentalists, human rights activists, women's organizations, and racial and ethnic groups.

Rice strongly criticizes Chavez for his "close ties to Cuba," the concern that current "Venezuelan law does not specifically mention crimes of terrorism," and his "ideological affinity" as proof of his uncooperative posture in the anti-terrorism campaign.[94] Cuba, of course, is even more heavily chastised given its remaining status by the department as a sponsor of terrorism. The country is seen as a global leader in the effort to oppose U.S. anti-terrorist activities. It also had the temerity to accuse the United States of aiding attacks on the country. The report states, "The Cuban Government claims, despite the absence of evidence, that it is a principal victim of terrorism sponsored by Cuban-Americans in the United States," an incredible denial of forty well-documented years of aggression against Cuba by every administration including that of George W. Bush.

Despite the soft ground upon which the administration is attempting to build its case, anti-terrorism remains a key element of the relationship between the United States and the region. As Adam Isacson notes, "[T]he word 'terrorism' appears as a justification for military aid in 16 of the Western Hemisphere country narratives in the State Department's 2005 congressional presentation document for foreign aid programs."[95] In this document, it is mentioned that "Argentine officials [were brought] to the United States for valuable counter-terrorism briefings and training," Bolivia has received "equipment and training for the Bolivian Army's new Counterterrorism Unit," and U.S. funding "will train Dominican forces capable of responding to terrorist threats."[96]

While the United States has sought to overplay an issue that is not really there, it has underplayed an issue that is: racism against people of African descent and indigenous populations. The Bush era of color blindness has coincided with the most determined period of resistance and dissent among the regions racial and ethnic marginalized communities in recent history. The irony is compounded by the fact that the two highest ranking officials in the administration, whose job entailed being aware of the political and social dynamics of other states and how those impacted on their foreign policy, were Powell and Rice.

Race in the Americas

While the administration has chosen to ignore issues of race in the Americas, activists in the region and in the United States have found solidarity with each other and become voices of resistance to discrimination, human rights violations, and neo-liberal policies. Across the region people of African descent and indigenous organizations have risen up and challenged structures and discourses of racism, and even some governments have acknowledged the impact of slavery and racialized colonialization, and continuing discrimination. It is estimated that people of African descent comprise about 29 percent (150 million) and indigenous people about 8 percent (40 million) of the region's population.[97]

Race consciousness among people of African descent has been expressed more publicly in recent years. This has manifested itself in the formation of networks, campaigns, educational materials, new policies, and national, regional, and international conferences. Histories, novels, and scholarly studies have also proliferated.

Continuing a long history of interaction, black Americans have engaged with contemporary anti-racist activists from the region, black and otherwise. During the preparation for the World Conference against Racism (WCAR), a caucus comprised of people of African descent was formed at the preparatory conference in Chile in December 2000 that included blacks from Canada, the United States, and all of Latin America and the Caribbean. In the declaration issued by the NGO Forum in Santiago, it was stated, "We call upon all persons of indigenous or African descent to recognize their cultural tradition that has until now been submerged or dominated, and to claim their place in the universal and American struggle against the racism and discrimination which impairs their rights, also, to identity and social and cultural equality."[98] These activists in particular felt angered at the negative position toward the conference taken by Rice (and later Powell) on behalf of the Bush administration.

An important symbolic act of recognition of the situation of Afro-Latinos took place on July 18, 2005. The U.S. House of Representatives passed H. Con. Res. 175 that "recognizes and honors African descendants in the Americas for their contributions to the economic, social, and cultural fabric of the countries in the Americas, particularly in Latin American and Caribbean societies" and "recognizes that as a result of their skin color and ancestry, African descendants in the Americas have wrongfully experienced economic, social, and political injustices." The vote was 382 to 6, the latter all Republicans. Rep. Charles Rangel, one of the founding members of the Congressional Black Caucus and the sponsor of the resolution, stated in a press release, "Passage of the resolution marks the long-awaited crossing of a threshold for the U.S. It signifies the recognition by the House of Representatives that race is an important issue in the Caribbean and Latin America. It acknowledges the impact of slavery in the region and encourages the U.S. and international community to work to address the issue of poverty among those populations."[99]

Many believe that a nodal point in the long history of struggle against racism in the region was the participation of blacks and indigenous peoples from the region in the WCAR. In Brazil, activists argue that the mobilization of civil society groups to participate in WCAR was significant and resulted in advancing the struggle against racism in their country. Scholars Luiz Barcelos and Rachel Menezes estimate that more than half of the nation's 180 million are of African descent. As they go on to note,[100]

> Brazilian black activists gathered enough human and financial resources to send one of the largest and most active groups of Afro-descendants to Durban. The government's official delegation was headed by the Minister of Justice. This successful mobilization had a very positive impact at home. For one, it helped raise public awareness to the many problems confronting Brazilians of African descent—including pervasive racial discrimination and limited access to education, health and other public services . . . the Conference acted as a welcome catalyst for a long overdue debate on how to effectively address racial inequality.[101]

Subsequent to WCAR, Brazil's black movement continued to grow and win victories in the battle for equality and ending racism. The momentum from the conference is seen as qualitatively contributing to the passage of affirmative action in a series of bills—Presidential Degree No. 4.228 (May 13, 2002); PL 650/99 (2002); and Federal Law No. 10.639 (January 9, 2003)—following several decades of frustration and rejection.[102] In April 2005, on a five-country trip to Africa, President Luiz Inacio Lula da Silva apologized for Brazil's role in the African slave trade and slavery. In a speech at a slave castle in Senegal, he stated, "I want to tell you . . . that I had no responsibility for what happened in the 16th, 17th and 18th Centuries but I ask your forgiveness for what we did to black people."[103]

The crisis situation faced by Afro-Colombians has been acknowledged by black American legislators who have united with their demands and for addressing the issues and the ways that they have been victimized by the U.S.-sponsored war on drugs. Black congressmember Sheila Jackson Lee has spoken out on this issue. In a statement on the Burton Amendment to H.R. 2601, "The Foreign Relations Authorization Act," she wrote, "To truly win the war on drugs we must take action to help sectors of Colombian society most adversely affected. These communities; the poor, indigenous, and afro-Colombians, are most often the worst affected from the violence associated with the drug trade. The social marginalization that these groups already face is exacerbated intensely by the conflict."[104]

In the name of the war on drugs, Afro-Colombians have been displaced from their land, kidnapped, murdered, and forced into both drug gangs and paramilitary organizations. The area of Choco, which is about 75 percent black, has the largest number of internally displaced persons in the country. People in the region have little or no access to good housing, schools, health care, or other basic services. Jackson Lee states, "We must insist that the U.S government provide more aid to Afro-Colombian regions. American resources must be used to help alleviate the pain and suffering on the part of Afro-Colombians and provide them access to a better, more stable, livelihood."[105]

On the issue of race, Venezuela stands out for a number of reasons not the least being that President Chavez is himself of African and indigenous background. He has been called "Venezuela's first multiracial president" and much worse by his enemies. Among Venezuela's elite and in the right-wing media, he has been referred to as a "mono" (monkey) and "Nigger."[106]

It is estimated that about 60 percent of the population of Venezuela are people of African descent, about 7 million people.[107] Under Chavez, Afro-Venezuelans and indigenous peoples have made some political and policy gains. In 2002, there were three black state governors, a black secretary of education, two indigenous Venezuelan congresspersons, and new laws were passed that protected the land rights of black and indigenous farmers.[108] And they are demanding more.

One organization, the Network of Afro-Venezuelan Organizations, made up of thirty groups in that country, is lobbying for a number of reforms that include:

[A] reform of the constitution, so that it recognizes the nation's multi-ethnicity and respects Afro-Venezuelan rights; the creation of a new census that categorizes and counts Venezuela's Black population; the acknowledgement of Afro-Venezuelan history in school curriculum; the creation of a federal-level ministry to implement the World Conference Against Racism's "Durban Plan of Action"; the creation of a ministry to implement UNESCO's Convention on Diversity; and the creation of an Afro-Venezuelan Ministry, to address the everyday lives of Blacks in the country.[109]

The activism of Afro-Venezuelans has paid off in a number of ways. The national assembly officially declared May 10 "Afro-Venezuelan Day," which commemorates the May 10, 1795, slave uprising led by black Venezuelan Jose Leonardo Chirino, and Chavez has formally established a Presidential Commission against Racism in Venezuela.[110]

In Mexico, black American solidarity with Afro-Mexicans emerged as a result of two back-to-back controversies. In May 2005, Mexican president Vincente Fox made the statement that, "There is no doubt that Mexicans, filled with dignity, willingness and ability to work are doing jobs that not even blacks want to do there in the United States." He was criticized severely by a number of black American leaders for perpetuating a stereotype that blacks are at the bottom and perhaps should be willing to take jobs that willing and dignified Mexicans are doing. Given that most poor people in the United States are white, a more appropriate comparison, if one was to be made at all, would have been to talk about the job situation of the poor overall. Fox met with Rev. Jesse Jackson and later acknowledged that his remarks may have been seen as offensive, but did not issue a full and unambiguous apology.

This incident was followed by the release of a stamp in June 2005 with the image of Memin Pinguin, a 1940s Mexican comic book character drawn with stereotypical thick lips and a large flat nose, caricatures long associated with racist portrayals of blacks. When the first known response of denunciation came from black Americans, Fox and other Mexican officials attempted to brush off the controversy by stating that Memin Pinguin is a lovable character that has no racial meaning and that no one in Mexico was offended. That argument was blown away when the Asociacion Mexico Negro (Association of Black Mexico), an organization representing more 50,000 black Mexicans, sent a letter to Fox stating, "Memin Pinguin rewards, celebrates, typifies and cements the distorted, mocking, stereotypical and limited vision of black people in general."[111] A number of black and Latino American activists including the NAACP, Rainbow/PUSH Coalition, National Council of La Raza, and National Urban League were offended at the image and called on Fox to apologize which he did not.[112] Again Rev. Jesse Jackson and also Rev. Al Sharpton both met separately with Fox in Mexico, who refused to rescind the stamp or acknowledge their criticisms. Although the White House ignored the first controversy, Press Secretary Scott McClellan made a general statement in reference to the controversy saying "racial stereotypes are offensive no matter what their origin."[113]

On both sides of the borders, activists note the long history of black American interactions and engagement with Mexico. In the latter years of slavery in the United States, decades after it had been outlawed in Mexico, many thousands of escaped blacks went to Mexico and formed maroon societies. As Elizabeth

Martínez writes, "One record shows 4,000 crossing in a relatively short period."[114] The coming of black Americans was preceded by a longer history of blacks in Mexico forming their own maroon societies, the most famous of which was founded by black Mexican Gaspar Yanga, who in 1570 led a band of escaped slaves into the mountains and, in 1609, negotiated an agreement with the Spanish to end their war and founded the first free town in the Americas today known as Yanga in the Veracruz region of Mexico.

While the usually outspoken Rice has responded to virtually every single utterance of Chavez in Venezuela, she remained silent on these two incidents with Mexico. Referring to the stamp incident, Rev. Jesse Jackson stated, "I would think Secretary Rice would be personally demeaned by such a character," and he called upon her to speak on the issue as a matter of national diplomacy.[115] If she was insulted, her views were kept private.

Even in Argentina, a nation that seems to epitomize white Latino-ness, its black past is emerging and finding political expression among Afro-Argentines. According to newly documented research, Argentina had a substantial black population in the early nineteenth century, as much 30 percent of the population was black. Yet, by 1887, according to official records, it had dropped to about 1.8 percent of the population. This figure has more or less been accepted since that period. However, according to private census research and even small representative DNA samples, 10 percent of the population is of African descent. Afro-Argentines are seeking to have a question on African ancestry placed on the 2011 national census.[116]

These issues of blackness underscore the racial dimensions of Latin American societies and the need to consider them as a critical dimension of U.S. foreign policy toward the region. While it should not be the only concern of black policy-makers and legislators, neither should it be ignored. By history and temper, black officials are in the best position to ensure that the wide range of concerns of citizens of the region, including racial ones, are addressed. During their tenure at the State Department, neither Powell nor Rice have spoken out on these issues and given hope to those who are most marginalized that there is a sympathetic ear in the Bush White House.

Conclusion

Close to home, the Bush administration has sought to squeeze further states that suffer from some of the worst poverty and wealth inequities in the world. Its agenda has been insensitive to the needs of the region, and it has forced economic policies that by many measures will continue the downward spiral that has existed for decades. Its call for democracy rings hollow as it has supported and even cheered undemocratic and anti-democratic political maneuvers and activities. And, finally, it has demonstrated an obsessive desire to foster a post–September 11 security framework on a region that needs jobs more than anti-terrorist training, fair immigration policies more than helicopters, and respect for international and regional law more than unilateralist demands for special treatment.

Powell and Rice helped to draft and implement these policies. When the administration, including them both, was not ignoring the real needs of the region, it was railing against its perceived enemies and threatening its potential allies. Even states that were pre-disposed to following U.S. dictates, such as Jamaica and Mexico, found themselves the target of U.S. hubris and harangues from Powell and Rice.

The rise of black movements in the region is remapping the politics of states in Central and South America. Marginalized for decades, if not centuries, new policy initiatives and greater unity by Afro-Latinos and indigenous peoples, which include support from outside the region, promises substantial changes in the years ahead. It is in the interest of the United States to understand and work with these communities as they struggle to bring genuine democracy into play. Powell failed to make that link, despite having a personal connection to the region, and, in the first year of her tenure as secretary of state, so has Rice.

Eight

Washed Up: The Legacies of Powell and Rice (and Bush)

It was as if all of us were already pronounced dead. As if somebody already had the body bags. Wasn't nobody coming to get us.

Tony Cash, one of thousands trapped at the New Orleans Convention Center after New Orleans flooded[1]

It would take an incident on the scale of an alien invasion to overshadow the political disaster and fallout that befell the Bush administration in the aftermath of Hurricane Katrina in August-September 2005. After spending four-and-a-half years either evading issues of race and poverty, at the domestic and global scale, or, worse, exacerbating the nation's racial divide under the cover of the ideology of color blindness, denials of the raw racial and class gaps of contemporary U.S. society were washed away in the flood waters that drowned both New Orleans and the Bush presidency. Before it was embarrassed into action, the Bush administration allowed the world to witness horrifying images of desperate, starving, and dying (and, indeed, dead) mostly black people begging for an assistance that came criminally late if at all. Cornered, Bush could no longer speak in the vagueness of "ownership society," "the soft bigotry of low expectations," and "look at Condi and Colin," media-ready spin that denies that racism and glaring class inequality exist and need to be addressed. As writer Mike Davis points out, "Disasters in American history have almost always been theaters of class struggle and racial struggle."[2]

September 11, the Iraq war, and the Katrina disaster are chain-linked events operating through the prism of a governing philosophy that seeks the end of the welfare state and the institutionalization of the corporate state and a global objective of unchallenged and unchallengeable hegemony. The undermining of the state's capacity to care effectively for and safeguard its citizens and residents was driven by the strategy of shifting funding away from social programs toward military and economic programs that furthered hegemonic aspirations and disproportionate benefits to the nation's elite. Central to this strategy was a requirement of winning popular domestic support for an anti-government agenda that assumed there was no longer a need for downward wealth redistribution and state social intervention. Within this context, conservative use of the race card manifest itself in two forms: racializing poverty and, paradoxically, promoting a thesis of color blindness. From Reagan to Bush to Clinton and to another Bush, the pervasive images of black "welfare queen" recipients have underscored studies that demonstrate that support or non-support for welfare is linked to perceptions of the racial identity of the recipients, that is, the more whites believe welfare recipients are black, they less they support welfare.[3] At the same time, however, it was necessary to promote the view that race no longer determined one's destiny or life chances. Thus, rather than confront the institutional nature of racism, phenotype diversity grew to be the racial strategy of choice for both parties as it became clear that they did not require ideological compromise with more than a few racial minorities willing to embrace any range of doctrines. Colin Powell and Condoleezza Rice not only sufficed the domestic dimension of this strategy but gave it an international cache given their expertise in international relations.

For nearly five years, the Bush administration was able to avoid the issues of racial and class inequality and suffering. Although substantial and in many instances growing inequities existed, they became invisible and erased. As noted earlier, when Bush mentioned race at all, it was to lambaste civil rights leaders, honor anti–civil rights black conservatives, or, most cynically, use race to promote a domestic policy agenda, such as proposals to change Social Security or bankruptcy laws, that actually would have the consequence of hurting the nation's poor or racial minorities. Although poverty has increased every year of the Bush tenure, mostly affecting poor whites, the administration has been able to deflect the issue because the popular face of poverty is black and urban, two characteristics that are demonized by Bush's constituency. While the Congressional Black Caucus and other black, Latino, Asian, and Native American leaders continued non-stop to raise these issues, Republicans on Capitol Hill united with the administration in excluding these concerns from the policy and political agendas. It was, therefore, with a great amount of confidence that Bush could certainly feel that he could continue his policy of criminal neglect of the plight of the country's poor and excluded while pressing a global agenda of hegemony.

And then came Hurricane Katrina. While one administration-fueled disaster—September 11—rescued Bush and allowed him to construct a myth of strong, nearly flawless leadership leading an efficient and capable administration, another would expose this façade, as well as the destructive and harmful limits of a governing philosophy that could not do what Bush counted on to be the cornerstone of his legacy: that his administration protected citizens against enemies from without and within. The Katrina fiasco demonstrated that for many U.S. citizens that what they needed most was protection from an uncaring and crony-packed administration whose priorities had little to due with meeting the genuine needs of the nation.

The post–Hurricane Katrina calamity was a history-changing event. It redefined the character of the Bush presidency exposing its lack of compassion, competence, integrity, strength, and ability to protect the people of the United States. It forced a heretofore non-existent debate within the anti-government Republican Party over its governing philosophy and strategy and what will be needed to maintain its political hegemony over the nation. It demonstrated, contrary to both Republican and Democratic conservative orthodoxy, that a sufficiently robust and responsive federal government is necessary. It generated an unprecedented international humiliation where offers of foreign aid from even the smallest countries and Bush's most hated enemies had to be acknowledged humbly. It solidified opposition to the Iraq war and the ability of the administration to launch further foreign military operations. It ignited the greatest full-scale humanitarian mobilization of the American people, and within the African American, Native American, Asian American, and Latino communities, perhaps ever attempted in the nation's history. It shook the nation out of a three-decade blindness regarding racial and class disparities that has come to dominate U.S. political culture since the end of the heyday of the civil rights era.

As had been the case on a number of earlier issues, in the aftermath of Hurricane Katrina, Bush was forced to bring race off the shelf and press Rice into race relations repair duty. With Powell banished and outside of the administration, and even (mildly) criticizing the administration, Bush relied on Rice to take a lead in defending the administration against charges of racial insensitivity, at best, and outright racial discrimination at worse raised by liberal black, Latino, and Native American leaders and activists, rapper Kayne West, many Democrats, and even some conservatives. Rice took to the airwaves and even went to Alabama, her birthplace (but not her residence since the mid-1960s), to explain why Bush was not a racist. Rather than explain how he had failed to address any of the concerns that had been raised for years by blacks and others, she argued against what she claimed were unfair statements that were never specifically attributed to anyone in particular. She stated, "I find it very strange to think that people would think that the president of the United States would sit deciding who ought to be helped on the basis of color, most especially this president. What evidence is there that this is the case? Why would you say such a thing?"[4] Setting aside the fact that she made up this argument and had no evidence that anyone made such a statement, Rice evaded the fundamental issue that her president had little to demonstrate that his administration had sought seriously to take on the nation's poverty or its racial divisions, both of which had grown under the Bush administration. When she was asked on the *Tavis Smiley Show*, whether she believed there were race and class dimensions related to Katrina, she stated,

> I do believe that we are dealing with the fact that there are pockets of America which are very poor and that some of those pockets of America have a bad combination of race and poverty. I do believe that. I'm from the South and I know that there are still vestiges of the Old South that have to be dealt with. And one of the questions is going to be, in the longer run, how, when we start to rebuild, do we address what was clearly an underlying social problem . . . we've always known that race and poverty is a particularly bad witches brew. We know that. But as we address rebuilding, how do we make certain that we don't rebuild on that basis but we rebuild on a new basis? That is a legitimate question for our future endeavors. But this idea that somehow there was a racial dimension to the rescue effort or to trying to help people, it's just not true. And if people are going to say it, they ought to be made to defend why they would say such a thing.[5]

Here Rice reduces race and poverty to basically a southern issue that is a lingering vestige of the old South. She speaks of "pockets" of poverty, a reductive term that elides the widespread and long-term nature of the nation's poor in urban and rural areas across the country. The "underlying problem" that Rice claims that the administration knows about has never made its way into a priority or seemingly even an afterthought for Bush. The number of people in the United States below the official poverty line was 37.0 million in 2004, 1.1 million more than in 2003, which constituted a poverty rate of 12.7 percent.[6] Poverty is defined by the Office of Management and Budget and updated for inflation using the Consumer Price Index, and, in 2003, was officially noted as $19,307 for a family of four; $15,067 for a family of three; $12,334 for a family of two; and $9,645 for unrelated individuals.

By race, the poverty rate for non-Hispanic whites was 8.6 percent, who constituted 44 percent of the poor; for blacks 24.7 percent; for Asians 9.8 percent, for Hispanics of all races 21.9 percent, and for American Indians and Alaska natives 23.2 percent.[7] One-third of America's poor are children reflecting significant increases since 2000. As the Children's Defense Fund notes,

The number of poor Latino children has increased by 774,000 (23%), the number of poor Black children increased by 293,000 (8.4%), and the number of poor White (non-Latino) children by 322,000 (7%). Nearly one million black children live not just in poverty, but in extreme poverty. That is the greatest number of black children trapped in dire poverty since the early 1980s. Extreme poverty is defined as living with an annual income that is less than $7,610 for a family of three.[8]

Bush's current agenda to privatize Social Security, which he vowed to revive just days before Katrina hit, would increase poverty among seniors of color. Without Social Security, fully 60 percent of African American seniors would be poor, along with 55 percent of Latinos and 26 percent of American Indians.[9]

The war in Iraq, although vehemently denied, also had a direct impact on the ability of the administration to respond to the Katrina crisis. The estimated $4-5 billion a month spent on the war absorbed badly needed funding to the poorest cities and states in the country. The National Priorities Project has estimated how much state and local communities are losing as a result of the Iraq war. For the states most severely devastated by the inadequate and incompetent response by the Bush administration, the costs were $2 billion for Alabama, $918.7 million for Mississippi, and $1.7 billion for Louisiana. This translated into $79.7 million for Baton Rouge and $151.6 million for New Orleans. Like Bush, Rice argued that the war was unrelated to the Katrina crisis. In addition, National Guard troops that should have been in the affected states assisting in evacuation, rescue, and restoration operations were in Iraq. More than 35 percent of Louisiana's National Guard were deployed as well as 40 percent of those from Mississippi.[10]

Further, her argument that Bush and the Bush administration cares about poor people was undermined as it was revealed that while the flood waters were rising dramatically in New Orleans and people were dying or caught up in life-threatening circumstances, images that were by then ubiquitous on all the television news shows, newspapers, and the Internet, she was in New York City taking in a Broadway play (*Spamalot*), where she was reportedly booed, and shopping for expensive shoes (Ferragamo); Bush was attending fundraisers; and Cheney was house-shopping.[11] This level of insensitivity fueled the rapid decline in Bush's popularity, already at its lowest point in the days before Katrina hit.

The vast racial divide that Rice, Bush, and the administration refuse to see is captured in polls taken in the wake of Katrina. Survey data demonstrated that whites and blacks had very different views on the racial dimensions of Katrina. According to a survey released by the Pew Research Center in early September

2005, while 66 percent of blacks thought the government response would have been faster if most of the victims had been white, only 17 percent of whites felt that way. Along these lines, only 19 percent of blacks felt the government response was excellent or good, while 41 percent of whites thought so. Another gap was identified when respondents were asked if racial inequality was still a major problem. Again, while 71 percent of blacks thought so, only 32 percent of whites did. Much of this divide translated into how respondents felt about Bush. With his overall approval ratings at a record low, Bush's approval rating among blacks was at 15 percent, 22 percent among other people of color, and 45 percent for whites.

Meanwhile, Powell was raising criticisms of the response by the administration no doubt reifying its decision to send him on his way. Consistent with the tentativeness that marked his tenure as secretary of state, he disclaimed any racial overtones to the response by the Bush administration and state and local officials as he chastised it for its slow response. He stated in an interview, "When you look at those who weren't able to get out, it should have been a blinding flash of the obvious to everybody that when you order a mandatory evacuation, you can't expect everybody to evacuate on their own. These are people who don't have credit cards; only one in 10 families at that economic level in New Orleans have a car. So it wasn't a racial thing—but poverty disproportionately affects African-Americans in this country. And it happened because they were poor."[12] Powell, as did Rice, lets the Bush administration off the hook, and does not explore why poverty disproportionately affects African Americans in the first place or the policies of the Bush administration that worsen the problems or failed to address the issue. However, Powell did recognize in a way that the administration did not, until it was forced to, that the evacuation essentially left people with no means to evacuate in distress, their lives changed forever, leaving many hundreds to die.

Global Perspective on the Legacy of Powell and Rice

The presence of Powell and Rice in the Bush administration not only (re)-raised the issue of race in the making of U.S. foreign policy, but the larger questions of race, class, and gender inequality in contemporary U.S. society. For many outside of the communities of color, these concerns have been dormant for the last quarter century as the ideology of color blindness has been accepted by most white Americans. Notwithstanding periodic eruptions such as the 1992 Los Angeles uprising, the Million Man March, the O. J. Simpson and Michael Jackson trials, the University of Michigan affirmative action case, and most recently the Hurricane Katrina disaster, race inequality has been pushed to the margins of U.S. policy concerns. Both major parties essentially nationalized the "southern strategy" of reaching out to middle-class, suburban whites while giving, at best, symbolic and rhetorical flourish to the ideas of ending across-the-board racial disparities. The color-blind society construct, while not necessarily winning the debate, provided sufficient political cover and confusion to allow public officials, journalists, scholars, and others to conclude that other than a few embittered and out-of-touch civil rights leaders, racism no longer shaped U.S. domestic or foreign policy. At the core of this trope, in the Bush administration was the view that phenotype (and gender) diversity constituted genuine racial progress and signaled that a racism-free America had arrived. And exhibits number one and two, for many, were Powell and Rice.

The legacy of Powell and Rice in the Bush administration is tied fundamentally to the success or failure of the administration itself. On the defining issues of the administration—the September 11 attacks, the Iraq war, and the Katrina fallout—the judgment on Bush is growing harsher by the day. Broad sectors of U.S. society including non-partisan scholars, policy-makers of both major parties, and surveys of popular opinion have reached a consensus that the Bush administration, for ideological purposes, did not do enough to prevent these disasters, reacted with political interests above all else when they occurred, and has attempted to construct revised narratives that distort the truth about its less than stellar role as the catastrophic dimensions became clear. Bush has appeared mostly hapless and robotic, and, has consciously slept through history to paraphrase Haynes Johnson's famous description of Ronald Reagan leaving the heavy lifting to Powell, Rice, and other administration officials. That Powell and Rice committed themselves to an administration that let blind ideological rigidity override competence, fairness, tolerance, and restraint, says much. More than innocent bystanders or dupes, both are implicated in Bush's failed presidency as part of the insider team and council that created and implemented his vision and agenda. Neither, to this day, has disavowed the Bush domestic and international doctrine of hegemony and power politics at the expense of domestic progress and global cooperation and development.

International opinion about the departure of Powell and elevation of Rice fell into five categories, which included: (1) those who saw Powell's resignation as a loss, (2) those who saw the end of Powell's tenure as having no impact on U.S. foreign policy, (3) those who believed that Powell's legacy was sealed by his February 2003 U.N. speech, (4) those who worried about Rice's elevation to secretary of state, and (5) those who believed that Rice's closeness to Bush would generate a more honest reading of U.S. foreign policy than Powell provided. There were those who argued that Powell's departure was a loss for the administration and the world. Many viewed him as the last savior—a lone dove—of a

U.S. administration whose foreign policy initiatives were alienating and destructive. An editorial in Israel's *Yediot Aharonot*, stated, "In this sense, it is not just Powell that is going home. He is taking with him an outlook that says that the unprecedented power America wields in the world means responsibility, and not just something to justify any forcible action. His departure marks the disappearance of the belief that the United States should lead wisely, in consent with and out of consideration for others, while insisting on domestic consensus and persuasive arguments."[13]

Some viewed Powell's resignation as a setback for their specific regional or national concerns. Grenada's prime minister Keith Mitchell, who is also chairman of CARICOM, stated, he believed that Powell is a "genuine friend of the region" and "we know his heart was in the Caribbean in a general sense and therefore we certainly see it as a loss for the region."[14] Germany's *Die Welt* wrote, "For Europeans, the US Secretary of State was the John Kerry of the Bush administration; the last hope on this side of the Atlantic and a man who stood for a reasonable and measured foreign policy."[15]

However, there were many others who contended that he was a marginalized and ultimately ineffective secretary of state and that his exit would have no impact on the direction of U.S. foreign policy. Kuala Lumpur's Berita Harian wrote, "The resignation of US Secretary of State Colin Powell, who strongly defended the lies of President George W Bush that Iraq had weapons of mass destruction (WMD) will not change the chaotic situation in Baghdad, the devastation of Al-Fallujah and the ruthless killings of Palestinian civilians by Israeli troops."[16]

Eventually most commentators made note of his February 5, 2003, speech at the United Nations and how it permanently tarnished his legacy and became a decisive and defining low point in his career. India's *The Statesman* stated, "In what was hardly his finest hour he was forced to make a fictitious case for Iraq's possession of WMD in front of the UN General Assembly, as part of Bush's drive to war."[17] South Africa's Barry Mthombothi was especially harsh in his criticisms of Powell referring to him as Bush's "useful idiot" and a "damaged man."[18]

While Powell received his share of praises and criticisms, views of Rice upon her coming into the office of secretary of state were decidedly more negative. Many argued that her elevation would strengthen the hand of hardliners. The *Beijing News* wrote, "Although Rice cannot simply be classed as a hard-liner, her taking up the post of secretary of state is undoubtedly a significant sign that the hard-liners are moving onto the diplomatic stage."[19]

Outside of Asia, many in the Middle East felt the same. In Oman, *Al-Watan* wrote, "The resignation of Powell and the appointment of Condoleezza Rice in his place strengthens the position of the New Conservatives in the Bush Administration which will be, according to observers, inclined to adopt more arrogant policies and likely to use excessive force like the storming of Al-Fallujah soon after Bush's reelection for a second term and Powell's resignation."[20]

Newspapers in the Middle East, in particular, viewed the elevation of Rice as detrimental to their interests. In Saudi Arabia, an editorial stated, "With the departure of US Secretary of State Colin Powell from the Bush Administration, the hawks will be exclusively in charge of the US foreign policies over the next four years. This should be seen as a bad omen not only for America but for the whole world, especially the Arab region.[21] Yet, it was also argued, however, that because Rice was so close to Bush she would be more reflective of the administration's politics as secretary becoming the world's "second strongest person in the U.S.,"[22] and that, unlike Powell, when she spoke she would truly represent Bush's views. South Africa's *The Star* wrote that Rice "sings from the same hymn sheet as her boss."[23]

The *Financial Times* (German edition) also expressed this more gracious view writing nicknames given by the media such as "Steel Magnolia," "Terminatrix," and "Warrior Princess," were unwarranted, and that Rice "though unpopular, can take the stage with her master's voice because, for years, Bush has kept her on a very short leash. . . . What the new secretary of state says will often bring displeasure to international dialogue partners, but at least they'll be able to assume the president has similar thoughts."[24]

Powell and Rice in Retrospect

> I want to be measured as Secretary of State, not as the black Secretary of State.
>
> Colin Powell[25]

And so he was. Domestic opinions on Powell's tenure during Bush's first term and Rice's role in both have focused mostly on their commitment to the Bush doctrine and their capabilities in implementing it. Like Bush, their political fates in the first term were sealed by the September 11 attacks and the subsequent war on terrorism and the Iraq war. For the most part, conservatives have worshiped the loyalty of Rice and winched at the mere mention of Powell and his time at the State Department.

Powell was also evaluated by some observers regarding his leadership at the State Department. Even those who disagreed with his support for Bush's policies regarding Iraq and other issues were praiseworthy of his management. As foreign policy expert Dennis Jett noted, "He was the kind of general who always took care of his troops. His stature helped boost State's budget, allowing equipment upgrades and additional hiring. He attended functions where secretaries had rarely been sighted."[26]

On his role in the administration, however, Jett states, "Powell moderated very little and stayed as long as he did out of self-interest, not national interest. . . . He lied about the justifications for the war just as often as other key administration officials did."[27]

Powell's role in the administration was a bad marriage from the beginning. In many ways, he displayed symptoms of the "battered wife syndrome." Though abused by the administration time and time again, he did not leave and deluded himself that his presence was having a qualitative impact on the administration's foreign policy direction. He tended to respond to differences by acting surreptitiously through back channels to inject his genuine opinion into the public debate. While Bush and Cheney had *Fox News*, Powell had Bob Woodward and other reporters through which he could leak his views. He was successful to some degree in implementing his policy options, in the face of White House opposition, in dealing with China, India, and Libya. But on a number of issues, such as six-party talks around North Korea or having a more balanced policy on the Palestinian-Israeli conflict, he was overruled by Bush. And on the defining issue of the day, the Iraq war, he was used, abused, and marginalized. Liberals have been pretty consistent in criticizing them both Powell and Rice, although fear of racism accusations seems to have muted those criticisms somewhat. While the blacks have split somewhat along ideological lines, Powell has certainly fared better than Rice in terms of reception within the broader black community overall.

The balance sheet on Powell may mellow over time, but overall many, if not most, commentators consider his tenure a disappointment by any set of measures. What was significant about the UN speech is not that it delivered false information, which is Powell's biggest regret, but that Powell delivered it in the first place. He has been equivocal in accepting responsibility for the role of the speech in justifying the launch of the U.S.-led invasion.

Powell, of course, vehemently defends his stature in the Bush administration. Being a moderate in an extremist administration, he wanted the impossible: a reputation for integrity and for loyalty. He challenges the popular notion that he and his views were irrelevant. He stated, somewhat desperately, in an interview in *The Crisis*, the magazine of the NAACP, "I can assure you that I make my voice heard, and if you wrote a balance sheet as to where my advice has been ignored and where my advice has essentially helped shape policy, I'll put money on it, my side."[28] Giving an interview in *The Crisis* guaranteed that one of

Powell's strongest bases of support would be stroked and be fed an alternative view of his position inside the administration.

Despite his efforts to strike a balance between his own moderate, traditional Republican views and the confrontational, anti-diplomatic style of the Bush foreign policy team in general, the short view of history on Powell has been harsh. He did play a key role on a number of foreign policy concerns including addressing the North Korean nuclear issue, Libya's disarmament, Russia's war in Chenchnya, and Iran's nuclear weapons program among others. Yet, even on these issues, he was overruled when he attempted to continue what he felt were solid policy initiatives started under the Clinton administration such as with North Korea.[29]

His moderating views were shelved and he was often on the bench, used only to defend the team. In practice, he was ultimately behind a president whose worldview seemed to conflict with his own. He was shrewd enough to find avenues that served as vehicles for his rebellious ideas but at the same time would not hold him completely accountable for his contradictory behavior. He was out maneuvered and out-powered by Cheney and his neo-con mob who, according to Woodward, he referred to as a "Gestapo office." In the final analysis, Powell has been complicit in diminishing his own stature and legacy. Entering the administration as perhaps the one individual with the most international standing and respect, he departed as a near tragic figure whose influence ebbed with each moment he remained in office.

For Rice, race is non-determinant. Along these lines, her views appear to be nearly identical to that of Bush. She clearly acknowledges her racial heritage and demonstrates, in a broad stroke, a historical awareness that is probably alien to most—if not all—of the Bush administration's top officials. However, she has employed that knowledge in the service of the administration and fails to connect ongoing racial disparities and inequality with the contemporary public policy priorities and perspective of the Bush administration, in the immediacy, and with U.S. policy frameworks by both major parties since the heyday of the civil rights movement. What Rice views as progress in the form of diversity appointments and individual achievements is assessed by others as a retreat from a serious examination of persisting racial disparities affecting millions of blacks and other people of color.

Like Powell, however, Rice will be and should be principally judged on her role as a foreign policy expert and leading member of the Bush inner circle. Unlike Powell, she has not been ambiguous in demonstrating her loyalty and enthusiasm for the Bush nee Rice doctrine. As noted throughout this work, Rice was as enthusiastic about going to war as anyone in the administration. If that meant presenting a distorted picture of the evidence, defending Bush's false-hoods, bullying allies, or rewriting the history of her role and others in the buildup for the war, then those were the tasks that had to be done.

Though few challenge her training, expertise, intellect, and scholarly capa-bilities, an assessment of work in the jobs and tasks she held in the Bush admin-istration raises serious questions about whether she was in a position actually to do the job and handle politically that role she was assigned. The September 11 attacks occurred during her tenure as national security advisor. And so did the develop-ment of arguments that proved totally to be false about going to war with Sadaam Hussein. After the war started, and chaos reigned, she was put in charge with great fanfare of the so-called "Iraq stabilization program," a project that came and went in a flash. Most observers felt that her position as national security advisor was overrun by Cheney and Rumsfeld. Perhaps most important, her understanding of the role of the national security advisor was to first and foremost give Bush a veneer of political protection, which may or may not have comported with accurate, though ideologically disappointing information.

She was no doubt conscious of the problems that came from national security advisors who demonstrated a great deal of independence, such as Henry Kis-singer, from the president they were supposed to serve. However, there were strong indications that perhaps Rice was too close to Bush and lost the ability to be objective and willing to deliver bad news. The issue of closeness should have not really mattered one way or the other though because the role of advisors should be first to serve the interests of the people of the United States. Another ex-planation is that Rice is a true believer. There is virtually no record of Rice demonstrating the slightest crack in implementing the Bush agenda. Indeed, much of the Bush agenda on foreign policy has Rice's imprint.

In her first year as secretary of state, Rice seemed re-energized. No longer under the direct authority or clout of Cheney and Rumsfeld, she threw herself into the broad array of U.S. foreign policy issues and hit the road. She traveled to Europe, Asia, Africa, and the Americas to meet with foreign leaders at a pace that will far outstrip Powell's four years of travel. Behind all of this activity, however, there was little evidence of fixing the problems that ostensibly Powell left behind. Iraq remained as intractable as ever with little sign that the insurgency was weakening, as Cheney and Rice declared on a regular basis. Broader Middle East policy was not advancing with any visible sign of significant engagement by the State Department. While relations with Europeans eased, none of the major policy differences were resolved and seemed to be languishing. Rice was finding it particularly difficult to find friends in Latin America.

Despite the damage control and rekindling efforts by Rice to smooth rela-tionships between the Bush administration and the world, little progress was made due to the fact that few changes occurred in the policies that the United States has attempted to force upon the world. The evidence that the second term was not going to be moderated was expressed in the nomination and later recess appointment of John Bolton, who had a long record of antagonism toward the United Nations, to the post as U.S. ambassador. Rice was one of Bolton's strongest backers and resisted calls to pull his nomination when both Democrats and even some Republicans questioned his selection.

Ultimately, the whims of Powell and Rice mattered little. The strategic objective of the furtherance of hegemony drove the foreign policy and political agenda. Both essentially agreed with that objective and carried it out with a strong sense of mission and purpose. To the degree that race was useful for this project, it was employed; to the degree it was not, it was not employed.

The Alternative to Hegemony: Human Security, Human Rights, and the Crisis of Racial Disparities

What is required to reverse the agenda of hegemony is a new and challenging vision of what U.S. society as a whole, including the objective of eradication of inequalities, must become and a political strategy that seeks nothing short of achieving that goal. Evolving such a vision requires both a national and global rethinking on the issue of security and the elements that shape it.

The paradigm of *human security* offers a way out of the limits of the current framework of national security (or state security) that is used to rationalize hegemony. Human security focuses on people rather than states. It has been defined by the UN Commission on Human Security as security "to protect the vital core of all human lives in ways that enhance human freedoms and human fulfillment. . . . It means creating political, social, environmental, economic, military, and cultural systems that together give people the building blocks of survival, livelihood, and dignity."[30] Fundamentally, human security is about the empowerment of people to control the decisions that affect their lives and possibilities. Whereas national security functions as a state-implemented process determined by elite political and military actors, human security is a democratic initiative by which its very essence involves civil society, as well as the public and private sectors. A vibrant human security creates the conditions under which national security is able to most ably function and maintain legitimacy.

Human security is also directly linked with human rights and social justice. A number of groups have, correctly, long called racism a violation of human rights.[31] In the international community, most scholars and activists promote a broad definition of human rights that covers not only race, ethnic, religious, gender, and other discriminations, but also includes political, civil, economic, social, and cultural rights. In the post–Cold War era, a third wave is cascading across the international community.[32] Third wave human rights—taking place in an era of muted ideologies, economic and socio-cultural globalization, and a belief that human rights values and responsibilities extend to non-state actors, such as corporations and individuals—goes much further than in the past. In the current period, human rights activists and scholars universally agree that not only states but also the private sector, civil society groups, and individual abusers are capable of committing violations and should be held accountable, thus the call for and establishment of the International Criminal Court, Truth Commission, special tribunals, and international law suits. Another feature of the third wave is the effort to transpose regional and international human rights instruments into domestic law as in the case of the UK's Human Rights Act, a modified version of the European Convention on Human Rights.[33]

Activists have also demanded, and succeeded in many instances, in advocating that domestic courts exercise their authority, given that nearly all states have signed and ratified them, to make reference to international human rights instruments. This tact is part of a broader strategy to mainstream human rights through codification into domestic law and legal codes of practice. Another manifestation of third wave human rights is the effort to include human rights provisions in bi-lateral and multi-lateral treaties. This strategy has become a norm in the battle over trade agreements such as the North American Free Trade Agreement and in negotiations with the World Trade Organization.

These developments are important for black American activists as the struggle for racial equality is increasingly bound to other cross-cutting concerns and issues including foreign policy. From voting rights to racial profiling, there are relevant and insightful international references, many of which are embodied in treaties and other instruments that the U.S. government has signed and ratified already, treaties that the United States ostensibly is committed to observe legally. Whether that commitment is acknowledged is somewhat irrelevant. What is more important is the global connection of rights that are value added to the struggle for justice and equal opportunity in the United States. There has been no time in history when the link between the black struggle and the global justice movements has been so salient and needed.

To call for a human security and human rights agenda is to include also more organically discrimination and exclusions based on other variables such as gender, sexual orientation, disability, religion, political beliefs, and age among others. The multiple identities and multiple discriminations that characterize modern societies are best addressed by a framework that does not artificially separate and rank differences in a hierarchal manner. Inequality does indeed manifest differently, and this must be recognized. At the same time, collaborative efforts to develop public policies that address all discriminations must be preffered. It must be stressed, however, that human rights, as recognized around the world, are much more inclusive than just around discrimination based on identities. A human security framework with human rights at the center, *inter alia*, includes the right not to be tortured, a right for a family to be together, freedom of movement, right to asylum, and much more. Only a security policy that addresses both the problem of terrorist activity *and* the causes of terrorism with its roots in global insecurity issues, can win the confidence of the global community that U.S. anti-terrorism initiatives are more than thinly veiled covers for advancing American corporate and political interests. More important, human security is not just defensive but also developmental. It lays the foundation for the forward movement of societies and people regardless of the terrorist threat.

The tasks ahead for building this movement are daunting. The Bush so-called "war on terror" has become a political trump card that has been and will be used time and again to thwart advances on human rights and social justice concerns both inside and outside the United States. In many key areas where progress was being made—death penalty, voting rights, immigrant rights, religious tolerance, and so forth—there have been setbacks due to the Patriot Act and civil liberties violations on the part of the U.S. government. Not only has the administration been brazenly unapologetic, it is inscribing as many of these features as possible into legal and administrative decrees to guarantee their endurance no matter who is in the White House or in Congress. A movement for a human security and human rights movement must unite with progressive and liberal policy-makers and change the tide of public policy. Black members of Congress, many of whom participated in WCAR, have shown a determination to embrace and must be drawn more organically into the movement to the degree possible. Challenging and eradicating the doctrine of "states' rights," the other side of the coin of Bush's anti-government philosophy, is the major obstacle to reform in the areas of voting rights, criminal justice, and other arenas as well as foreign policy. Such a movement must revolutionize the current philosophy of public policy.

Human rights violations, by many names and in the form of economic, social, cultural, political and civil abuses, occur on a daily basis in the United States. We need to call them such. In retelling the history of black politics, particularly the history of the civil rights period, the battle for human rights must be given a more central role. The goal of mainstreaming human rights is a necessary step if the United States and the international community are to avoid Dr. King's uncharacteristically bleak prediction of a doomed world and instead achieve his hope of a world house "in which we have to live together—black and white, Easterner and Westerner, Gentile and Jew, Catholic and Protestant, Moslem and

Hindu—a family unduly separated in ideas, culture and interest, who, because we can never again live apart, must learn somehow to live with each other in peace."

Conclusion

> In practice, much of the international community would find it difficult
> to stand in the way of the determined course of the U.S. hegemon.
>
> From a July 21, 2002, briefing paper for a meeting
> two days later between Prime Minister Tony Blair
> and his top foreign policy advisors.[34]

In *2001: A Space Odyssey*, a battle erupts between rival apes over water. The battle is relatively equal until one of the apes grabs a big stick and changes the balance of power. In the end, it is the monkey with the big stick and his allies that assert hegemony over the others.

In 2001, the reality, George W. Bush became the latest U.S. president to wield the big stick. In political affairs, global and domestic, confrontation and partisanship were the operating principles. Brute force, political or military, was the option of choice for the administration. The politics of polarization, despite a sham claim of self-identification as a "uniter," characterized Bush and his habits. The big stick of the U.S. military was on display as it stretched across around the world. And Bush demonstrated more than a healthy enthusiasm in employing it. At his side, on more occasions than not, were Colin Powell and Condoleezza Rice.

Powell and Rice represent a historic breakthrough in terms of black American involvement in U.S. foreign policy. The confluence of their appointments, the ascendancy of the neo-conservatives, and the changes wrought by the events of September 11, the Iraq war, and the Katrina fiasco, presents a complicated reading of their representational significance regarding their racial identities. Despite the fact that neither Powell nor Rice have ever stated that their roles were influenced by racial considerations, publics in the United States and globally have attempted to discern such deliberations.

They will not find them. At least not in the substantive and discernible manner in which some hope—or fear. Neither Powell nor Rice, unlike many black conservative Republicans who focus on domestic issues, deny or distance themselves from their racial identity or the country's racial past. In fairly sophisticated ways, they have linked their race and racial experiences to their political roles. As noted, Rice regularly links the war against contemporary terrorists—and even the Bush response to Katrina—with her experiences growing up in Jim Crow

Alabama and the terrorist activities of the Ku Klux Klan. Powell views himself as a black American but is careful to draw the line at being an African American. He is much more comfortable with his black Jamaican (or "Jamerican") identity, and as he stated, he wanted to be measured as secretary of state, not as the black secretary of state. Yet, much more than Rice, he reaches out to black civil society, and it reaches back with honors, awards, and muted criticism.

These excursions into racial talk notwithstanding, Powell and Rice are fiercely resolute that they are individual Americans first and foremost. The politics of U.S. hegemony would demand nothing less. Powell and Rice rose to their positions not because of race but neither in spite of it. Their clarity on who they are and what they seek to represent ideologically and politically has escaped many of their observers who seek fruitlessly any identifiable expression of strategic racial consideration in their constructing of U.S. foreign policy and defending hegemony. The exigencies of projecting U.S. power, conditioned by the ever-present rhetoric of the threat of terrorism, but not determined by it, transcends party and racial affiliations and ensures that those black Americans—and for that matter other people of color and women—who rise to positions of strategic foreign policy construction will substantially represent state interests above all others.

Notes

Introduction

1. From "A Rare Glimpse Inside Bush's Cabinet," an interview with Bob Woodward on *60 Minutes*, November 17, 2002. Also cited in Bob Woodward, *Plan of Attack* (New York: Simon & Schuster, 2005), 79, 149.

2. Following these announcements, a string of articles appeared heralding the "inclusiveness" of the incoming administration. See Timothy J. Burger, "Two More Minorities Named As His Aides," *Daily News*, December 18, 2000; Toby Harnden, "Bush Tries to Heal the Wounds as He Names His Team," *Daily Telegraph*, December 18, 2000; Michael Ellison, "Bush Reaches out to Minorities: Anger Lingers Among America's Black and Hispanic Voters over the Republican Victory," *Guardian*, December 18, 2000; Mary Dejevsky, "Bush Names Diverse Team for the White House," *Independent*, December 18, 2000; "Powell to Rice to Gonzales; In His First Batch of Choices For High-Level Jobs, President-Elect Bush Combines Diversity with Determination," *The Oregonian*, December 19, 2000; "Diversity, and Then Some," *St. Louis Post-Dispatch*, December 19, 2000; Anne E. Kornblut, "Transition 2000; Another First in Store as Rice Gets Nod for National Security Post," *Boston Globe*, December 18, 2000; Anand Vaishnav, "Blacks Reflect on Bush Choices Powell, Rice Seen as Models," *Boston Globe*, December 18, 2000; Edward Smith, "Republicans Have a Place in Black History," *Wall Street Journal*, December 20, 2000; and Mary A. Mitchell, "Powell, Rice Should Silence Critics of Black Republicans," *Chicago Sun-Times*, December 19, 2000.

3. "The 43rd President; Remarks at Announcement of Powell's Nomination as Secretary of State," *New York Times*, December 17, 2000.

4. Condoleezza Rice, remarks following her nomination to become national security advisor, Austin, Texas, December 17, 2000.

5. See James Steele, "The 2004 Democratic Mobilization: Historic, But Not Enough," *New Labor Forum*, December 2004/5.

6. Ibid.

7. "Condoleezza Rice: The Devil's Handmaiden," *The Black Commentator* 26, January 23, 2003, www.blackcommentator.com and Manning Marable, http://www.manningmarable.net/.

8. Hall argues that reading race is a contingent and unstable variable. Such readings rarely exhibit consistency across social groups and time and space. These interpretations or signifiers float from one assessment to the next. See video *Stuart Hall: Race, the Floating Signifier* (Northampton, MA: Media Education Foundation, 1996).

9. Randolph B. Persaud, "Shades of American Hegemony: The Primitive, the Enlightened, and the Benevolent," *Connecticut Journal of International Law* (spring 2004): 263.

10. Ibid., 266.

11. Ibid.

12. See Condoleezza Rice, testimony before the Senate Foreign Relations Committee, January 18, 2005.

13. *International Narcotics Control Strategy Report, Volume I, Drug and Chemical Control* (Washington, DC: United States Department of State, Bureau for International Narcotics and Law Enforcement Affairs, March 2005), 265.

14. Rod Nordland, Babak Dehghanpisheh, and Michael Hirsh, "Hell to Pay," *Newsweek International*, November 8, 2004.

15. Richard Morin and Dan Balz, "Political Divisions Persist After Election," *Washington Post*, January 18, 2005.

16. Laura Flanders, *Bushwomen: Tales of a Cynical Species* (New York: Verso, 2004), 14.

17. John F. Harris and Paul Farhi, "Kerry Pulls Out the Clinton Card," *Washington Post*, October 21, 2004; and Warren Vieth and Ricardo Alonso-Zaldivar, "Bush's Cabinet Members Pay Visits to Swing States," *Los Angeles Times*, October 21, 2004.

18. Lee Hockstader, "Israel's Sharon Met U.S.'s Rice, and Their Encounter Had Legs," *Washington Post*, February 4, 2001.

19. Robin Givhan, "Condoleezza Rice's Commanding Clothes," *Washington Post*, February 25, 2005, C1; Dale Russakoff, "Team Rice, Playing Away; Will State's Head Coach Miss Her First Kickoff?," *Washington Post*, February 6, 2005, D01; and Robin Wright, "The Secretary of State Spreads Her Wings," *Washington Post*, February 10, 2005, C01.

20. Givhan, "Condoleezza Rice's Commanding Clothes."

21. http://www.presidentialprayerteam.org/aiaward/2002_august.php.

22. See Stephen Mansfield, *The Faith of George W. Bush* (New York: Jeremy P. Tarcher, 2003).

Chapter 1

1. Horace R. Cayton, "An Awakening: The Negro Now Fights for Democratic Rights of All the World's Peoples," *Pittsburgh Courier*, February 27, 1943, 14.

2. Gary Younge, "Different Class," *The Guardian*, November 23, 2002.

3. Fran Scott and Abdulah Osman, "Identity, African-Americans, and U.S. Foreign Policy: Differing Reactions to South African Apartheid and the Rwandan Genocide," in Thomas Ambrosio, ed., *Ethnic Identity Groups and U.S. Foreign Policy* (Westport, CT: Praeger, 2002), 72.

4. "Black American" is an inclusive descriptive term used here to mean all those blacks of African descent in the United States whether they are descendants of those who were enslaved, those who were "free," or those who came more recently from Africa, the Caribbean, Latin America, North America, Europe, or elsewhere. When a particular group of black Americans is referred to, their specific categorization will be noted.

5. Scott and Osman, "Identity, African-Americans, and U.S. Foreign Policy," 73.

6. See Azza Salama Layton, *International Politics and Civil Rights Policies in the United States, 1941–1960* (New York: Cambridge University Press, 2000); Carol Anderson, *Eyes Off the Prize: The United Nations and the African American Struggle for Human Rights, 1944–1955* (New York: Cambridge University Press, 2003); Penny M. Von Eschen, *Race Against Empire: Black Americans and Anticolonialism, 1937–1957* (Ithaca, NY: Cornell University Press, 1997); and Brenda Gayle Plummer, *Rising Wind: Black Americans and U.S. Foreign Affairs, 1935–1960* (Chapel Hill: University of North Carolina Press, 1996).

7. Charles P. Henry, "Introduction: Black Global Politics in a Post–Cold War World," in Charles P. Henry, ed., *Foreign Policy and the Black (Inter)National Interest* (Albany: State University of New York Press, 2000), 1.

8. Frederick Douglass, *My Bondage and My Freedom* (New Haven, CT: Yale University Press, 2003).

9. On Haitian history, see C.L.R. James, *The Black Jacobins: Toussaint L'Ouverture and the San Domingo Revolution* (London: Allison & Busby, 1980); and David Nicholls, *From Dessalines to Duvalier: Race, Colour, and National Independence in Haiti* (New Brunswick, NJ: Rutgers University Press, 1995). On Liberian history, see Claude A. Clegg III, *The Price of Liberty: African Americans and the Making of Liberia* (Chapel Hill: University of North Carolina Press, 2004); Amos Claudius Sawyer, *The Emergence of Autocracy in Liberia* (San Francisco: Institute for Contemporary Studies, 1992); Stephen Ellis, *The Mask of Anarchy: The Destruction of Liberia and the Religious Dimension of an African Civil War* (New York: New York University Press, 1999); and John Peter Pham, *Liberia: Portrait of a Failed State* (New York: Reed Press, 2004).

10. Michael L. Krenn, "Black Diplomacy: African Americans and the State Department," presentation to Secretary's Open Forum, U.S. State Department, March 1, 2000.

11. Ibid.

12. U.S. Department of State, www.state.gov.

13. Krenn, "Black Diplomacy."

14. Seymour Maxwell Finger, *American Ambassadors at the UN: People, Politics, and Bureaucracy in Making Foreign Policy* (New York: Holmes & Meier, 1988), 262.

15. Ibid., 264.

16. Colin Powell, *My American Journey* (New York: Ballantine, 1995), 477.

17. Finger, *American Ambassadors*, 283.

18. See Robert C. Smith, "The Political Behavior of Black Presidential Appointees, 1960–1980," *Western Journal of Black Studies* 8 (1984): 139–147; and Clark Mollenhoff, *The President Who Failed: Carter Out of Control* (New York: Macmillan, 1980).

19. Bruce Shapiro, "A House Divided: Racism at the State Department," in Ernest J. Wilson III, ed., *Diversity and U.S. Foreign Policy: A Reader* (New York: Routledge, 2004), 93.

20. Ibid.

21. Ronald Walters, "The Africa Growth and Opportunity Act: Changing Foreign Policy Priorities Toward Africa in a Conservative Political Climate," in Charles P. Henry, ed., *Foreign Policy and the Black (Inter)National Interest* (Albany: State University of New York Press, 2000), 17–36.

22. "Gravely Lauded for His Work Recruiting Blacks for U.S. Foreign Service," *Jet*, October 18, 1993.

23. "Madeleine Albright is First U.S. Secretary of State to Address Black Diplomat Group—Thursday Luncheon Group," *Jet*, August 3, 1998.

24. "Powell Addresses Blacks in Foreign Service," *Jet*, July 16, 2001.

25. The Association of Black American Ambassadors is an organization of current and former black American ambassadors that is "working to enhance public understanding of foreign affairs, to strengthen the Foreign Service through improved diversity, and to document African American achievements in diplomacy. Founded in 1983, this organization works to advance public understanding of diplomacy and to provide a forum for an exchange of views between its members and the governmental bodies responsible for shaping foreign policy."

26. According to its website, "BPIA was established in 1989 to increase the involvement of African Americans and other people of African heritage in international affairs. BPIA implements its educational, economic, cultural exchange, and human resource development objectives through public education programs and conferences, a newsletter, professional networking and outreach activities, a mentors' forum and a scholarship program." www.iabpia.org.

27. Charles Hays Burchfield, "Powell Announces $1 Million U.S. Grant for Minority Diplomats," International Information Programs, U.S. Department of State, May 20, 2002.

28. Ibid.

29. See Charles Henry, ed., *Ralph J. Bunche: Selected Speeches & Writings* (Ann Arbor: University of Michigan Press, 1995); Charles Henry, *Ralph Bunche: Model*

Negro or American Other? (New York: New York University Press, 1999); and Brian Urquhart, *Ralph Bunche: An American Odyssey* (New York: W. W. Norton & Company, 1993).

30. Gunnar Myrdal, *An American Dilemma: The Negro Problem & Modern Democracy*, 2 vols. (New York: Pantheon Books, 1944).

31. http://www.cia.gov/cia/publications/oss/art02.htm.

32. Urquhart, *Ralph Bunche*, 389.

33. Karin L. Stanford, *Beyond the Boundaries: Reverend Jesse Jackson in International Affairs* (Albany: SUNY Press, 1997).

34. Karin L. Stanford, "Citizen Diplomacy and Jesse Jackson: A Case Study for Influencing U.S. Foreign Policy Toward Southern Africa," in Ernest J. Wilson III, ed., *Diversity and U.S. Foreign Policy: A Reader* (New York: Routledge, 2004), 263.

35. See Lisa Brock and Digna Castaneda Fuerte, eds., *Between Race and Empire: African Americans and Cubans Before the Cuban Revolution* (Philadelphia: Temple University Press, 1998).

36. Richard Wright, *The Color Curtain: A Report on the Bandung Conference* (Jackson, MS: Banner Books, University Press of Mississippi, 1956/1995), 12.

37. Ibid., 11.

38. Cary Fraser, "An American Dilemma: Race and Realpolitik in the American Response to the Bandung Conference, 1955," in Brenda Gayle Plummer, ed., *Window on Freedom: Race, Civil Rights, and Foreign Affairs, 1945–1988* (Chapel Hill: University of North Carolina Press, 2003), 123–124.

39. Sylvia Hill, "The Free South Africa Movement," presentation, Durban, South Africa, October 10–13, 2004.

40. See Barbara Lee, "Speech Before the House of Representatives—September 16, 2001," in Julianne Malveaux and Reginna A. Green, eds., *The Paradox of Loyalty: An African American Response to the War on Terrorism* (Chicago: Third World Press, 2002), 76.

41. Maya Rockeymoore, Kenya Covington, Gerald Ford, and Elias Mageto, *Issues Facing African Americans Over the Next Four Years: A Critical Analysis* (Washington, DC: Congressional Black Caucus Foundation, 2004), 29.

42. Ibid.

43. Ibid., 31–32.

44. See "How to Fix the Fractured Black Caucus," *The Black Commentator* 136, April 28, 2005, www.blackcommentator.com.

45. "Congressional Black Caucus Reiterates Call for the Immediate Resignation of Secretary of Defense Donald Rumsfeld," Congressional Black Caucus, Washington, DC, December 17, 2004.

46. See Black Voice for Peace, http://www.bvfp.org/AboutUs.htm.

47. See Zogby International poll, September 20, 2002, cited in Karin Stanford, "The War Within: African American Public Opinion on the War Against Terrorism," in Julianne Malveaux and Reginna A. Green, eds., *The Paradox of Loyalty: An African American Response to the War on Terrorism* (Chicago: Third World Press, 2002), 105.

48. Ibid., 107.

49. See *Time*/CNN poll, February 19–20, 2003, at http://www.pollingreport.com/iraq7.htm.

50. "Poll: Blacks Favor Kerry, 8 to 1," CBS News Polls, www.cbsnews.com/stories/2004/07/21/opinion/polls/main630986.shtml.

51. Jesse Jackson, "London Peace Rally," speech, February 15, 2003.

52. Bill Fletcher, Jr., "Statement Regarding the US Attack on Iraq," *TransAfrica Forum Newsletter*, March 20, 2003.

53. www.blackradicalcongress.org/opposition.htm.

54. "From Haiti to Iraq and Beyond," *The Black Commentator* 125, February 10, 2005, www.blackcommentator.com/125/125_pirates.htm.

55. *The McNeil-Lehrer NewsHour*, May 12, 2005.

56. See Tony Blair, speech to Labour Party conference, October 2, 2001.

Chapter 2

1. Lawrence Oland Christensen, "Black St. Louis: A Study in Race Relations, 1865–1916" (Ph.D. dissertation, University of Missouri, 1972), 211.

2. Cecil Brown, *Stagolee Shot Billy* (Cambridge, MA: Harvard University Press, 2003), 21–36.

3. Office of the Press Secretary, July 23, 2004, President Emphasizes Minority Entrepreneurship at Urban League, Remarks by the President to the 2004 National Urban League Conference, Detroit Marriott Renaissance Hotel, Detroit, Michigan.

4. James Steele, *Freedom's River: The African-American Contribution to Democracy* (New York: Franklin Watts, 1994), 49.

5. Abraham Lincoln, "The Gettysburg Address," Gettysburg, Pennsylvania, November 19, 1863.

6. See Peter Camejo, *Racism, Revolution, Reaction, 1861–1877: The Rise and Fall of Radical Reconstruction* (New York: Monad Press, 1976).

7. See Taylor Branch, *Parting the Waters: America in the King Years 1954–63* (New York: Simon and Schuster, 1988).

8. David Bositis, *Blacks and the 1992 Republican National Convention* (Washington, DC: Joint Center for Political and Economic Studies, 1992), 6.

9. Joseph A. Aistrup, *The Southern Strategy Revisited: Republican Top-Down Advancement in the South* (Lexington: University of Kentucky Press, 1996); Earl Black and Merle Black, *The Rise of Southern Republicans* (Cambridge, MA: Harvard University Press, 2002); and Dan T. Carter, *From George Wallace to Newt Gingrich: Race in the Conservative Counterrevolution, 1963–1944* (Baton Rouge: Louisiana State University Press, 1996).

10. Speech at Republican National Convention, August 1, 2000.

11. Colin Powell, *My American Journey* (New York: Ballantine, 1995), 600.

12. Ibid., 602.

13. Ibid., 388.

14. Ibid., 598.

15. *Wolf Blitzer Reports*, CNN, December 13, 2002.

16. Joshua Holland, "Blackwashing," July 26, 2004, http://www.alternet.org/story/19331.

17. www.aarlc.org/index.shtml.

18. www.aarlc.org.

19. www.nationalcenter.org/p21index.html.

20. "Black Activists Commend Secretary Powell, Bush Administration for Trying to Curb Ethnic Violence in Sudan," press release, Project 21, July 1, 2004.

21. "Black Activists Denounce Jesse Jackson for Calling U.S. Military Action in Iraq 'Murder,'" press release, Project 21, April 26, 2004.

22. "Black Groups Call for Investigation of Congressional Black Caucus," press release, Project 21, April 7, 2004.

23. www.bampac.org.

24. Ibid.

25. Janice Rogers Brown, "'A Whiter Shade of Pale': Sense and Nonsense—The Pursuit of Perfection in Law and Politics," speech to the Federalist Society, University of Chicago Law School, April 20, 2000.

26. "Jurist Defends Record, Vows to Rule Fairly," *Washington Post*, October 23, 2003.

27. "Administration Agitprop," *Washington Post*, January 9, 2005.

28. Ibid.

29. George Curry, "Williams 'Payola' Was Part of a Covert Propaganda Campaign," *Seattle Medium*, January 11, 2005.

30. Armstrong Williams, "Armstrong Williams Offers Readers an Apology," *Afro-American*, January 13, 2005.

31. George Curry, "Armstrong Williams: No Money Left Behind," *Afro-American*, January 13, 2005.

32. Kiron Kanina Skinner, "Ronald Reagan and the Road to Ending the Cold War," speech to the Commonwealth Club, San Francisco, June 16, 2004.

33. Kenneth O'Reilly, *Nixon's Piano: Presidents and Racial Politics from Washington to Clinton* (New York: The Free Press, 1995), 350.

Chapter 3

1. World Social Forum in Mumbai, January 16, 2004.

2. See Toni Morrison, CBS News Polls, "Poll: Blacks Favor Kerry, 8 to 1," July 21, 2004.

3. *Redefining Rights in America: The Civil Rights Record of George W. Bush Administration, 2001–2004*, Draft Report for Commissioner's Review, U.S. Commission on Civil Rights, Office of Civil Rights Education, September 2004, vii.

4. Michael K. Brown, Martin Carnoy, Elliot Currie, Troy Duster, David B. Oppenheimer, Marjorie M. Shultz, and David Wellman, *Whitewashing Race: The Myth of a Color-Blind Society* (Berkeley: University of California Press, 2003), 5.

5. Ibid., 6–7.

6. Ibid., 37.

7. George Will, "Race and 'Rights,'" *Washington Post*, March 11, 2005.

8. Antonia Felix, *Condi: The Condoleezza Rice Story* (New York: Newmarket Press, 2002), 47; and David Roth, *Sacred Honor: A Biography of Colin Powell* (San Francisco: HarperSan Francisco, 1993), 53–55, 62–63.

9. Jane Perlez, "How Powell Decided to Shun Racism Conference," *New York Times*, September 5, 2001.

10. http://academic.udayton.edu/race/02rights/repara23.htm.

11. Gay McDougall, "The World Conference Against Racism: Through a Wider Lens," *Fletcher Forum of World Affairs* (summer/fall 2002).

12. See Zapiro cartoon, *Sowetan*, August 29, 2001.

13. See interview on Africana.com, http://www.africana.com/articles/daily/index_20010905.asp.

14. Gay McDougall, "The World Conference against Racism: Through a Wider Lens," *The Fletcher Forum of World Affairs* (summer/fall 2002): 135.

15. See "Statement by Secretary of State Colin Powell on the Withdrawal of the USA from the WCAR," statement issued by the U.S. Department of State, September 3, 2001.

16. This call was expressed by the International Human Rights Group (now Group Rights) and other groups in the United States. On the international level, the World Council of Churches led a campaign in the 1990s titled, "Racism is a Violation of Human Rights," and the argument has been made by the International Labour Organization. The phrase is also the slogan of the London-based, the 1990 Trust, an anti-racism and human rights organization. See websites Group Rights (www.globalrights.org), World Council of Churches (www.wcc-coe.org/wcc/assembly/hr-e.html), International Labour Organization (www.ilo.org), and the 1990 Trust (www.blink.org.uk).

17. The United States has not ratified CEDAW, ICESCR, and CRC.

18. In the ICERD, racial discrimination is defined as "any distinction, exclusion, restriction or preference based on race, color, descent, or national or ethnic origin which has the purpose or effect of nullifying or impairing the recognition, enjoyment or exercise, on an equal footing, of human rights and fundamental freedoms in the political, economic, social, cultural or any other field of public life." While politically useful, the broad inclusiveness of the definition makes it difficult to use as a policy guideline. In addition, the ICERD and other documents avoid the all-important issue of racial definition, that is, exactly who are we talking about. This is due, in part, to the fact that the UN recognizes that race is a social construction that differs in each in society and in different times.

19. The non-binding resolution, which did not passed, was prompted by the Supreme Court case, *Lawrence v. Texas*, a case involving sodomy, where a reference was made by Justice Kennedy to a decision by the European Court of Human Rights. See Supreme Court of the United States, *Lawrence et al. v. Texas*, June 26, 2003.

20. See "WCAR NGO Forum Declaration," September 3, 2001, www.un.org/wcar.

21. See "WCAR NGO Forum Programme of Action," September 3, 2001, www.un.org/wcar.

22. See "WCAR Declaration," www.unchr.ch/pdf/durban.pdf.

23. Ibid.

24. Ibid.

25. Isabel Hilton, "The 800 lb. Gorilla in American Foreign Policy," *The Guardian*, July 28, 2004.

26. "Harper's Index," *Harper's Magazine*, September 1999, www.harpers.org.

27. Adam Liptak, "$5 Million Settlement Ends Case of Tainted Texas Sting," *New York Times*, March 11, 2004.

28. Lawrence Weschler, "He's the Picture of Racial Compassion," *Los Angeles Times*, May 13, 2004.

29. Brown et al., *Whitewashing Race*, 54.

30. Julianne Malveaux, "Recession, Affirmative Action, Trickery: Reflections on a Bush Appointment," *Black Issues in Higher Education* (April 25, 2002).

31. Betsy Leondar-Wright, Meizhu Lui, Gloribell Mota, Dedrick Muhammad, and Mara Youkydis, *State of the Dream 2005: Disowned in the Ownership Society* (Boston: United for a Fair Economy, January 10, 2005), 1.

32. Ibid., 6.

33. The "Three Strikes" provisions, at the state and federal level, mandate that anyone convicted of three felonies will serve life in prison without the possibility of parole. Federal law punishes those caught with crack cocaine, disproportionately young black men, much more severely than those caught with cocaine power. Offenders who possess five grams of crack receive a mandatory five-year sentence. It takes 500 grams of cocaine power to receive such a sentence.

34. Paige M. Harrison and Jennifer C. Karberg, "Prison and Jail Inmates at Midyear 2003," *Bureau of Justice Statistics Bulletin*, U.S. Department of Justice, Washington, DC, May 2004, 11.

35. Deborah Fins, "Death Row U.S.A.," quarterly report, NAACP Legal Defense and Educational Fund, April 1, 2004, 1.

36. See Jamie Fellner and Marc Mauer, *Losing the Vote: The Impact of Felony Disenfranchisement Laws in the United States*, Human Rights Watch and The Sentencing Project, Washington, DC, October 1998, 2, 17; and *Felony Disenfranchisement Laws in the United States*, The Sentencing Project, Washington, DC, May 2004, 1–3.

37. Ibid.

38. Associated Press, October 25, 2000.

39. *Regents of the University of California v. Bakke*, 438 U.S. 265 (1978).

40. Redefining Rights in America, 11. Brief of Amicus Curiae for the United States Supporting Petitioner at 13, Gratz v. Bollinger, et al., 539 U.S. 244 (2003) (No. 02-516), and Brief of Amicus Curiae for the United States Supporting Petitioner at 10, Grutter v. Bollinger, et al., 539 U.S. 306 (2003) (No. 02-241).

41. Mike Allen and Charles Lane, "Rice Helped Shape Bush Decision on Admissions," *Washington Post*, January 17, 2003.

42. Ibid.

43. Statement by the National Security Advisor Dr. Condoleezza Rice on the Michigan decision, January 17, 2003.

44. Mike Allen, "Rice: Race Can Be Factor in College Admissions," *Washington Post*, January 18, 2003.

45. Diane Manuel, "Senators, Others Debate Status of Women Faculty," *Stanford On-line Report*, May 20, 1998, http://news-service.stanford.edu/news/1998/may20/facsen520.html.

46. Mark Z. Barabak, "Condoleezza Rice at Stanford," *Los Angeles Times*, January 16, 2005.

47. Allen, "Rice: Race Can Be Factor in College Admissions."

48. Nicholas Lemann, "The Three Cushion Shot That Won Colin Powell's Support for Affirmative Action in Higher Education," *Journal of Blacks in Higher Education* (winter 1999–2000): 104.

49. Ibid.

50. See U.S. Commission on Civil Rights, *Beyond Percentage Plans: The Challenge of Equal Opportunity in Higher Education*, staff report, November 2002; The Civil Rights Project, *Percent Plans in College Admissions: A Comparative Analysis of Three States' Experiences*, Harvard University, February 2003; The Civil Rights Project, *Appearance and Reality in the Sunshine State: The Talented 20 Program in Florida*, Harvard University, February 2003; Marta Tienda et al., "Closing the Gap?: Admissions & Enrollment at the Texas Public Flagships Before and After Affirmative Action," *Policy Brief*, Woodrow Wilson School of Public Affairs, Princeton University, January 2003; and Tomas Rivera Policy Institute, *The Reality of Race Neutral Admissions for Minority Students at the University of California: Turning the Tide or Turning Them Away?*, March 2003.

51. "President Applauds Supreme Court for Recognizing Value of Diversity," June 23, 2003, www.whitehouse.gov/news/releases/2003/06/20030623/htm.

52. See "Harry Belafonte on Colin Powell," *Larry King Live*, CNN, October 15, 2002.

53. Condoleezza Rice Discusses Foreign Policy at the 28th Annual Convention of the National Association of Black Journalists, August 7, 2003.

54. See "Remarks by Condoleezza Rice," International Institute for Strategic Studies, London, June 26, 2003; and "Condoleezza Rice Speaks at Los Angeles Town Hall," The Westin Bonaventure Hotel, June 12, 2003.

55. Remarks by Condoleezza Rice, International Institute for Strategic Studies, London, June 26, 2003.

56. Condoleezza Rice Discusses the President's Trip to Africa, press briefing, July 3, 2003.

57. Remarks by Condoleezza Rice at Mississippi College School of Law, Commencement Ceremony, First Baptist Church, Jackson, Mississippi, May 19, 2003.

58. Ibid.

59. Christopher M. Hamlin, *Behind the Stained Glass: A History of Sixteenth Street Baptist Church* (Birmingham, AL: Crane Hill, 1998); Elizabeth H. Cobbs and Petric J Smith, *Long Time Coming: An Insider's Story of the Birmingham Church Bombing that Rocked the World* (Birmingham, AL: Crane Hill, 1994); Frank Sikora, *Until Justice Rolls Down: The Birmingham Church Bombing Case* (Tuscaloosa: University of Alabama Press, 2005).

60. "In Race for White House, the 'Cult of Condi' Plays Growing Role," *Los Angeles Times*, May 28, 2000.

61. Condoleezza Rice Discusses Foreign Policy, August 7, 2003.

62. Remarks by Condoleezza Rice at Mississippi College School of Law.

63. Colin Powell, *My American Journey* (New York: Ballantine, 1995), 19.

64. Ibid., 21–22.

65. Ibid., 22.

66. Ibid., 121.

67. Ibid.

Chapter 4

1. George Herbert Walker Bush, "Toward a New World Order," address to a joint session of Congress, September 11, 1990.

2. The most explicit elaboration of the doctrine is contained in the 2002 National Security Strategy drafted by the office of the national security advisor. See *The National Security Strategy of the United States*, The White House, 2002.

3. James Mann, *Rise of the Vulcans: The History of Bush's War Cabinet* (New York: Penguin, 2004), xv.

4. George W. Bush, "Graduation Speech at West Point Academy," June 1, 2002, http://www.whitehouse.gov/news/releases/2002/06/20020601-3.html.

5. See Patrick E. Tyler, "Pentagon Drops Goal of Blocking New Superpowers," *New York Times*, May 24, 1992; and Barton Gellman, "Keeping the US First; Pentagon Would Preclude a Rival Superpower," *Washington Post*, March 11, 1992.

6. Frontline website, http://www.pbs.org/wgbh/pages/frontline/shows/iraq/etc/wolf.html.

7. Gellman, "Keeping the US First."

8. Project for the New American Century, http://newamericancentury.org/.

9. See Letter to President Clinton, http://www.newamericancentury.org/iraqclintonletter.htm.

10. Thomas Donnelly, *Rebuilding America's Defenses: Strategy, Forces and Resource for a New Century*, Project for the New American Century, Washington, DC, September 2000, i, 2.

11. Jason Vest, "Coming Soon: 'Total War' on the Middle East," *The Nation*, August 29, 2002.

12. Ibid.

13. Zbigniew Brzezinski, *The Grand Chessboard: American Primacy and Its Geo-strategic Imperatives* (New York: Basic Books, 1997), xiv.

14. Ibid., 211.

15. See Zbigniew Brzezinski, *The Choice: Global Domination or Global Leadership* (New York: Basic Books, 2004), 37.

16. See Brent Scowcroft, "Don't Attack Saddam," *Wall Street Journal*, August 15, 2002, A12.

17. Condoleezza Rice, "National Security Advisor Condoleezza Rice Interview with German Television," Office of the Press Secretary, White House, July 31, 2003.

18. Robert Kagan, "The Problem with Powell," *Washington Post*, July 23, 2000.

19. Ibid.

20. Colin Powell, *My American Journey* (New York: Ballantine Books, 1995), 452.

21. "Powell's Doctrine, in Powell's Words," *Washington Post*, October 21, 2001.

22. The remarks were allegedly made during a phone conversation between Powell and British foreign secretary Jack Straw. Both Powell and Straw deny the conversation, but did not seek legal action to prevent the book's publication. See James Naughtie, *The Accidental American: Tony Blair and the Presidency* (New York: Public Affairs, 2004).

23. Lawrence F. Kaplan, "Colin Powell's Out-of-Date Foreign Policy," *The New Republic*, January 1, 2001.

24. This is a criticism that actually carries some merit. Powell certainly found ways to "leak" his disagreement with some of the policies coming out of George W. Bush's White House. See Bob Woodward, *Plan of Attack* (New York: Simon & Schuster, 2004).

25. Hans J. Morgenthau, *Politics among Nations: The Struggle for Power and Peace* (New York: Knopf, 1978), 267.

26. Ibid., 273–326.

27. Condoleezza Rice, "Campaign 2000—Promoting the National Interest," *Foreign Affairs* (January/February 2000).

28. Morgenthau, *Politics among Nations*, 40.

29. Ibid.

30. Speech at the Republican National Convention, August 1, 2000.

31. Robin Wright, "Top Focus Before 9/11 Wasn't on Terrorism," *Washington Post*, April 1, 2004.

32. "Rice on Iraq, War and Politics," *NewsHour with Jim Lehrer*, PBS, September 25, 2002.

33. Ibid.

34. Indeed, their appointments were celebrated by even some of the civil rights organizations. On February 23, 2002, Rice was awarded the President's Award by the NAACP, the civil rights group most vocal in its opposition to the Bush administration.

35. Full Spectrum Dominance is military parlance meaning "the ability of U.S. forces, operating unilaterally or in combination with multinational and interagency partners, to defeat any adversary and control any situation across the full range of

military operations. . . . Additionally, given the global nature of our interests and obligations, the United States must maintain its overseas presence forces and the ability to rapidly project power worldwide in order to achieve full spectrum dominance." See *Joint Vision 2000* (Washington, DC: Government Printing Office, June 2000), 8–9.

36. "Power's Paper Trail," *Foreign Policy* (November/December 2002): 53.

37. *A National Security Strategy for a New Century*, The White House, December 1999, iii.

38. Ibid., 2–3.

39. Ibid., 5.

40. Ibid., iv.

41. Ibid., 3.

42. "Rice on Iraq, War and Politics."

43. See Rahul Mahajan, *Full Spectrum Dominance: U.S. Power in Iraq and Beyond* (New York: Seven Stories Press, 2003), 112–113; Brzezinski, *The Choice*, 35–37; and Michael E. O'Hanlon, Susan E. Rice, and James B. Steinberg, *The New National Security Strategy and Preemption* (Washington, DC: Brookings Institution, December 2002), 3–5.

44. Ralph Bunche, "Nobel Lecture," delivered at the University of Oslo, December 11, 1950.

45. Colin L. Powell, "A Strategy of Partnerships," *Foreign Affairs* (January/February 2004).

46. Ibid.

47. Charles Lane, "Refusal to Testify Has Precedent," *Washington Post*, March 27, 2004.

48. Alberto R. Gonzales, "Letter to 9-11 Commission," The White House, March 30, 2004.

49. Ibid.

50. Ibid.

51. Richard A. Clarke, *Against All Enemies: Inside America's War on Terror* (New York: Free Press, 2004).

52. Dana Milbank and Mike Allen, "White House Counters Ex-Aide," *Washington Post*, March 23, 2004.

53. National Commission on Terrorist Attacks, *The 9/11 Commission Report: Final Report of the National Commission on Terrorist Attacks Upon the United States* (New York: W. W. Norton & Company, 2004), 255.

54. Ibid., 256.

55. Ibid., 257.

56. Presidential Daily Briefing, August 6, 2001.

57. Ibid.

58. See David Corn, "Capital Games," *The Nation*, April 8, 2004, www.thenation.com.

59. National Commission on Terrorist Attacks, *The 9/11 Commission Report*, 260.

60. Condoleezza Rice testimony before National Commission on Terrorist Attacks, April 8, 2004.

61. Ibid.

62. Michael Isikoff, "In the Months Before 9/11, Justice Department Curtailed Highly Classified Program to Monitor Al Qaeda Suspects in the US," *Newsweek*, March 21, 2004.

63. Adam Clymer, "How Sept. 11 Changed Goals of Justice Dept.," *New York Times*, February 28, 2002.

Chapter 5

1. Chip Berlet, "Condi's Dad and the Lessons of War," October 27, 2004, www.publiceye.org/frontpage/OpEds/berlet_condi_dad_html.

2. "Rice on Iraq, War and Politics," *NewsHour with Jim Lehrer*, PBS, September 25, 2002.

3. David Rose, "Bush and Blair Made Secret Pact for Iraq War," *Observer*, April 4, 2004.

4. "Secret 23 July 2002 Downing Street Memo," *Sunday Times* (London), May 1, 2005. The full memo is available at the Justice not Vengence website, www.j-n-v.org.

5. See Steven Kull, Clay Ramsay, Evan Lewis, and Phil Warf, *Misperceptions, the Media, and the Iraq War*, Program on International Policy Attitudes/Knowledge Networks, October 2, 2003, www.pipa.org.

6. Ibid., 2.

7. Ibid., 4.

8. Sheldon Rampton and John Stauber, *Weapons of Mass Deception: The Uses of Propaganda in Bush's War on Iraq* (New York: Penguin, 2003), 6.

9. Jim Lobe, "Bush Falls from Favor Abroad, too," *Asia Times*, October 30, 2003.

10. Ibid.

11. Ibid.

12. Ibid.

13. "Air Force Intelligence and Security Doctrine: Psychological Operations (PSYOP)," Air Force Instruction 10-702, Secretary of the Air Force, July 19, 1994, www.fas.org/irp/doddir/usaf/10-702.htm.

14. Ibid.

15. Ibid., 168.

16. Colin L. Powell, "Speech to the UN Security Council," February 5, 2003.

17. Interview on *Meet the Press with Tim Russert*, NBC, December 16, 2001.

18. Remarks with French Foreign Minister Hubert Vedrine, Paris, France, December 11, 2001.

19. Bob Woodward, *Plan of Attack* (New York: Simon & Schuster, 2004), 269.

20. Mark Danner, "Secret Way to War," *New York Times Review of Books*, May 17, 2005.

21. Evgenia Peretz, David Rose, and David Wise, "The Path to War," *Vanity Fair*, May 2004, 102.

22. See Glenn Kessler and Walter Pincus, "A Flawed Argument in the Case for War," *Washington Post*, February 1, 2004; and "Looking Back at Powell's Claims," *Washington Post*, February 1, 2004.

23. Glenn Kessler, "Powell Expresses Doubts About Basis for Iraqi Weapons Claim," *Washington Post*, April 3, 2004.

24. www.electroniciraq.net/news/1946.shtml.

25. Peretz, Rose, and Wise, "A Flawed Argument," 102.

26. *Iraq on the Record: The Bush Administration's Public Statements on Iraq*, U.S. House of Representatives, Committee on Government Reform—Minority Staff, Special Investigations Division, prepared for Rep. Henry A. Waxman, Washington, DC, March 16, 2004.

27. Condoleezza Rice, "National Security Advisor Condoleezza Rice Interview with ZDF German Television," ZDF German Television, July 31, 2003.

28. Powell, "Speech to the UN Security Council."

29. *Iraq on the Record: The Bush Administration's Public Statements on Iraq*; and "Iraq Trailers Said to Make Hydrogen, Not Biological Arms," *New York Times*, August 9, 2003.

30. See Interview, *Sean Hannity Show,* ABC Radio Network, July 2, 2003; *Press Briefing*, State Department, July 10, 2003; Interview, *Today Show with Katie Couric*, NBC, June 30, 2003; Interview, *All Things Considered*, NPR, June 27, 2003; Interview with *Al Arabiyya Television*, Al Arabiyya, June 23, 2003; and Interview by the Associated Press, State Department, June 12, 2003.

31. Remarks at stakeout following Fox News interview, *Fox News*, June 8, 2003.

32. Interview, *Late Edition with Wolf Blitzer*, CNN, June 8, 2003.

33. Kessler, "Powell Expresses Doubts."

34. Powell, "Speech to the UN Security Council."

35. David Leigh and John Hooper, "Britain's Dirty Secret," *Guardian*, March 6, 2003; David Leigh, "The Strange Case of Falluja 2," *Guardian*, March 6, 2003; David Leigh, "How Deal Got the Green Light Despite Nerve Gas Warning," *Guardian*, March 6, 2003.

36. Stephen Zunes, "Mr. Powell, You're No Adlai Stevenson," *Foreign Policy in Focus*, February 6, 2003.

37. Luke Harding, "Revealed: Truth Behind U.S. 'Poison Factory' Claim," *Observer*, February 9, 2003.

38. *This Week with George Stephanopolous*, ABC, June 8, 2003.

39. *Meet the Press*, NBC, June 8, 2003.

40. See *Capital Report*, CNBC, June 3, 2003; *Dr. Rice Previews the President's Trip to Europe and the Middle East*, White House, May 28, 2003.

41. Condoleezza Rice, "Why We Know Iraq is Lying," *New York Times*, January 23, 2003.

42. George W. Bush, "State of the Union," speech, January 28, 2003.

43. *This Week with George Stephanopolous*, June 8, 2003.

44. *Face the Nation*, July 13, 2003.

45. Joseph Wilson, "What I Didn't Find in Africa," *New York Times*, July 6, 2003.

46. Dana Milbank and Walter Pincus, "Bush Aides Disclose Warnings from CIA," *Washington Post*, July 23, 2003.

47. Timothy Noah, "Did Condi Give the Game Away," *Slate*, July 31, 2003.

48. *Meet the Press*, NBC, June 8, 2003.

49. Ibrahim al-Marashi, "Iraq's Security and Intelligence Network: A Guide and Analysis," *Middle East Report of International Affairs* (September 2002).

50. Joseph Fitchett, "Washington's Best Ally: An American Poodle or a Modern Churchill?," *International Herald Tribune*, January 24, 2003.

51. *Late Edition with Wolf Blitzer*, CNN, September 8, 2002.

52. See *Comprehensive Report of the Special Advisor to the DCI [Director of Central Intelligence] on Iraq's WMD* (Washington, DC: CIA), September 30, 2004.

53. Dana Priest and Walter Pincus, "U.S. 'Almost All Wrong' on Weapons," *Washington Post*, October 7, 2004.

54. See *NewsHour with Jim Lehrer*, PBS, July 30, 2003.

55. *Iraq on the Record: The Bush Administration's Public Statements on Iraq*.

56. *Fox News Sunday*, Fox News, February 16, 2003.

57. See Walter Pincus, "No Link Between Hijacker, Iraq Found, U.S. Says," *Washington Post*, May 1, 2002; and James Risen, "Prague Discounts an Iraq Meeting," *New York Times*, October 21, 2002. ·

58. Rampton and Stauber, *Weapons of Mass Deception*, 93–95.

59. *Fox News Sunday*, Fox News, September 7, 2003.

60. Bush, "State of the Union" speech.

61. "Show Us the Proof," editorial, *New York Times*, June 19, 2004.

62. See National Commission on Terrorist Attacks, *The 9/11 Commission Report: Final Report of the National Commission on Terrorist Attacks Upon the United States* (New York: W. W. Norton & Company, 2004).

63. Remarks after Meeting with Hungarian foreign minister Laszlo Kovacs, State Department, October 3, 2003.

64. Stephen Pelletiere, "A War Crime or an Act of War?," *New York Times*, January 31, 2003.

65. Dana Milbank, "Stabilization Is its Middle Name," *Washington Post*, May 18, 2004.

Chapter 6

1. George Kennan, "Review of Current Trends: U.S. Foreign Policy," in Thomas H. Etzold and John Lewis Gaddis, eds., *Containment: Documents on American Policy and Strategy, 1945–1950* (New York: Columbia University Press, 1978).

2. *The National Security Strategy of the United States of America* (Washington, DC: The White House, September 2002), 2.

3. Condoleezza Rice, "Opening Statement," U.S. Senate confirmation hearing, U.S. Senate, Washington, DC, January 18, 2005.

4. "Implications of Gen. Powell's Call," *The Nation* (Kenya), June 3, 2001.

5. Charles Cobb, Jr., "Considering Colin Powell and Africa," *Foreign Service Journal* (March 29, 2003).

6. "Condoleezza Rice Discusses the President's Trip to Africa," White House Press Briefing, July 3, 2003.

7. Colin L. Powell, Remarks to University of Witwatersrand, Johannesburg, South Africa, May 25, 2001.

8. "Condoleezza Rice Discusses the President's Trip to Africa."

9. Salih Booker, William Minter, and Ann-Louise Colgan, "America and Africa," *Current History* (May 2003).

10. *Human Development Report 2003* (New York: Oxford University Press, 2003), 1–2, 7.

11. Patrick Wintour and Larry Elliott, "Debt Deal in Pipeline After US Visit," *The Guardian*, June 9, 2005.

12. *Human Development Report 2004* (New York: United Nations, 2005).

13. Ibid.

14. *Human Development Report 2003*, 37.

15. Booker, Minter, and Colgan, "America and Africa."

16. Marina Ottaway, "Africa's 'New Leaders': African Solution or African Problem," *Current History* (May 1998).

17. Salih Booker and Ann-Louise Colgan, "'Compassionate Conservatism' Comes to Africa, *Current History* (May 2004).

18. Powell, Remarks to University of Witwatersrand.

19. "Humilation for Powell at Earth Summit," *The Guardian*, September 4, 2002.

20. Austin Mbozi, "Powell: Please Speak for Black Africa," *The Post*, September 16, 2002.

21. "Glad You Could Come...," *The Star*, May 25, 2001.

22. "Hands Across the Water," *The Star*, May 26, 2001.

23. George Monbiot, "A Truckload of Nonsense," *The Guardian*, June 14, 2005.

24. Andrew Buncombe, "Global Spending on Arms Tops $1 Trillion," *The Independent*, June 9, 2005.

25. Booker and Colgan, "'Compassionate Conservativism' Comes to Africa."

26. Ibid.

27. Ann-Louise Colgan, "Africa Policy Outlook 2005," *Foreign Policy in Focus*, January 1, 2005.

28. Paul Blustein, "Debt Cut Is Set for Poorest Nations," *Washington Post*, June 12, 2005.

29. Larry Elliott and Ashley Seager, "£30 bn Debts Write-off Agreed," *The Guardian*, June 11, 2005.

30. Booker and Colgan, "'Compassionate Conservativism' Comes to Africa."

31. Wintour and Elliott, "Debt Deal in Pipeline After US Visit."

32. Norm Dixon, "Debt Cancellation: Africa Needs Justice, Not Charity," *Green Left Weekly* (Australia), June 28, 2005, www.worldpress.org/africa/2107.cfm.

33. "G8 Finance Ministers' Conclusions on Development," statement, June 10–11, 2005, London, UK.

34. Dixon, "Debt Cancellation."

35. Gideon Mendel, "Eight Women One Voice," *The Guardian Weekend*, June 11, 2005.

36. Booker and Colgan, " 'Compassionate Conservativism' Comes to Africa."

37. FAO, http://www.fao.org/documents/show_cdr.asp?url_file=/docrep/005/ac735e/ac735e00.htm.

38. Jim Lobe, "Bush Exaggerates Increase in U.S. Aid to Africa," *Inter Press Service*, June 28, 2005.

39. Elizabeth Becker and David E. Sanger, "Bush Maintains Opposition to Doubling Aid to Africa," *New York Times*, June 2, 2005.

40. "Transcript: Joint Press Conference with President Bush and Prime Minister Blair," *Washington Post*, June 7, 2005.

41. Susan Rice, *U.S. Foreign Assistance to Africa: Claims vs. Reality* (Washington, DC: Brookings Institution, June 29, 2005), 1.

42. Ibid., 2.

43. "G8 Finance Ministers' Conclusions on Development."

44. John Feffer, ed., *Power Trip: U.S. Unilateralism and Global Strategy After September 11* (New York: Seven Stories Press, 2003), 144–145.

45. South Africa was mentioned once in passing. See Condoleezza Rice, "Campaign 2000: Promoting the National Interest," *Foreign Affairs* (January/February 2000).

46. Ann-Louise Colgan, "The State of U.S. Africa Policy," *Africa Action*, December 3, 2004, www.africaaction.org.

47. Derrick Z. Jackson, "Powell's Oil Quest," *Boston Globe*, September 6, 2002.

48. Ibid.

49. Gilbert Da Costa, "Securing Africa Oil," *Washington Times*, July 13, 2004.

50. Ibid.

51. Colgan, "Africa Policy Outlook 2005," 6.

52. Booker and Colgan, " 'Compassionate Conservativism' Comes to Africa."

53. Salih Booker, "Bush's AIDS Plan: More Smoke and Mirrors," *Economic Justice News*, March 28, 2003.

54. Booker and Colgan, " 'Compassionate Conservativism' Comes to Africa."

55. "Helping Poor Countries," *New York Times*, February 17, 2003.

56. "UN's Darfur Death Estimate Soars," BBC news, http://news.bbc.co.uk/2/hi/africa/4349063.stm; and Colgan, "Africa Policy Outlook 2005," 7.

57. Colin Powell, "The Crisis in Darfur," testimony before the U.S. Senate Foreign Relations Committee, Washington, DC, September 9, 2004.

58. "President's Statement on Violence in Darfur, Sudan," press statement, the White House, Washington, DC, September 9, 2004.

59. Jamal Jafari, " 'Never Again,' Again: Darfur, the Genocide Convention, and the Duty to Prevent Genocide," *Human Rights Brief* (Fall 2004), 8–10, 21.

60. Powell, "The Crisis in Darfur."

61. See "100 Days of Slaughter: A Chronology of U.S/U.N. Actions," PBS, www.pbs.org.

62. Ibid.

63. Nicholas D. Kristof, "Sudan's Policy of Systematic Rape," *International Times Herald*, June 6, 2005.

64. Elijah E. Cummings, "CBC Chairman Elijah E. Cummings Comments on Meeting with Secretary Powell Regarding Sudan Crisis," U.S. House of Representatives, July 23, 2004.

65. Ibid.

66. Ken Silverstein, "Official Pariah Sudan Valuable to America's War on Terrorism," *Los Angeles Times*, April 29, 2005.

67. Ibid.

68. Ibid.

69. Larry Elliott and Patrick Wintour, "Broken Promises Leave Three Million Children to Die in Africa," *The Guardian*, June 8, 2005; and Larry Elliott, "Africa Still on Road to Disaster Says UN," *The Guardian*, June 8, 2005.

Chapter 7

1. Rickey Singh, "Our Caribbean: Our Interest Under Bush," *Daily Nation* (Barbados), September 3, 2004.

2. Laura Carlsen, "Ad Hoc Interventions?: Bush, Rice and Latin America," *Counterpunch*, February 5/6, 2005.

3. Colin Powell, "En Route to College Station," press briefing, U.S. Department of State, Washington, DC, November 4, 2003.

4. John Williamson, "What Should the World Bank Think About the Washington Consensus?," *World Bank Research Observer*, Washington, DC, August 2000, 251.

5. James Monroe, speech to Congress, December 2, 1823.

6. Condoleezza Rice, "Remarks at the Council of Americas Annual Meeting," U.S. Department of State Washington, DC, May 3, 2005.

7. For more on the Bolivarian Revolution, see Richard Gott, *Hugo Chavez: The Bolivarian Revolution in Venezuela* (New York: Verso, 2005).

8. Conn Hallinan, "U.S. Shadow Over Venezuela," *Foreign Policy in Focus*, April 17, 2002, www.fpif.org.

9. "Chavez and Venezuelan Officials React to US Remarks on Referendum and Relations with Cuba," January 11, 2004, www.venezuelanalysis.com.

10. Colin Powell, "Statement on President Bush's Budget Request for FY 2003," U.S. Senate Foreign Relations Committee, February 5, 2002.

11. Linda Robinson, "Terror Close to Home," *U.S. News & World Report*, October 6, 2003.

12. Condoleezza Rice, U.S. Senate Confirmation hearing testimony, U.S. Department of State, January 19, 2005.

13. Juan Forero, "Documents Show CIA Knew of a Coup Plot in Venezuela," *New York Times*, December 3, 2004.

14. Mike Ceaser, "As Turmoil Deepens in Venezuela, Questions Regarding NED Activities Remain Unanswered," December 9, 2002, http://americas.irc-online .org/articles/2002/0212venezuela_body.html.

15. Ibid.

16. "Venezuela: Change of Government," press statement, U.S. State Department, Washington, DC, April 12, 2002.

17. Ibid.

18. Ibid.

19. George A. Folsom, "IRI President Folsom Praises Venezuelan Civil Society's Defense of Democracy," press statement, International Republican Institute, Washington, DC, April 12, 2002.

20. Ibid.

21. "Hugo Chavez Departs," editorial, *New York Times*, April 13, 2002.

22. Charter of the Organization of American States, http://www.oas.org/juridico/ english/charter.html.

23. Ibid.

24. *Meet the Press*, April 14, 2002.

25. Ed Vulliamy, "Venezuela Coup Linked to Bush Team," *Observer*, April 21, 2002.

26. Forero, "Documents Show CIA Knew of a Coup Plot in Venezuela."

27. Martin Sanchez, "Venezuela Officials Praise Colin Powell's Statements on Signature Repair for Recall," May 29, 2004, venezuelanalysis.com.

28. Ronald Sanders, "Rice and Zoellick: Not Rice and Peas," January 18, 2005, www.caribbeannetnews.com.

29. Bill Clinton, "Remarks by the President in Television Address to the Nation," White House, Washington, DC, September 15, 1994.

30. Ibid.

31. Ibid.

32. Lisa McGowan, "Democracy Undermined, Economic Justice Denied: Structural Adjustment and the Aid Juggernaut in Haiti, the Development Group for Alternative Policies," Washington, DC, January 1997, http://www.developmentgap.org/.

33. Ibid.

34. John Canham-Clyne, "U.S. Policy on Haiti: Selling Out Democracy," *Covert Action* 48 (spring 1994): 8.

35. McGowan, "Democracy Undermined."

36. Ibid.

37. Maxine Waters, "Statement by Rep. Maxine Waters on the Overthrow of the Democratically-Elected Government of Haiti," U.S. House of Representatives, Washington, DC, March 4, 2004.

38. "Report of the Commission of Inquiry into the Events of December 17, 2001 in Haiti," OAS, July 1, 2002.

39. Colin Powell, "Testimony Before the U.S. Senate Committee on Foreign Relations," U.S. Senate, Washington, DC, February 12, 2004.

40. Kevin Pina, "Godfather Colin Powell: The Gangster of Haiti," *The Black Commentator*, March 4, 2004, www.blackcommentator.com.

41. Kevin Sullivan, Scott Wilson, and Fred Barbash, "Aristide Bows to Pressure, Leaves Haiti," *Washington Post*, February 29, 2004; and Peter Slevin and Mike Allen, "Former Ally's Shift in Stance Left Haiti Leader No Recourse," *Washington Post*, March 1, 2004.

42. Ibid.

43. Colin Powell, "Remarks with Prime Minister Gerard Latortue of Haiti After Their Meeting," Port-au-Prince, Haiti, U.S. Department of State, Washington, DC, April 5, 2004, www.state.gov/secretary/former/powell/remarks/31186.htm.

44. Interview, *American Morning with Bill Hemmer*, CNN, Washington, DC, March 1, 2004, www.state.gov/secretary/former/powell/remarks/30002.htm.

45. "Noriega, Bolton and Condoleezza Rice's New Financial Subsidy to Right-wing Cuban America," press release, Council on Hemispheric Affairs, Washington, DC, August 3, 2004.

46. Slevin and Allen, "Former Ally's Shift."

47. *Meet the Press*, March 14, 2004.

48. Sullivan, Wilson, and Barbash, "Aristide Bows to Pressure."

49. Maxine Waters, "Congresswoman Maxine Waters' Statement on Kidnapping of Haitian President Aristide," U.S. House of Representatives, Washington, DC, March 1, 2004.

50. Wayne Washington, "Bush Administration Assailed as Withholding Support," *Boston Globe*, March 1, 2004.

51. Randall Robinson, "Haiti: Bushwhacked in the Caribbean," *MITF Report*, Marin Interfaith Task Force on the Americas, summer 2004.

52. Avi Steinberg, "Haiti Update VI: Out with the Bad, in with the Worse," March 31, 2004, www.africana.com.

53. "Shots fired as Powell visits Haiti palace," *CNN*, December 1, 2004, http://www.cnn.com/2004/WORLD/americas/12/01/powell.shooting.

54. "Fact Sheet: Report of the Commission for Assistance to a Free Cuba," White House, Washington, DC, May 6, 2004, www.whitehouse.gov/news/releases/2004/05/20040506-7.html.

55. "Noriega, Bolton and Condoleezza Rice's New Financial Subsidy to Right-wing Cuban America."

56. Ann Louise Bardach, "Our Man's in Miami. Patriot or Terrorist?," *Washington Post*, April 17, 2005.

57. Jacqueline Charles, "Caribbean Leaders, Rice Discuss Haiti," *Miami Herald*, June 7, 2005.

58. Michael Weinstein, "Washington Loses Control of the O.A.S.," *Power and Interest News Report*, May 9, 2005, www.pinr.com.

59. Ibid.

60. "Rice Got Burned," *Progreso Weekly*, May 26–June 1, 2005, www.progresoweekly.com.

61. See Interview between Condoleezza Rice and Giuliana Morrone, U.S. Department of State, Office of the Spokesman, Washington, DC, April 27, 2005.

62. "Rice Got Burned."

63. Weinstein, "Washington Loses Control."

64. Rice, "Remarks at the Council of Americas Annual Meeting."

65. Condoleezza Rice, "Remarks before the OAS," Ft. Lauderdale, FL, June 5, 2005.

66. Weinstein, "Washington Loses Control."

67. Larry Rother, "O.A.S. to Pick Chile Socialist U.S. Opposed as Its Leader," *New York Times*, April 30, 2005.

68. Laura Carlsen, "Continental Drift: Latin America Shifts Left," *Counterpunch*, December 4–6, 2004.

69. Juan Forero, "Bush's Aid Cuts on Court Issue Roil Latin American Neighbors," *New York Times*, August 19, 2005.

70. Colin Powell, "At Last, Some Good News for Central America," *Houston Chronicle*, November 11, 2003.

71. Ibid.

72. Fred Rosen, "Ms. Rice Goes to Mexico," *NACLA Report on the Americas*, May/June 2005.

73. Ibid.

74. *Life and Debt*, Stephanie Black, A Tuff Gong Pictures Production, © 2001.

75. The North American Free Trade Agreement went into effect on January 1, 1994.

76. For a survey of pro-NAFTA media exposure, see Jim Naureckas, "Happily Ever NAFTA?," *Extra!*, October 1993.

77. "Top Ten Reasons to Oppose the Free Trade Area of the Americas," press release, Global Exchange, San Francisco, undated.

78. Ibid.

79. "Frequently Asked Questions About the Free Trade Area of the Americas (FTAA)," Global Exchange, undated.

80. Manuel Castells, *The Power of Identity* (Maiden, MA: Blackwell Publishers, 1997), 74.

81. Larry Rohter, "Backlash from Nafta Batters Economies of Caribbean," *New York Times*, January 30, 1997.

82. Ibid.

83. Ibid.

84. "Top Ten Reasons to Oppose the Free Trade Area of the Americas."

85. Ed Matthew, "European League Table of Imports of Illegal Tropical Timber," Briefing Paper, Friends of the Earth, London, England, August 2–3, 2001.

86. Lee Sustar, "Defying the Police State in Miami," *Counterpunch*, December 6–7, 2003, http://www.counterpunch.org/sustar12062003.html.

87. See *A Fair Globalization: Creating Opportunities for All*, World Commission on the Social Dimension of Globalization, International Labour Office, Geneva, Switzerland, February 2004.

88. Joseph Stiglitz, "The Social Costs of Globalisation," *Financial Times,* February 25, 2004.

89. Deborah James, "CAFTA: Democracy Sold Out," July 29, 2005, www.alternet.org/story/23788.

90. Colin Powell, Press Briefing, En Route to College Station, Texas, November 4, 2003.

91. Rice, "Remarks at the Council of Americas Annual Meeting."

92. Mark Weisbrot, "Economic Arguments Surrounding CAFTA Remain Misunderstood," press release, Center for Economic and Policy Research, July 14, 2005.

93. *Country Reports on Terrorism*, Office of the Coordinator for Counterterrorism, U.S. State Department, April 27, 2005, http://www.state.gov/s/ct/rls/45392.htm.

94. Ibid.

95. Adam Isacson, "Closing the 'Seams': U.S. Security Policy in the Americas," NACLA, May 2005.

96. Ibid.

97. John Zoninsein, "The Economic Case for Combating Racial and Ethnic Exclusion in Latin America and Caribbean Countries," paper presentation, Towards a Shared Vision of Development: High Level Dialogue on Race, Ethnicity and Inclusion in Latin America and the Caribbean Conference, Inter-American Development Bank, Washington, DC, 2001, 4.

98. "Declaration," Conference of Citizens Against Racism, Xenophobia, Intolerance and Discrimination, Forum of NGOs and Civil Society Organizations of the Americas, Santiago, Chile, December 2000.

99. Charles Rangel, "Blacks in the Western Hemisphere: 'We Are All From Africa,' " press release, U.S. House of Representatives, Washington, DC, July 18, 2005.

100. Luiz Barcelos and Rachel Menezes, "Afro-Brazilians and the UN World Conference against Racism," Inter-Agency Consultation on Race in Latin America, undated, www.thedialogue.org/iac/eng/pubs/other_pubs.html.

101. Ibid.

102. Sergio da Silva Martins, Carlos Alberto Medeiros, and Elisa Larkin Nascimento, "Paving Paradise: The Road From 'Racial Democracy' to Affirmative Action in Brazil," *Journal of Black Studies,* July 2004, 787–816.

103. "Brazil's Lula 'Sorry' for Slavery," BBC, April 14, 2005, www.bbc.co.uk.

104. Sheila Jackson Lee, "Statement on the Burton Amendment to H.R. 2601, 'The Foreign Relations Authorization Act,' " press release, U.S. House of Representatives, Washington, DC, July 19, 2005.

105. Ibid.

106. Alejandro Correa and Willie Thompson, "African Venezuelans Fear New U.S. Coup Against President Chavez," December 18, 2002, www.trinicenter.com; and Karen Juanita Carrillo, "Completing the Chavez Revolution," July 1, 2005, http://www.seeingblack.com/2005/x070105/garcia.shtml.

107. Correa and Thompson, "African Venezuelans Fear New U.S. Coup."

108. Ibid.

109. Carrillo, "Completing the Chavez Revolution."

110. Ibid.

111. "Mexican Blacks Demand Stamp Apology," *CNN News Online*, July 5, 2005, www.cnn.com.

112. Darryl Fears, "Mexican Stamps Racist, Civil Rights Leaders Say Images Feature Popular Cartoon Character," *Washington Post*, June 30, 2005.

113. "Mexico Denies Stamps Are Racist," *CBS News*, June 30, 2005, http://www.cbsnews.com/stories/2005/06/30/world/main705522.shtml.

114. Elizabeth (Betita) Martínez, "Looking at the Mexican Stamp and Beyond," *Portside*, July 21, 2005, http://www.zmag.org/content/showarticle.cfm?SectionID=30&ItemID=8349.

115. "Mexico Defends Stamp of Black Character," *WJLA News*, Detroit, MI, June 30, 2005, http://www.wjla.com/news/stories/0605/239795.html.

116. Monte Reel, "In Buenos Aires, Researchers Long-Unclaimed African Roots," *Washington Post*, May 5, 2005.

Chapter 8

1. Wil Haygood and Ann Scot Tyson, " 'It Was as if All of Us Were Already Pronounced Dead,' " *Washington Post*, September 15, 2005.

2. Mike Davis, "The Struggle over the Future of New Orleans," September 23, 2005, www.socialistworker.org/2005-2/558/558_04_MikeDavis.shtml.

3. See Martin Gilens, *Why Americans Hate Welfare* (Chicago: University of Chicago Press, 1999).

4. Steven R. Weisman, "Rice Defends Bush's Race Record and Calls for Rebuilding Fairly," *New York Times*, September 13, 2005.

5. Condoleezza Rice, interview, *Tavis Smiley Show*, Washington, DC, September 8, 2005.

6. "Income Stable, Poverty Rate Increases, Percentage of Americans Without Health Insurance Unchanged," U.S. Census Bureau News, U.S. Department of Commerce, Washington, DC, August 30, 2005, http://www.census.gov/Press-Release/www/releases/archives/income_wealth/005647.html.

7. Ibid.

8. "Poverty Increase for Fourth Year in a Row in 2004; 1.5 Million More Children are Poor Than in 2000," press release, Children's Defense Fund, Washington, DC, August 30, 2005.

9. Rinku Sen, "Katrina and the Inequality President," September 15, 2005, www.alternet.org/story/25486.

10. See Molly Ivins, "Why New Orleans is in Deep Water," *Chicago Tribune*, September 1, 2005; and Ann Scott Tyson, "Strain of Iraq War Means the Relief Burden Will Have to Be Shared," *Washington Post*, August 31, 2005.

11. Jo Piazza and Chris Rovzar, "As South Drowns, Rice Soaks in N.Y.," *New York Daily News*, September 2, 2005.

12. "Colin Powell on Iraq, Race, and Hurricane Relief," *ABC News*, http://abc news.go.com/2020/Politics/story?id=1105979&page=1.

13. Ofer Shelah, "The Departure of a Doctrine," *Yediot Aharonot*, November 16, 2004.

14. Caribbean Media Corporation, Bridgetown, Barbados, November 17, 2004.

15. Von Schuster Jacques, "Powell Geht, Mehr Nicht," *Die Welt*, November 16, 2004.

16. Kuala Lumpur's Berita Harian in Malay, www.bharian.com.my (Editorial) (17).

17. "Powell Resigns Couldn't Live up to His Own Doctrine," *The Statesman* (India), November 19, 2004.

18. Barry Mthombothi, "Powell Leaves the Bush Administration a Damaged Man," *Pretoria News*, November 18, 2004.

19. Wang Yiwei, "Rice Comes to Power," *Beijing's Xin Jing Bao* (*The Beijing News*), November 18, 2004, www.thebeijingnews.com.

20. Commentary by Fa'iz Sarah, "Powell's Resignation Helps Conservatives Regain Their Homogeneity," *Oman Al-Watan*, www.alwatan.com, 18.

21. Editorial, "American Hawks and Gloomy Future," *Saudi Al-Watan*, www.alwatan.com.sa, 17.

22. Kuala Lumpur's *China Press* in Chinese, www.chinapress.com.my.

23. "Condoleezza the Saviour?," *The Star* (Johannesburg), November 18, 2004.

24. "End of the Duplicity," *Financial Times Deutschland*, November 17, 2004.

25. George Gedda, "Colin Powell: Four Tumultuous Years," *Foreign Service Journal* (February 2005): 40.

26. Dennis Jett, "The Failure of Colin Powell," *Foreign Service Journal* (February 2005): 22.

27. Ibid., 23–24.

28. Joe Davidson, "The General Gets Specific," *The Crisis* (September/October 2004): 41.

29. John Newhouse, *Imperial America* (New York: Knopf, 2003), 130–132.

30. *Human Security Now*, Commission on Human Security, UN Commission on Human Security, Washington, DC, 2003, 4.

31. This call was expressed by the International Human Rights Group (now Group Rights) and other groups in the United States. On the international level, the World Council of Churches led a campaign in the 1990s titled, "Racism is a Violation of Human Rights," and the argument has been made by the International

Labour Organization. The phrase is also the slogan of the London-based, the 1990 Trust, an anti-racism and human rights organization. See websites Group Rights (www.globalrights.org), World Council of Churches (www.wcc-coe.org/wcc/assembly/hr-e.html), International Labour Organization (www.ilo.org), and the 1990 Trust (www.blink.org.uk).

32. First wave human rights were limited to the prevention of state abuse against its citizens. With the emergence of the United Nations at the end of World War II, a second wave witnessed a more expansive conception of human rights that demanded that states not only not abuse people's rights but also adopt an obligation to protect those rights. And the notion of rights extended beyond civil and political rights to economic, social, and cultural rights.

33. A major weakness of this particular transposition is that policy-makers in England, Wales, and Scotland are allowed to derogate and declare that a new law is not compatible with the HRA. In Northern Ireland, legislators must make primary legislation compatible.

34. "Cabinet Office Paper: Conditions for Military Action," *Sunday London Times*, June 12, 2005.

Select Bibliography

Books, Monographs, and Scholarly Studies

Anderson, Carol. *Eyes Off the Prize: The United Nations and the African American Struggle for Human Rights, 1944–1955*. New York: Cambridge University Press, 2003.

Bositis, David. *Blacks and the 1992 Republican National Convention*. Washington, DC: Joint Center for Political and Economic Studies, 1992.

Branch, Taylor. *Parting the Waters: America in the King Years 1954–63*. New York: Simon and Schuster, 1988.

Brock, Lisa, and Digna Castaneda Fuerte, eds. *Between Race and Empire: African Americans and Cubans Before the Cuban Revolution*. Philadelphia: Temple University Press, 1998.

Brown, Cecil. *Stagolee Shot Billy*. Cambridge, MA: Harvard University Press, 2003.

Brown, Michael K., Martin Carnoy, Elliot Currie, Troy Duster, David B. Oppenheimer, Marjorie M. Shultz, and David Wellman. *Whitewashing Race: The Myth of a Color-Blind Society*. Berkeley: University of California Press, 2003.

Brzezinski, Zbigniew. *The Grand Chessboard: American Primacy and Its Geostrategic Imperatives*. New York: Basic Books, 1997.

Brzezinski, Zbigniew. *The Choice: Global Domination or Global Leadership*. New York: Basic Books, 2004.

Camejo, Peter. *Racism, Revolution, Reaction, 1861–1877: The Rise and Fall of Radical Reconstruction*. New York: Monad Press, 1976.

Castells, Manuel. *The Power of Identity*. Maiden, MA: Blackwell Publishers, 1997.

Christensen, Lawrence Oland. "Black St. Louis: A Study in Race Relations, 1865–1916." Ph.D. dissertation, University of Missouri, 1972.

Clarke, Richard A. *Against All Enemies: Inside America's War on Terror*. New York: Free Press, 2004.

Clegg, Claude A., III. *The Price of Liberty: African Americans and the Making of Liberia*. Chapel Hill: University of North Carolina Press, 2004.

Ellis, Stephen. *The Mask of Anarchy: The Destruction of Liberia and the Religious Dimension of an African Civil War*. New York: New York University Press, 1999.

Feffer, John, ed. *Power Trip: U.S. Unilateralism and Global Strategy After September 11*. New York: Seven Stories Press, 2003.

Finger, Seymour Maxwell. *American Ambassadors at the UN: People, Politics, and Bureaucracy in Making Foreign Policy*. New York: Holmes & Meier, 1988.

Flanders, Laura. *Bushwomen: Tales of a Cynical Species*. New York: Verso, 2004.

Fraser, Cary. "An American Dilemma: Race and Realpolitik in the American Response to the Bandung Conference, 1955." In Brenda Gayle Plummer, ed., *Window on Freedom: Race, Civil Rights, and Foreign Affairs, 1945–1988*. Chapel Hill: University of North Carolina Press, 2003.

Henry, Charles P. *Ralph Bunche: Model Negro or American Other?* New York: New York University Press, 1999.

Henry, Charles P., ed. *Ralph J. Bunche: Selected Speeches & Writings*. Ann Arbor: University of Michigan Press, 1995.

Henry, Charles P., ed. "Introduction: Black Global Politics in a Post–Cold War World." In Charles P. Henry, ed., *Foreign Policy and the Black (Inter)National Interest*. Albany: State University of New York Press, 2000.

Kennan, George. "Review of Current Trends: U.S. Foreign Policy." In Thomas H. Etzold and John Lewis Gaddis, eds., *Containment: Documents on American Policy and Strategy, 1945–1990*. New York: Columbia University Press, 1978.

Layton, Azza Salama. *International Politics and Civil Rights Policies in the United States, 1941–1960*. New York: Cambridge University Press, 2000.

Leondar-Wright, Betsy, Meizhu Lui, Gloribell Mota, Dedrick Muhammad, and Mara Youkydis. *State of the Dream 2005: Disowned in the Ownership Society*. Boston: United for a Fair Economy, January 10, 2005.

Mahajan, Rahul. *Full Spectrum Dominance: U.S. Power in Iraq and Beyond*. New York: Seven Stories Press, 2003.

Malveaux, Julianne, and Reginna A. Green, eds. *The Paradox of Loyalty: An African American Response to the War on Terrorism*. Chicago: Third World Press, 2002.

Mann, James. *Rise of the Vulcans: The History of Bush's War Cabinet*. New York: Penguin, 2004.

Mansfield, Stephen. *The Faith of George W. Bush*. New York: Jeremy P. Tarcher, 2003.

Mollenhoff, Clark. *The President Who Failed: Carter Out of Control*. New York: Macmillan, 1980.

Morgenthau, Hans J. *Politics among Nations: The Struggle for Power and Peace*. New York: Knopf, 1978.

Myrdal, Gunnar. *An American Dilemma: The Negro Problem & Modern Democracy*. 2 vols. New York: Pantheon Books, 1944.

National Commission on Terrorist Attacks. *The 9/11 Commission Report: Final Report of the National Commission on Terrorist Attacks Upon the United States*. New York: W. W. Norton & Company, 2004.

Newhouse, John. *Imperial America*. New York: Knopf, 2003.

Nicholls, David. *From Dessalines to Duvalier: Race, Colour, and National Independence in Haiti*. New Brunswick, NJ: Rutgers University Press, 1995.

O'Hanlon, Michael E., Susan E. Rice, and James B. Steinberg. *The New National Security Strategy and Preemption*. Washington, DC: The Brookings Institution, December 2002.

O'Reilly, Kenneth. *Nixon's Piano: Presidents and Racial Politics from Washington to Clinton*. New York: The Free Press, 1995.

Pham, John Peter. *Liberia: Portrait of a Failed State*. New York: Reed Press, 2004.

Plummer, Brenda Gayle. *Rising Wind: Black Americans and U.S. Foreign Affairs, 1935–1960*. Chapel Hill: University of North Carolina Press, 1996.

Rampton, Sheldon, and John Stauber. *Weapons of Mass Deception: The Uses of Propaganda in Bush's War on Iraq*. New York: Penguin, 2003.

Rice, Susan. *U.S. Foreign Assistance to Africa: Claims vs. Reality*. Washington, DC: Brookings Institution, June 29, 2005.

Rockeymoore, Maya, Kenya Covington, Gerald Ford, and Elias Mageto. *Issues Facing African Americans Over the Next Four Years: A Critical Analysis*. Washington, DC: Congressional Black Caucus Foundation, 2004.

Sawyer, Amos Claudius. *The Emergence of Autocracy in Liberia*. San Francisco: Institute for Contemporary Studies, 1992.

Scott, Fran, and Abdulah Osman. "Identity, African-Americans, and U.S. Foreign Policy: Differing Reactions to South African Apartheid and the Rwandan Genocide." In Thomas Ambrosio, ed., *Ethnic Identity Groups and U.S. Foreign Policy*. Westport, CT: Praeger, 2002.

Stanford, Karin L. *Beyond the Boundaries: Reverend Jesse Jackson in International Affairs*. Albany: SUNY Press, 1997.

Stanford, Karin L. "Citizen Diplomacy and Jesse Jackson: A Case Study for Influencing U.S. Foreign Policy Toward Southern Africa." In Ernest J. Wilson III, ed., *Diversity and U.S. Foreign Policy: A Reader*. New York: Routledge, 2004.

Steele, James. *Freedom's River: The African-American Contribution to Democracy*. New York: Franklin Watts, 1994.

Tienda, Marta, et al. "Closing the Gap?: Admissions & Enrollment at the Texas Public Flagships Before and After Affirmative Action." *Policy Brief*, Woodrow Wilson School of Public Affairs, Princeton University, January 2003.

Urquhart, Brian. *Ralph Bunche: An American Odyssey*. New York: W. W. Norton & Company, 1993.

Von Eschen, Penny M. *Race Against Empire: Black Americans and Anticolonialism, 1937–1957*. Ithaca, NY: Cornell University Press, 1997.

Walters, Ronald. "The Africa Growth and Opportunity Act: Changing Foreign Policy Priorities Toward Africa in a Conservative Political Climate." In Charles P. Henry, ed., *Foreign Policy and the Black (Inter)National Interest.* Albany: State University of New York, 2000.

Woodward, Bob. *Plan of Attack.* New York: Simon & Schuster, 2004.

Wright, Richard. *The Color Curtain: A Report on the Bandung Conference.* Jackson, MS: Banner Books, University Press of Mississippi, 1956/1995.

Zoninsein, John. "The Economic Case for Combating Racial and Ethnic Exclusion in Latin America and Caribbean Countries." Paper presentation, Towards a Shared Vision of Development: High Level Dialogue on Race, Ethnicity and Inclusion in Latin America and the Caribbean Conference, Inter-American Development Bank, Washington, DC, 2001.

Journals and Magazines

al-Marashi, Ibrahim. "Iraq's Security and Intelligence Network: A Guide and Analysis." *Middle East Report of International Affairs* (September 2002).

Booker, Salih, and Ann-Louise Colgan. "'Compassionate Conservatism' Comes to Africa." *Current History* (May 23, 2004).

Booker, Salih, William Minter, and Ann-Louise Colgan. "America and Africa." *Current History* (May 2003).

Canham-Clyne, John. "U.S. Policy on Haiti: Selling Out Democracy." *Covert Action* 48 (spring 1994).

Cobb, Charles, Jr. "Considering Colin Powell and Africa." *Foreign Service Journal* (March 29, 2003).

Davidson, Joe. "The General Gets Specific." *The Crisis* (September/October 2004).

Lemann, Nicholas. "The Three Cushion Shot That Won Colin Powell's Support for Affirmative Action in Higher Education." *Journal of Blacks in Higher Education* (winter 1999–2000).

Malveaux, Julianne. "Recession, Affirmative Action, Trickery: Reflections on a Bush Appointment." *Black Issues in Higher Education* (April 25, 2002).

Martins, Sergio da Silva, Carlos Alberto Medeiros, and Elisa Larkin Nascimento. "Paving Paradise: The Road From 'Racial Democracy' to Affirmative Action in Brazil." *Journal of Black Studies* (July 2004): 787–816.

McDougall, Gay. "The World Conference against Racism: Through a Wider Lens." *The Fletcher Forum of World Affairs* (summer/fall 2002).

Ottaway, Marina. "Africa's 'New Leaders': African Solution or African Problem." *Current History* (May 1998).

Persaud, Randolph B. "Shades of American Hegemony: The Primitive, the Enlightened, and the Benevolent." *Connecticut Journal of International Law* (spring 2004).

Smith, Robert C. "The Political Behavior of Black Presidential Appointees, 1960–1980." *Western Journal of Black Studies* 8 (1984): 139–147.

Print, Electronic, Internet Media

Allen, Mike. "Rice: Race Can Be Factor in College Admissions." *Washington Post*, January 18, 2003.

Allen, Mike, and Charles Lane. "Rice Helped Shape Bush Decision on Admissions." *Washington Post*, January 17, 2003.

Barabak, Mark Z. "Condoleezza Rice at Stanford." *Los Angeles Times*, January 16, 2005.

Blustein, Paul. "Debt Cut Is Set for Poorest Nations." *Washington Post*, June 12, 2005.

Booker, Salih. "Bush's AIDS Plan: More Smoke and Mirrors." *Economic Justice News*, March 28, 2003.

Cayton, Horace R. "An Awakening: The Negro Now Fights for Democratic Rights of All the World's Peoples." *Pittsburgh Courier*, February 27, 1943, 14.

Clymer, Adam. "How Sept. 11 Changed Goals of Justice Department." *New York Times*, February 28, 2002.

"Condoleezza Rice: The Devil's Handmaiden." *The Black Commentator* 26, January 23, 2003. Available: www.blackcommentator.com.

Corn, David. "Capital Games." *The Nation*, April 8, 2004. Available: www.thenation.com.

Curry, George. "Williams 'Payola' Was Part of a Covert Propaganda Campaign." *Seattle Medium*, January 11, 2005.

Da Costa, Gilbert. "Securing Africa Oil." *Washington Times*, July 13, 2004.

Fears, Darryl. "Mexican Stamps Racist, Civil Rights Leaders Say Images Feature Popular Cartoon Character." *Washington Post*, June 30, 2005.

Forero, Juan. "Bush's Aid Cuts on Court Issue Roil Latin American Neighbors." *New York Times*, August 19, 2005.

Forero, Juan. "Documents Show CIA Knew of a Coup Plot in Venezuela." *New York Times*, December 3, 2004.

Givhan, Robin. "Condoleezza Rice's Commanding Clothes." *Washington Post*, February 25, 2005.

Haygood, Wil, and Ann Scot Tyson. "'It Was as if All of Us Were Already Pronounced Dead.'" *Washington Post*, September 15, 2005.

Hockstader, Lee. "Israel's Sharon Met U.S.'s Rice, and Their Encounter Had Legs." *Washington Post*, February 4, 2001.

Holland, Joshua. "Blackwashing." July 26, 2004. Available: http://www.alternet.org/story/19331.

Isikoff, Michael. "In the Months Before 9/11, Justice Department Curtailed Highly Classified Program to Monitor Al Qaeda Suspects in the US." *Newsweek*, March 21, 2004.

Ivins, Molly. "Why New Orleans is in Deep Water." *Chicago Tribune*, September 1, 2005.

Jackson, Derrick Z. "Powell's Oil Quest." *Boston Globe*, September 6, 2002.

James, Deborah. "CAFTA: Democracy Sold Out." *Alternet*, July 29, 2005. Available: www.alternet.org/story/23788.

Kagan, Robert. "The Problem with Powell." *Washington Post*, July 23, 2000.

Kaplan, Lawrence F. "Colin Powell's Out-of-Date Foreign Policy." *The New Republic*, January 1, 2001.

Kessler, Glenn. "Powell Expresses Doubts About Basis for Iraqi Weapons Claim." *Washington Post*, April 3, 2004.

Kessler, Glenn, and Walter Pincus. "A Flawed Argument in the Case for War." *Washington Post*, February 1, 2004.

Kessler, Glenn, and Walter Pincus. "Looking Back at Powell's Claims." *Washington Post*, February 1, 2004.

Kull, Steven, Clay Ramsay, Evan Lewis, and Phil Warf. *Misperceptions, the Media, and the Iraq War.* Program on International Policy Attitudes/Knowledge Networks, October 2, 2003. Available: www.pipa.org.

Lehrer, Jim. "Rice on Iraq, War and Politics." *NewsHour with Jim Lehrer*, PBS, September 25, 2002.

Martínez, Elizabeth (Betita). "Looking at the Mexican Stamp and Beyond." *Portside*, July 21, 2005. Available: http://www.zmag.org/content/showarticle.cfm?SectionID=30&ItemID=8349.

"Mexican Blacks Demand Stamp Apology." *CNN News Online*, July 5, 2005. Available: www.cnn.com.

"Mexico Denies Stamps Are Racist." *CBS News*, June 30, 2005. Available: http://www.cbsnews.com/stories/2005/06/30/world/main705522.shtml.

Milbank, Dana. "Stabilization Is Its Middle Name." *Washington Post*, May 18, 2004.

Milbank, Dana, and Mike Allen. "White House Counters Ex-Aide." *Washington Post*, March 23, 2004.

Milbank, Dana, and Walter Pincus. "Bush Aides Disclose Warnings from CIA." *Washington Post*, July 23, 2003.

Mitchell, Mary A. "Powell, Rice Should Silence Critics of Black Republicans." *Chicago Sun-Times*, December 19, 2000.

Morin, Richard, and Dan Balz. "Political Divisions Persist After Election." *Washington Post*, January 18, 2005.

Noah, Timothy. "Did Condi Give the Game Away." *Slate*, July 31, 2003.

Pelletiere, Stephen. "A War Crime or an Act of War?" *New York Times*, January 31, 2003.

Peretz, Evgenia, David Rose, and David Wise. "The Path to War." *Vanity Fair*, May 2004, 102.

Perlez, Jane. "How Powell Decided to Shun Racism Conference." *New York Times*, September 5, 2001.

Piazza, Jo, and Chris Rovzar. "As South Drowns, Rice Soaks in N.Y." *New York Daily News*, September 2, 2005.

Pincus, Walter. "No Link Between Hijacker, Iraq Found, U.S. Says." *Washington Post*, May 1, 2002.

"Powell's Doctrine, In Powell's Words." *Washington Post*, October 21, 2001.

Priest, Dana, and Walter Pincus. "U.S. 'Almost All Wrong' on Weapons." *Washington Post*, October 7, 2004.

Reel, Monte. "In Buenos Aires, Researchers Long-Unclaimed African Roots." *Washington Post*, May 5, 2005.

Risen, James. "Prague Discounts an Iraq Meeting." *New York Times*, October 21, 2002.

Rohter, Larry. "Backlash from Nafta Batters Economies of Caribbean." *New York Times*, January 30, 1997.

Rohter, Larry. "O.A.S. to Pick Chile Socialist U.S. Opposed as Its Leader." *New York Times*, April 30, 2005.

Russakoff, Dale. "Team Rice, Playing Away; Will State's Head Coach Miss Her First Kickoff?" *Washington Post*, February 6, 2005, D01.

Sen, Rinku. "Katrina and the Inequality President." *AlterNet*, September 15, 2005. Available: http://www.alternet.org/story/25486.

"Shots Fired as Powell Visits Haiti Palace." *CNN News Online*, December 1, 2004. Available: http://www.cnn.com/2004/WORLD/americas/12/01/powell.shooting.

Slevin, Peter, and Mike Allen. "Former Ally's Shift in Stance Left Haiti Leader No Recourse." *Washington Post*, March 1, 2004.

Smith, Edward. "Republicans Have a Place in Black History." *Wall Street Journal*, December 20, 2000.

Steele, James. "The 2004 Democratic Mobilization: Historic, But Not Enough." *New Labor Forum*, December 2004/5.

Stiglitz, Joseph. "The Social Costs of Globalisation." *Financial Times*, February 25, 2004.

Sullivan, Kevin, Scott Wilson, and Fred Barbash. "Aristide Bows to Pressure, Leaves Haiti." *Washington Post*, February 29, 2004.

Sustar, Lee. "Defying the Police State in Miami." *Counterpunch*, December 6/7, 2003. Available: http://www.counterpunch.org/sustar12062003.html.

Tyler, Patrick E. "Pentagon Drops Goal of Blocking New Superpowers." *New York Times*, May 24, 1992.

Tyson, Ann Scott. "Strain of Iraq War Means the Relief Burden Will Have to Be Shared." *Washington Post*, August 31, 2005.

Vest, Jason. "Coming Soon: 'Total War' on the Middle East." *The Nation*, August 29, 2002.

Vieth, Warren, and Ricardo Alonso-Zaldivar. "Bush's Cabinet Members Pay Visits to Swing States." *Los Angeles Times*, October 21, 2004.

Weschler, Lawrence. "He's the Picture of Racial Compassion." *Los Angeles Times*, May 13, 2004.

Will, George. "Race and 'Rights.'" *Washington Post*, March 11, 2005.

Williams, Armstrong. "Armstrong Williams Offers Readers an Apology." *Afro-American*, January 13, 2005.

Wilson, Joseph. "What I Didn't Find in Africa." *New York Times*, July 6, 2003.

WJLA News. "Mexico Defends Stamp of Black Character." Detroit, MI, June 30, 2005. Available: http://www.wjla.com/news/stories/0605/239795.html.

Wright, Robin. "The Secretary of State Spreads Her Wings." *Washington Post*, February 10, 2005.

Wright, Robin. "Top Focus Before 9/11 Wasn't on Terrorism." *Washington Post*, April 1, 2004.

Zunes, Stephen. "Mr. Powell, You're No Adlai Stevenson." *Foreign Policy in Focus*, February 6, 2003.

International Media Coverage

"American Hawks and Gloomy Future." *Al-Watan* (Saudi Arabia). Available: http://www.alwatan.com.sa.

Buncombe, Andrew. "Global Spending on Arms Tops $1 Trillion." *The Independent*, June 9, 2005.

Carrillo, Karen Juanita. "Completing the Chavez Revolution." *SeeingBlack*, July 1, 2005. Available: http://www.seeingblack.com/2005/x070105/garcia.shtml.

"Condoleezza the Saviour?" *The Star* (Johannesburg), November 18, 2004.

Correa, Alejandro, and Willie Thompson. "African Venezuelans Fear New U.S. Coup Against President Chavez." *Trinicenter*, December 18, 2002. Available: http://www.trinicenter.com.

Dixon, Norm. "Debt Cancellation: Africa Needs Justice, Not Charity." *Green Left Weekly* (Australia), June 28, 2005. Available: www.worldpress.org/africa/2107.cfm.

Elliott, Larry. "Africa Still on Road to Disaster Says UN." *The Guardian*, June 8, 2005.

Elliott, Larry, and Ashley Seager. "£30 bn Debts Write-off Agreed." *The Guardian*, June 11, 2005.

Elliott, Larry, and Patrick Wintour. "Broken Promises Leave Three Million Children to Die in Africa." *The Guardian*, June 8, 2005.

"Europe Has Lost a Friend with Powell's Departure." *Agence France Presse*, November 16, 2004.

"Glad You Could Come . . ." *The Star* (Johannesburg), May 25, 2001.

"Hands Across the Water." *The Star* (Johannesburg), May 26, 2001.

Harding, Luke. "Revealed: Truth Behind U.S. 'Poison Factory' Claim." *Observer*, February 9, 2003.

Hilton, Isabel. "The 800 lb. Gorilla in American Foreign Policy." *The Guardian*, July 28, 2004.

"Humilation for Powell at Earth Summit." *The Guardian*, September 4, 2002.

"Implications of Gen. Powell's Call." *The Nation* (Kenya), June 3, 2001.

Kristof, Nicholas D. "Sudan's Policy of Systematic Rape." *International Times Herald*, June 6, 2005.

Leigh, David. "How Deal Got the Green Light Despite Nerve Gas Warning." *The Guardian*, March 6, 2003.

Leigh, David. "The Strange Case of Falluja 2." *The Guardian*, March 6, 2003.

Leigh, David, and John Hooper. "Britain's Dirty Secret." *The Guardian*, March 6, 2003.

Lobe, Jim. "Bush Exaggerates Increase in U.S. Aid to Africa." *Inter Press Service*, June 28, 2005.

Lobe, Jim. "Bush Falls from Favor Abroad, Too." *Asia Times*, October 30, 2003.

Mbozi, Austin. "Powell: Please Speak for Black Africa." *The Post*, September 16, 2002.

Mendel, Gideon. "Eight Women One Voice." *The Guardian Weekend*, June 11, 2005.

Monbiot, George. "A Truckload of Nonsense." *The Guardian*, June 14, 2005.

Mthombothi, Barry. "End of an Unhappy Marriage." *The Star* (Johannesburg), November 17, 2003.

Nordland, Rod, Babak Dehghanpisheh, and Michael Hirsh. "Hell to Pay." *Newsweek International*, November 8, 2004.

"Powell Resigns Couldn't Live up to His Own Doctrine." *The Statesman* (India), November 19, 2004.

Rose, David. "Bush and Blair Made Secret Pact for Iraq War." *The Observer*, April 4, 2004.

Sanders, Ronald. "Rice and Zoellick: Not Rice and Peas." *Caribbeannetnews*, January 18, 2005. Available: http://www.caribbeannetnews.com.

Sarah, Fa'iz. "Powell's Resignation Helps Conservatives Regain their Homogeneity." *Al-Watan* (Oman). Available: http://www.alwatan.com.

Shelah, Ofer. "The Departure of a Doctrine." *Yediot Aharonot* (Israel), November 16, 2004.

Singh, Rickey. "Our Caribbean: Our Interest Under Bush." *Daily Nation* (Barbados), September 3, 2004.

Steinberg, Avi. "Haiti Update VI: Out With the Bad, In With the Worse." *Africana*, March 31, 2004. Available: http://www.africana.com.

Vulliamy, Ed. "Venezuela Coup Linked to Bush Team." *Observer*, April 21, 2002.

Wintour, Patrick, and Larry Elliott. "Debt Deal in Pipeline after US Visit." *The Guardian*, June 9, 2005.

Zapiro. Political cartoon. *Sowetan*, August 29, 2001.

Statements by the Bush Administration

"Fact Sheet: Report of the Commission for Assistance to a Free Cuba." White House, Washington, DC, May 6, 2004. Available: http://www.whitehouse.gov/news/releases/2004/05/20040506-7.html.

Gonzales, Alberto R. "Letter to 9-11 Commission." The White House, March 30, 2004.

Iraq on the Record: The Bush Administration's Public Statements on Iraq. United States House of Representatives, Committee on Government Reform—Minority Staff, Special Investigations Division, prepared for Rep. Henry A. Waxman, Washington, DC, March 16, 2004.

National Security Strategy for a New Century, A. The White House, December 1999.

"Venezuela: Change of Government." Press statement, U.S. State Department, Washington, DC, April 12, 2002.

Writings and Statements by Colin Powell

Powell, Colin. "At Last, Some Good News for Central America." *Houston Chronicle*, November 11, 2003.

Powell, Colin. "The Crisis in Darfur." Testimony before the U.S. Senate Foreign Relations Committee, Washington, DC, September 9, 2004.

Powell, Colin. "En Route to College Station." Press briefing, U.S. Department of State, Washington, DC, November 4, 2003.

Powell, Colin. *My American Journey.* New York: Ballantine, 1995.

Powell, Colin. "Remarks to University of Witwatersrand." Johannesburg, South Africa, May 25, 2001.

Powell, Colin. "Remarks with Prime Minister Gerard Latortue of Haiti After Their Meeting." Port-au-Prince, Haiti, U.S. Department of State, Washington, DC, April 5, 2004. www.state.gov/secretary/former/powell/remarks/31186.htm.

Powell, Colin. "Speech to the UN Security Council." February 5, 2003.

Powell, Colin. "Statement by Secretary of State Colin Powell on the Withdrawal of the USA from the WCAR." U.S. Department of State, September 3, 2001.

Powell, Colin. "Statement on President Bush's Budget Request for FY 2003." U.S. Senate Foreign Relations Committee, February 5, 2002.

Powell, Colin. "A Strategy of Partnerships." *Foreign Affairs*, January/February 2004.

Powell, Colin. "Testimony Before the U.S. Senate Committee on Foreign Relations." U.S. Senate, Washington, DC, February 12, 2004.

Writings and Statements by Condoleezza Rice

Rice, Condoleezza. "Campaign 2000—Promoting the National Interest." *Foreign Affairs*, January/February, 2000.

Rice, Condoleezza. "Condoleezza Rice Discusses Foreign Policy at the 28th Annual Convention of the National Association of Black Journalists." August 7, 2003.

Rice, Condoleezza. "Condoleezza Rice Discusses the President's Trip to Africa." White House Press Briefing, July 3, 2003.

Rice, Condoleezza. "Condoleezza Rice Speaks at Los Angeles Town Hall." The Westin Bonaventure Hotel, June 12, 2003.

Rice, Condoleezza. "Interview between Condoleezza Rice and Giuliana Morrone." U.S. Department of State, Office of the Spokesman, Washington, DC, April 27, 2005.

Rice, Condoleezza. "Interview on *The Tavis Smiley Show*." Washington, DC, September 8, 2005.

Rice, Condoleezza. "National Security Advisor Condoleezza Rice Interview with German Television." Office of the Press Secretary, White House, July 31, 2003.

Rice, Condoleezza. "Opening Statement." U.S. Senate Confirmation Hearings, U.S. Senate, Washington, DC, January 18, 2005.

Rice, Condoleezza. "Remarks at the Council of Americas Annual Meeting." U.S. Department of State, Washington, DC, May 3, 2005.

Rice, Condoleezza. "Remarks before the OAS." Ft. Lauderdale, Florida, June 5, 2005.

Rice, Condoleezza. "Remarks by Condoleezza Rice." International Institute for Strategic Studies, London, June 26, 2003.

Rice, Condoleezza. "Remarks by Condoleezza Rice at Mississippi College School of Law." Commencement Ceremony, First Baptist Church, Jackson, Mississippi, May 19, 2003.

Rice, Condoleezza. "Remarks Following her Nomination to become National Security Advisor." Austin, TX, December 17, 2000.

Rice, Condoleezza. "Statement by the National Security Advisor Dr. Condoleezza Rice on the Michigan Decision." January 17, 2003.

Rice, Condoleezza. "Testimony before the Senate Foreign Relations Committee." January 18, 2005.

Rice, Condoleezza. "U.S. Senate Confirmation Hearings Testimony." U.S. Department of State, January 19, 2005.

Rice, Condoleezza. "Why We Know Iraq is Lying." *New York Times*, January 23, 2003.

Film

Black, Stephanie. *Life and Debt*. A Tuff Gong Pictures Production, © 2001.

Index

domestic policy of, 8, 93, 182, 183, 185, 187
economic conditions under, 184–85
education of, 75
election campaign of, 89
environmental policies of, 147
family background of, 75
on foreign aid, 135
foreign policy of, 11, 31, 32, 45–46, 57, 84, 91, 93–94, 97–98, 127, 145, 186
Haiti policy of, 156
Iraq war leadership of, 107, 121, 187, 189
lies of, 113–14, 116, 119, 188
media coverage on, 110–11, 190
in National Guard, 75
national security policy of, 95, 96
post-September 11 agenda of, 4, 94, 102–3, 105, 109, 179, 182–83
quoted statements by, 39, 75, 84, 94, 123
race record of, 2–3, 4, 11, 59–60, 69–71, 73–74, 182, 185–86
reelection of, 1, 8, 74, 188
religious beliefs of, 10
as Texas governor, 60, 69–70, 78
trade policies of, 171
U.S. public opinion regarding, 110, 186, 187
Venezuela policy of, 149–54
on World Conference against Racism (WCAR), 2001, 11, 64, 65
world opinion regarding, 109–10
Bush, Jeb, 78, 160
Bush, Prescott, 75
Byrd, James, Jr., 70

CAFTA (Central America-Dominican Republic Free Trade Agreement), 171–72
California Civil Rights Initiative (CCRI), 53, 77–78

Campbell, Alastair, 107
Caribbean
  black views on, 15, 93
  intervention in, 148
  NAFTA (North American Free Trade Agreement), impact on, 169
  Powell and Rice, views on, 64, 126–27
Caribbean Basin Initiative (CBI), 169
CARICOM (Caribbean Community), 157, 163, 164, 188
Carlsen, Laura, 145
Carmichael, Stokely, 82
Carmona, Pedro, 151
Carnegie Corporation, 25
Carter, Jimmy
  advisors of, 87, 98
  black appointments under, 19, 20, 21
  economic conditions under, 57
  foreign policy of, 45
  Haiti mission, participation in, 155
  race record of, 72
Cartwright, Margaret, 29
Carvajal, Leonardo, 151
Cash, Tony, 181
Castells, Manuel, 168–69
Castle Rock Foundation, 48
Castro, Fidel, 149, 150, 159, 160, 161, 162
"Catcher's Mitt" program, 102
Cayton, Horace R., 13, 14
CBC. See Congressional Black Caucus (CBC)
CBCF. See Congressional Black Caucus Foundation (CBCF)
CEDAW (International Convention on the Elimination of All Forms of Discrimination Against Women), 67–68
Cedras, Raoul, 154, 155
Center for Economic and Policy Research, 172
Center for Equal Opportunity, 72

Haiti policy of, 154–55
national security policy of, 95–96
race record of, 64, 72, 182
trade policies of, 169
Coalition of Black Trade Unionists, 30
Cold War, 148
Cold War mentality, 145
Coleman, Tom, 70
Colgan, Ann-Louise, 130, 132, 137
Collins, Addie Mae, 80
Colombia
conflict in, 172
drug war in, 148, 176
U.S. black views on, 32
as U.S. ally, 164
weak government of, 7
colonization, racialized, 174
color-blindness, 4, 72, 181, 182,
186, 187
See also black Republicans: on racial
disparities; racial realism
commonality of circumstances, 14
Communist movement, 15
Community of Democracies, 164
Community of South American
Nations, 166
Comprehensive Anti-Apartheid Act, 30
Confederation of Venezuelan
Workers, 151
Congressional Black Caucus (CBC), 20,
22, 32, 33, 51, 141, 157–58, 159,
175, 182
Congressional Black Caucus Foundation
(CBCF), 32
Congressional Human Rights
Foundation, 52
Congressional Research Service, 132
Congress of Racial Equality (CORE), 81
Connerly, Ward, 47, 53–54, 60–61
Connor, "Bull," 81
constructive engagement, 129
consumer groups, 170
"Contract on America," 47

Contras, Nicaraguan, 146, 162, 167
Convention Against Torture and Other
Cruel, Inhumane or Degrading
Treatment or Punishment
(CAT), 68
Convention on the Rights of the Child
(CRC), 68
Conyers, John, 65
Corral, Oscar, 163
Council of Americas, 165
counter-hegemonic movements,
16, 123
Counterterrorism Security Group, 100
counter-terrorism training and exercises,
173
criminal justice, 195
CSP (Center for Security Policy), 86
Cuba
supporters of, 163, 166
terrorism, sponsoring, alleged,
161, 162t
U.S. policy on, 20, 159–62, 173
Venezuelan ties to, 150, 173
Cuban airliner, bombing of, 161–62
Cuban Americans, 161, 162, 174
"Cuban Liberty and Democratic
Solidarity Act of 1996," 161
Cummings, Elijah, 159
Custred, Glynn, 53

Darfur, Sudan, war in, 50, 139–40,
141–42, 143
Davis, Mike, 181
Davis, William B., 22
Dawkins, Marcus, 31
Dearlove, Richard, 107
death penalty, 195
debts, international, cancelling, 129,
132–35, 143
decolonization, 27
Defense Intelligence Agency, 114, 120
"Defense Planning Guidance" (DPG)
document, 85

tactics, 8
U.S. black views on, 15, 31, 32
Washington, Booker T., 17, 37
Washington Concensus, 146
Washington-Williams, Essie Mae, 56
Watergate hearings, 98
Waters, Maxine, 159
Waxman, Henry, study of, 113,
    115, 118
WCAR, 2001. *See* World Conference
    against Racism (WCAR), 2001
wealth redistribution, 182
weapons of mass destruction (WMD),
    92, 95, 96, 105, 107, 108–9,
    112–13, 114–18, 120, 121, 188
Weaver, Jay, 163
Weber, Vin, 151
welfare queens, 57, 182
welfare state, 43
Wesley, Charles, 25
Wesley, Cynthia, 80
West, Kayne, 183
Western states, 124
Weyrich, Paul, 49
Wharton, Clifton R., 17, 18
Wharton, Clifton R., Jr., 18–19
Wilkins, Roy, 29
Will, George, 60
William Donner Foundation, 53
Williams, Armstrong, 54, 55–56

Williams, Henry Sylvester, 28
Williamson, John, 146
Wilson, Joseph, 116, 117
Wilson, Valerie Plame, 116, 117
Wolfowitz, Paul, 85, 86, 94, 119
women in foreign service, 9, 19, 21–22,
    23, 135
women's rights, 15, 72
Wood, Tom, 53
Woodward, Bob, 111, 190, 191
World Affairs Council of Pittsburgh, 57
World Bank, 124, 133–34, 155
World Commission on the Social
    Dimension of Globalization, 171
World Conference against Racism
    (WCAR), 2001, 8, 11, 16, 52,
    63–67, 69, 131, 174, 175,
    176, 195
World Trade Organization, 7, 32, 124,
    138, 194
Wright, Richard, 29

Yanga, Gaspar, 178
Young, Andrew, 19–21, 22
Younge, Gary, 13, 14

Zapatista National Liberation Army,
    168
Zarqawi, Abu Musab, 118–19
Zenawi, Meles, 129

About the Author

CLARENCE LUSANE is Associate Professor at the School of International Service, American University, where he teaches courses in global race relations, anti-discrimination policy, and international drug politics. He is the author of six previous books, including *Hitler's Black Victims* (2002), *Race in the Global Era* (1997), and *The Struggle for Equal Education* (1992). He is a recipient of the prestigious British Council Atlantic Fellowship in Public Policy and a board member of the Institute for Policy Studies.